What People Are Saying About
3 KEYS TO KEEPING YOUR TEEN ALIVE

"In life we make many investments. This investment you don't want to miss! Every year, more teens die in car crashes than from anything else. Most crashes are preventable. Research proves that informed and involved parents make a difference. ***3 Keys to Keeping Your Teen Alive*** *is a great resource to help parents coach, monitor and support their teens."*

Michelle Anderson, Director of Operations,
National Road Safety Foundation–New York

"Both teen drivers and parents will benefit from this compelling survival blueprint to safe driving practices. Those parents like myself who lost their teen-child in their first year of driving feel this life-saving book is the best gift you can give your teen."

Laura Marchetti, Katie's Mom–Florida

"This book is a must read for all teens and new drivers. As a mother who lost her daughter in a car accident, I think Anne Marie covers all the risks out there for new drivers."

Linda Mulkey, Lauren's Mom–Salt Lake City, Utah

"I am very honored to be a small part of the creation of such an important resource for teen drivers. I strongly encourage parents to go through this book with your teens because it not only contains practical advice about what to do while driving, but also true stories about regular people who have suffered tragedy because of poor decisions. I believe there can be some productive discussions as teens and their parents open the lines of communication about driving safety. We should never assume our children learn everything they need to know in Driver's Ed. We are their role models and they learn the most from us. Thanks, Anne Marie, for caring enough to undertake such a huge task to help keep our young drivers as well as their parents safe while driving."

Renee Napier, Meagan's Mom–Florida

"Designed with parental involvement in mind, ***3 Keys to Keeping Your Teen Alive*** *is a comprehensive instruction manual designed to give all new drivers a solid foundation of driving skills, based upon proven safe-driving principles. I highly recommend its use in the instruction of inexperienced drivers, and as a future reference guide, for a lifetime of safe driving."*

Dean T. Johnson, President, The Sandy Johnson Foundation:
Making Our Roads Safer–Ohio

*"**3 Keys to Keeping Your Teen Alive** is a great tool for our new drivers, their parents—and all ages. It will make a difference in how we drive and make us all better drivers."*

Barry Marcone, DrivingSober.net–Florida

*"**3 Keys to Keeping Your Teen Alive** is a must-have for every informed parent who seeks to have their son or daughter return home safely each time they use the car or even enter a friend's car. You will want to be assured that not only have you read it, but also the other young drivers and parents with whom your youth associates. There are never guarantees, but reducing risk is always worth the effort!"*

Gary Direnfeld, MSW, RSW,
Parent-Child Relationship Expert & Founder of the I Promise Program–Canada

"As a trauma nurse, I've seen too many teens suffer and die because of car crashes that didn't have to happen. Do everything you can to keep your teen out of the emergency room—starting with using this book."

Sheila MacDonell, RN, MICN, TNCC–California

*"**3 Keys to Keeping Your Teen Alive** by Anne Marie Hayes is a comprehensive resource that fills a tremendous need for parents to work through guiding their child to become a safe driver. The interactive style of this resource between teen and parent provides a tool for families to work together through the teen driver experience. National Organizations for Youth Safety (NOYS) believes that all work done to address youth safety should be done with youth and not to youth. This resource supports that model and supports parent/teen learning relationships."*

Sandy Spavone, Executive Director of
National Organizations for Youth Safety (NOYS)–Washington, D.C.

"As a police officer but more importantly as a parent I have one thing to say—outstanding! This is a true hands-on tool which should be used by all parents and new teen drivers. I am confident that if the parent and teen work through the book and multi-media program together they will not only enhance their driving but their relationship as well. (Anne Marie Hayes) has obviously put a lot of hard work and research into creating a quality product and should be commended for (her) efforts. The 3 Keys methodology is a nice touch to the novel concept of actively engaged parenting ... I tried to find something (she) might have overlooked but came away empty handed."

Police Officer

"What Anne Marie Hayes has put together in the '3 Keys' program is a comprehensive guide for parents, new drivers, and anyone with a student at the wheel. From navigating your first day out, to understanding your vehicle, this is the one publication to keep handy at all times—especially in your first year of driving."

Karen & Alan Klayman–Pennsylvania

*"I highly recommend, **3 Keys to Keeping Your Teen Alive** to any parent or teenager who is considering getting a learner's driving permit. As the mother of three teens, I especially appreciated the checklists and quizzes included in this book. Also invaluable were the links to related videos, which capture the attention of tech savvy teens. Thanks Anne Marie, you have helped with my own bad (speeding when late) driving habits as well!"*

Leslie Hustins–Ontario, Canada

3 KEYS TO KEEPING YOUR TEEN ALIVE

Lessons for Surviving the First Year of Driving

Anne Marie Hayes

NEW YORK

3 KEYS TO KEEPING YOUR TEEN ALIVE

Lessons for Surviving the First Year of Driving

Anne Marie Hayes

ISBN 978-1-60037-884-3 Paperback
ISBN 978-1-60037-885-0 e-Pub Version
Library of Congress Control Number: 2010939483

Published by:

Morgan James Publishing
The Entrepreneurial Publisher
5 Penn Plaza, 23rd Floor
New York City, New York 10001
(212) 655-5470 Office
(516) 908-4496 Fax
www.MorganJamesPublishing.com

Cover Design by:
Rachel Lopez
rachel@r2cdesign.com

Interior Design by:
Bonnie Bushman
bbushman@breanan.net

Photography Credits
Page 15 © FLASHON/Veer
Page 66 © IOFOTO/Veer
Page 120 ©DEKLOFENAK/Veer
Page 175 ©AVAVA/Veer
Page 198 ©COREPICS VOF/Veer
Page 201 ©ROBERT CRUM/Veer
Page 3 ©ELENA ELISSEEVA/Veer
Page 69 ©Robert Adrian Hillman/Dreamstime.com
Page 69 ©Robert Adrian Hillman/Dreamstime.com

Clipart Credits
Clipart images are ©2010 Jupiterimages Corporation

Other Images
My special thanks to Sydney Stone, Erica Riedy, Eric Venuto, Joshua-Martin Lederman, Lucas Pinheiro, Richard Brady, Kenneth Svensson, Andrea Agostini, Samantha Garrett and all the other talented young artists who contributed their illustrations to this workbook. You can see what great work they do—so hire them if you get the chance. For information about how to reach them, please send me an email at AMHayes@TeensLearntoDrive.com.

In an effort to support local communities, raise awareness and funds, Morgan James Publishing donates one percent of all book sales for the life of each book to Habitat for Humanity.

Get involved today, visit

www.HelpHabitatForHumanity.org.

Special thanks to:

My beautiful daughter, Emily, who inspired me to write this book. I love her and need her and want her to live to be a happy, healthy old lady. I wrote this book because statistics show—*if I lose her as a teenager*—it will most likely be in a car crash and I can't let that happen.

My wonderful husband, Al, who has supported everything I do for more than twenty years. He has helped me with this project in more ways than I can say. I love him and need him and look forward to being a happy, healthy old lady at his side.

And my mom, Mary Ellen, the English teacher who gave me a love for learning and writing. She's also supported me and my brothers and sister throughout the stages of our lives. I am grateful that she is happy and healthy but she will never be old to me.

Author's Note

The English language is outdated.

Traditionally our language has preferred boys. "He" and "him" were used as the neutral pronouns as in: "Talk to your teen and ask him what he wants."

That might have worked a hundred years ago when men still ruled the world, but it doesn't work now. If I picked up a book and read 'he—he- he' I'd think, "This book isn't for me at all!"

So I consulted grammatical experts. It seems I'm not the first person to have this problem. They unanimously offered 4 options:

1. I could go with tradition, use 'he' and 'him' (and alienate all teen girls)
2. I could use "s/he" or "he or she" and "him or her" (which is lengthy and cumbersome)
3. I could alternate between male and female pronouns in different sections (which is confusing but alienates everyone equally).
4. I could use 'they' and 'them' as singular pronouns as in, "Ask your teen what they want."

I opted for the last. It sounds a little awkward at first but you'll get used to it.

Foreword

By Sandy Spavone,
Executive Director of National Organizations for Youth Safety (NOYS)–Washington, DC

As parents, we spend months preparing for the births of our children. We guide them through the "terrible twos" and prepare them for that first day of school. We help them deal with the challenges of middle school and spend hours in sports camps and practices for the various activities that help them become well-rounded children. Until, one day we turn the corner to find ourselves in the unique new role of 'driver educator.'

Teaching a teen to drive safe and be safe on the road is one of the most important roles and interactions a parent will have with their teen. For too long, parents have had few resources to guide them through this awesome responsibility.

3 Keys to Keeping Your Teen Alive is a comprehensive resource that fills a tremendous need for parents to work through guiding their child to become a safe driver.

The interactive style of this resource between teen and parent provides a tool for families to work together through the teen driver experience. National Organizations for Youth Safety (NOYS) believes that all work done to address youth safety should be done with youth and not to youth. This resource supports that model and supports parent/teen learning relationships.

Preface

This workbook is part of a multimedia program for teaching teens to become safe drivers. It is the result of thousands of hours of research and incorporates tips and recommendations based on the best practices of leading safety organizations across North America. The developer is a professional trainer who has used those skills to present the information in ways that will interest teens and make the process simple for parents to follow.

This program includes:

- 20 Fundamental Driving Lessons that are critical for every new driver to master. These lessons include skills like backing up, various types of parking, right & left turns, driving on country roads, passing, high-speed highways and more.
- 5 Advanced Lessons to help new drivers cope with combinations of hazards like highway driving at night.
- Free access to the video library at TeensLearntoDrive.com. The videos are arranged to accompany the lessons. Links to professional driving videos show how to execute road maneuvers correctly. Youtube videos underscore the tragic consequences that can occur when drivers make mistakes or are distracted.
- The 3 key elements necessary for successful driver training programs. (Actively Involved Parents, Need-to-Know-Info and Structured Practice)
- Facts, opportunities for discussion and stories about real teens who made tragic mistakes—to help teen drivers make good decisions.
- Quizzes, activities and games to keep teens interested and reinforce the lessons.
- Tips, tools and checklists to help parents & coaches be successful and ensure they cover critical skills and techniques during practice driving sessions.
- The most current information from trusted sources like The National Highway Traffic Safety Administration (NHTSA), the Insurance Institute for Highway Safety (IIHS), The Governor's Highway Safety Administration (GHSA) and other road-safety focused organizations.
- Information about the latest products and safety features available to help keep teen drivers safe.
- A structure that complements Graduated Driver Licensing (GDL) programs

Some of the tools that are provided in this program include:

- Driving Logs to ensure drivers get sufficient practice and cover all the bases
- A Customizable Teen Passenger Contract to keep your teen safe when they ride as passengers with other teen drivers
- A Customizable Teen-Parent Driving Contract
- Checklists for Basic, Intermediate and Advanced Driving Skills
- Checklists to cover various road, weather, and light conditions
- Basic vehicle maintenance information and checklists
- The "Accident Report" Checklist
- And more!

Acknowledgments

A Note of Thanks to My Heroes:

My heroes are not mountain climbers or sports figures or actors. They are ordinary people who try to make the world a better, safer place for all of us. All the people who helped me with this book are my heroes.

Some are parents who, despite their own unbearable losses, work every day to make sure other families won't have to suffer the way theirs does.

Others are talented people who do jobs that are often underpaid and thankless. They do their chosen work with grace and diligence because they know that what they do benefits and protects the rest of us.

Thank you all—

Renee Napier of the Meagan Napier Foundation; Phillip and Mary Dickson, Gary, Raine and Eric Smallridge, Mark Cox of the Bridgestone Winter Driving School; Gary Direnfeld of Ipromise.com; S/Sgt. Don C. Fawcett of the Ontario Provincial Police; Dick and Jonathon Fischer of LiveFastDriveSlow.com; Jennifer Smith of FocusDriven.com, Denise Gallagher, Matt McIntyre, Tim Hollister of fromReidsDad.org, Lauren Pearce (the Driving Instructor Extraordinaire!); Barry and Chris Marcone; Carole McDonnell of "Maggie's Law"; Linda Mulkey of HangUpSaveaLife.com; Officer Al Perez of the Start Smart Program, California Highway Patrol in Los Angeles County, CA; Sergeant Gus Ramirez of the Highway Patrol in Sante Fe County New Mexico; Dianne Sipe and Laura &Vincent Marchetti of the Katie Marchetti Memorial Foundation; Lyndsay Atkinson, Darrel Drobnich of the National Sleep Foundation, Dr. David Strayer of the University of Utah; Sandy Spavone of National Organizations for Youth Safety, Aaron Chatten, Shannon Campbell and Amber Rollins of KidsandCars.org, Alan and Karen Klayman, Erin Meluso of RADD, Jacqueline Hackett, Roy Bavaro, John Graham, Dean Johnson of The Sandy Johnson Foundation, Trevor Hoff and Ruth Kristi of Farm Safety 4 Just Kids, Bill Combs of Driver Education and Training Administrators and Dr. Dale Wisely.

Thanks to Fred Manocherian and Ralph Nader for being the pioneers in car safety advocacy—and never giving up. Their work has saved countless lives.

Thanks to all the friends and relatives who jumped on my bandwagon and supported me throughout this journey. Special thanks to Shannon and Bob Hogan, and Philip van Munching who helped me more than he knows.

A Message from Meagan Napier's Mom

End every conversation and meeting with "I love you" because you never know …

Those were the last words I said to Meagan and that gives me peace.

Introduction

Countless governments, police departments and private safety organizations have done dozens of studies and reports that focused on 1 thing—***keeping teen drivers safe***. All the information they compiled can be boiled down into 3 key elements that are critical to helping teens become responsible, safe drivers.

The 3 key elements are:

1. **Actively Involved Parents**—to coach & support teens and monitor their driving behavior
2. **'Need-to-Know' Info**—solid information teens can use to make wise choices
3. **Structured Practice**—to develop good habits, reinforce learning and help create solid reflexive driving skills.

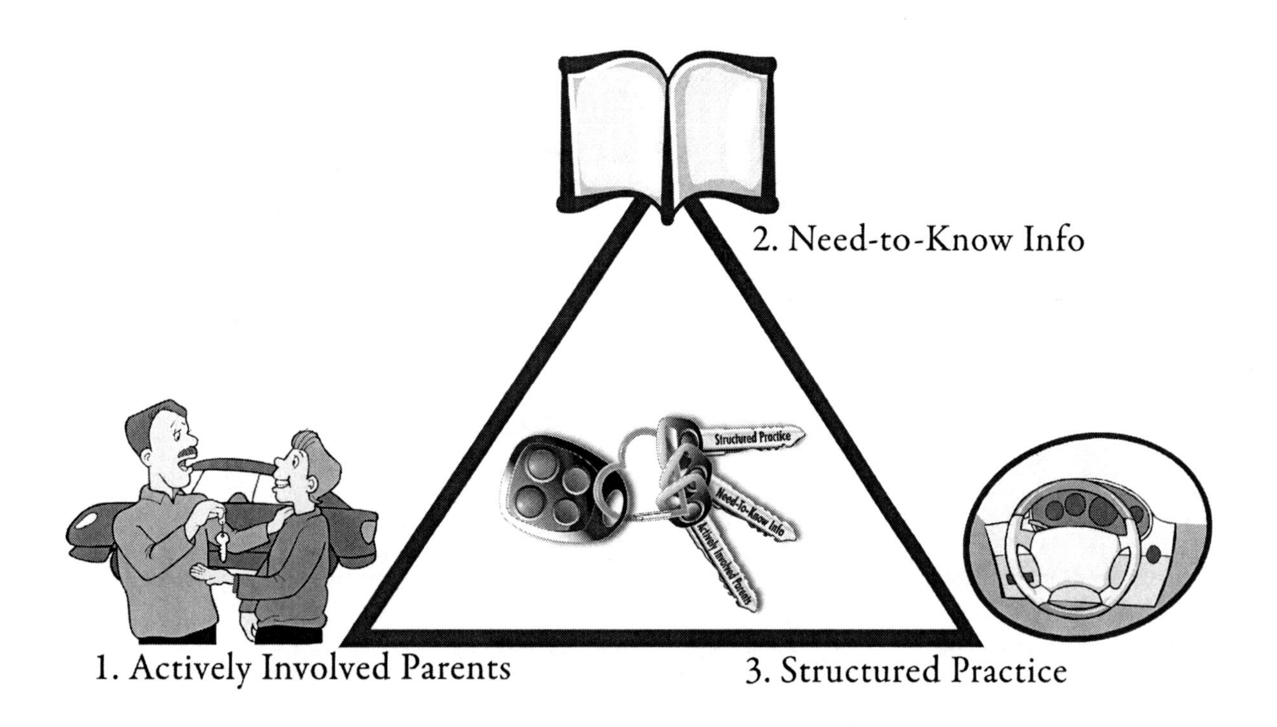

The 3 Keys

At every stage of driver-training programs, all 3 'Keys' are necessary. This program is designed to provide important information, tips and tools for each of the 3 Keys, at the appropriate time for teens progressing through Graduated Driver Licensing Programs.

Table of Contents

Overview of The 3 Keys:

Key #1 

This section provides important information to help parents understand and perform their roles as coaches and monitors during each stage of their teen driver's development.

Key #2 

Every new driver should start with an excellent professional driver-training program, (you'll find some tips on how to choose the right one for you on page 266.) but that's not nearly enough. There are so many things to know that even the best courses can't cover everything.

This book contains crucial information on topics including:

- Driving skills
- Dealing with distractions
- How to develop safe driving habits
- Car operation and basic maintenance
- What to do in an emergency
- Common problems and how to avoid them
- Driving etiquette
- Insurance tips
- Parking lot and roadside safety
- And more!

The lessons in this book are reinforced through fun activities, true stories and quizzes. Even parents who've been driving for years will learn some things they didn't know.

Key #3 

New drivers need lots of practice—at least 100 hours on the road in the first year. (State/provincial requirements vary but experts recommend 100 hours.)

That works out to about 2 hours every week, which isn't easy in our world of long workdays and extracurricular activities.

That's why driving practice must be scheduled and consistent. This book includes a Driver's Log (page 268) to help you keep track.

In addition, the practice sessions must begin with basics and gradually include new information and techniques. It must cover all kinds of roads, different times of day, and various weather conditions. The 'Structured Practice' sections include 20 comprehensive driving lessons that cover basic skills plus 5 more lessons that feature advanced driving skills. They also provide lots of valuable information and tools to make sure you cover all the bases. There are lots of tips for making the most of your coaching sessions and checklists to help you introduce new skills at the right time.

How This Program is Organized

There are 2 elements to the "3 Keys" program:

A. This workbook
B. The companion website at TeensLearntoDrive.com

A. This Workbook

This workbook provides a step-by-step plan for preparing teens to be safe drivers. The diagram below shows how each section is organized and when you should begin working on it.

NOTE: If your area has only 2 levels of licensing, combine the Provisional License section and the Final License section.

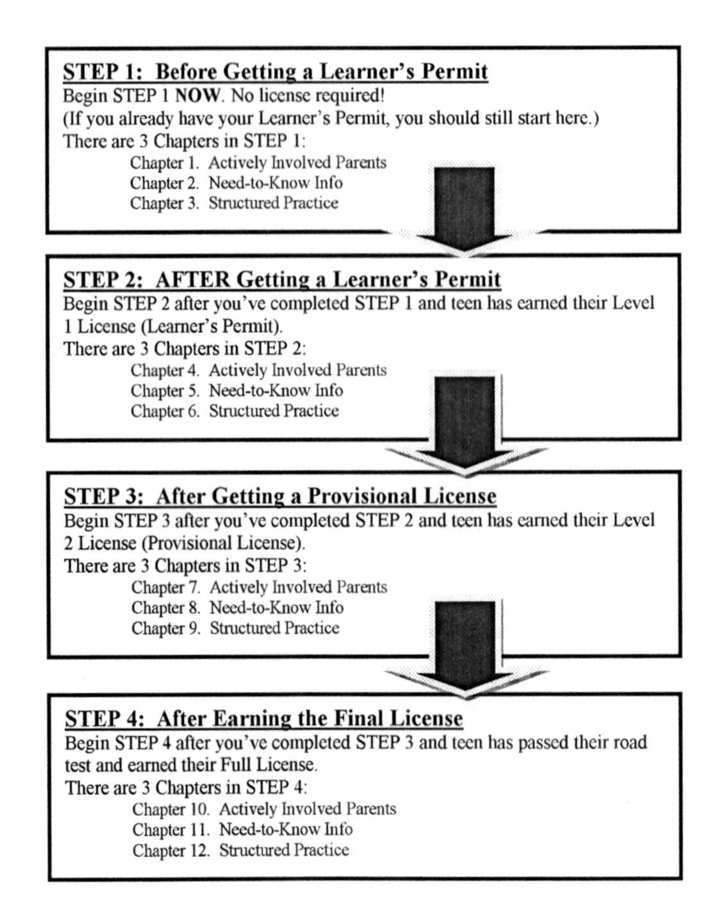

B. The Companion Website at:

http://TeensLearntoDrive.com

This may look like a regular workbook, but it's also your free ticket to the best driving resources on the web!

Take a look around the site now. You'll find lots of great resources including articles, games, videos and information about driving laws in your state or province.

To access the complete free video library, go to the home page and enter your name, email address and city in the boxes under "Free Video Library". A new page called "Full Video Library" will open. (*Don't forget to add this page to your "Favorites".)

On the "Full Video Library" page, you'll find links to all 25 of the Structured Driving lessons that are included in this workbook. Each lesson-link takes you to great instructional videos and online resources to accompany the topics in that lesson.

Everything's been organized for you, so it follows the Graduated Driver Licensing (GDL) program formats. The advantage of this system allows parents and teens to receive information and tools when they need them instead of being overloaded with information they won't need for another 6 months or a year.

TIP: Don't forget to add this site to your favorites because you'll be returning often.

Before Getting a Learner's Permit

In This Section:

- Parents—Seize the Day!
- Which Parent Are You?
- How to Be a Great Role Model
- Preparing Your Teen to be a Passenger
- The Teen Passenger Contract
- Teen—Are You Ready to Learn to Drive?
- Test Your Driving Knowledge Quiz
- True or FOAF Quiz
- Graduated Driver Licensing 101
- Responsibilities of the Passenger
- Getting Your Local Driver Training Manual
- Maintenance Basics Everyone Needs to Know
- Your Car's Fluids
- Your Tires: Where the Rubber Meets the Road!
- Saturday with Dad* Checklist
- Chapter Review Crossword Puzzle

Chapter 1
Actively Involved Parents
Before Getting a Learner's Permit

Seize the Day!

Every parent remembers the day their child mastered the 2-wheeler. Perhaps there were a few preliminary lessons, maybe even a few skinned knees, but on that momentous day—

You gripped the back of the seat to help them get their balance and offered a few words of encouragement like "I know you can do it!"

Then you jogged alongside until their balance was firm and let go without saying a word.

You watched and held your breath.

They began steadily, believing you were still by their side, and then suddenly realized they were on their own! For a moment—a look of panic replaced the smile. They wobbled a bit and then abruptly regained their balance and forged ahead—solo!

You beamed from the sidelines—the proud parent of the smartest kid in the world! *You're smiling even now—aren't you?* Those memories are powerful! The experience of teaching them to ride bonded you together.

Being able to ride a 2-wheeled bike is a big step for a kid. It gives them instant self-confidence, status among their friends and expands their world. Helping them get there is rewarding in a way only a parent can appreciate.

But your job wasn't over. Once they graduated to 2-wheeled rider-status you imposed strict rules regarding where & when they could go, helmet use, no passengers and other rules with one object in mind—to keep them safe. When they went too far or removed their helmet they lost their riding privileges for a week or two, until they could prove they were responsible enough to get the bike back. Their safety was the most important thing!

Your next challenge looms!

Now as that child approaches sixteen—your next challenge looms. You've got to up your game this time because the stakes are much higher. A powerful vehicle weighing two tons or more has replaced the bike, and the Band-Aids & kisses could be replaced by a wheelchair or even a headstone.

A Car is Not a Bike with 4 Wheels

A car is not a bike with 4 wheels, so a few spur-of-the-moment trips around the parking lot won't do to prepare your teen to drive a car. They need a professional driving program and lots of structured driving practice so they can gain the experience they need to survive on the road.

Every Trip is Different

Every trip in a car is different. There are so many variables: the weather, the road conditions, the other drivers …

This program provides lots of tools, tips and checklists to make sure you cover all the bases.

Bike Rules—Car Rules

Just like the 'bike rules,' you need to talk with your teen about your family rules for driving. Review the sections in this book that outline potential dangers—together. Talk about them and do the activities. This is one case where "I thought you meant" really won't do.

Use the contract to put your rules and the consequences for breaking them—in writing. Both of you sign it. Then monitor your teen's adherence to them and enforce the consequences immediately if the rules are broken.

Trading Blocks for Miles

And whereas that bike expanded your child's world by blocks, a car explodes their world by miles! That distance and independence expose your teen to situations and potential dangers they've never before encountered. This book provides information and tools to help you prepare your teen to make wise decisions there as well.

The Motivated Learner

Being able to ride a 2-wheeler was important to your child. Teaching them how made you godlike in their eyes. By the time they've reached their teens, however, that glow of admiration has faded. Now they know you aren't perfect, and they are. And they challenge most of what you say!

The great thing is that they need you again. They can't get their license without you (their permit requires your signature). So once again, you have a truly motivated student who will linger on your every word—until they get the keys.

Seize the Day!

Your window of opportunity is brief. Don't wait until it's too late!

You Will Make a Difference

Research shows that teens pay a lot more attention to what parents say than we think they do. They may roll their eyes and look like they want the ground to open under us.

They may stomp their feet and slam the door behind them. But then they go away and think about what we said. Our words and example do make a difference.

Years from now they may even appreciate it. You'll know for sure when it comes time for them to teach their own teens to drive.

Parents: Are You Up to the Challenge?

Imagine lying awake in bed, waiting to hear the front door open so you'll know your teen is home safely.

But tonight, the doorbell rings instead. Your heart stops when you see the police officers in the doorway, and you know instantly that your life will never be the same again.

Wouldn't you do ANYTHING to go back and change things? By then it will be too late. The time to prepare your teen to drive and survive is NOW!

This book provides a simple step-by-step plan to prepare teens to become safe, responsible drivers. It's straightforward and easy to follow but will take a lot of time, patience and dedication from both of you—parent and teen.

Isn't it worth it?

You have to decide now. After the crash will be too late. Before you say you'd do ***anything***, figure out—

Which Parent are You?

When it comes to parenting teens, there are 5 types of parents:

1. The BFF Parent—Best Friend Forever Parent
2. The DADT—Don't Ask, Don't Tell Parent
3. The "I Would if I had Time" Parent
4. The "Gotcha" Parent
5. The "Whatever it Takes" Parent

1. The BFF Parent—(Best Friend Forever)

This parent tries to be cool and wants to be their teen's best buddy. They'd love to be voted "Most Popular Parent." Popularity means everything to them so they encourage their teen to do things just to be popular.

BFF parents may allow things other parents don't—like drinking alcohol underage at home because "they're going to drink anyway and at least I know what's going on."

The BFF parent is afraid to make rules or enforce consequences because they don't want their teen to get mad at them. They may threaten from time to time, but give in easily. Their teen knows exactly what buttons to push and plays them like a song.

Sadly, when the teen gets older, they'll probably equate that permissiveness with not caring.

2. The DADT Parent—(Don't Ask, Don't Tell)

This parent makes threats and sets consequences but never follows through. They'd rather not know about problems because doing something about them is inconvenient.

They were thrilled when their teens learned to drive because it meant ***they*** could finally stop running a taxi service and get on with their own lives.

They may set consequences for driving infractions but really don't want to enforce them—especially if that means suspension of driving privileges for the offender. If their teen stops driving, ***they'll*** have to start taking the kids to lessons and activities again—and there's no way they're going back to that!

You'll often hear them say things like:

"If you do that again, we aren't going swimming."

Followed by:

"I told you not to do that! If you do it again—we're not going swimming!"

Followed by:

"What is wrong with you? I told you not to do that. If you do it again—we're ***really*** not going swimming!"

Followed by:

"Hurry up. It's time to go swimming."

3. The "I Would if I had Time" Parent

These parents probably make a lot of money and spend a lot of time on their cell phones. When it comes to family—they spend money instead of time. Their kids have lots of stuff. They understand their family has needs and hire the best people to take care of them.

Image is important to them—and that includes their family. If their son loses his license for speeding—that will look bad—so they'll hire a lawyer to make the tickets go away instead. They don't really think about what they're teaching their teens until it's too late.

Note: Some parents work long hours or shifts because of the jobs they do. Others are single parents or have other challenges. There aren't enough hours in the day for them to do all the things they'd like to do with their families. They do not belong in this group. They are "Whatever It Takes" Parents (Group 5). It might be necessary for them to find a different driving coach for their teen.

4. The "Gotcha" Parent

This parent believes in enforcing consequences when rules are disobeyed. The problem is that they don't always make the rules clear upfront. So, even when their kids try to do the right thing, they sometimes misinterpret fuzzy rules. Then they get punished for their mistakes and that's unfair.

Eventually those teens might think, "Who cares? I might as well take risks and break the rules because I'm going to get punished anyway."

5. The "Whatever it Takes" Parent

This Mom or Dad knows that being a parent is the toughest job in the world. They love their kids unconditionally but understand that taking care of them can be inconvenient, frustrating and even—infuriating! They routinely sacrifice their own comfort for them and accept that there will still be times when their kids think they're the meanest parents in the world.

They think twice before making rules and ensure the punishments for infractions fit the crimes and provide a deterrent. Then they make sure their teens understand exactly what will happen if they break the rules.

They follow through with the stated punishment even though it breaks their hearts when their teens miss out on fun, as a result. But they know that unless they follow through every time, their kids won't take the rules seriously. And they know that in the end—keeping them safe and teaching them how to thrive in the world are ***their*** most important goals.

How to Be a Great Role Model

Now is a great time to review your own driving habits too. Take a look around you on the road any day and you'll see drivers—over 30—doing all kinds of things while they're driving. We eat, drink, smoke, talk, play with the GPS, consult our shopping lists, change radio stations, etc. We do these things because we take driving for granted.

Our teens are watching. They believe if *we* can do it—*they* can do it too. They don't realize we have more experience behind the wheel and that—*so far*—we've been very, very lucky!

Need to Brush-up Your Skills?

If you feel your skills need a brush-up, many driving schools provide excellent courses for parent co-pilots who are teaching their teens to drive. Check them out. You don't want to pass your bad habits on to your teen. (Updating your skills can't hurt either.)

Teaching your teens to drive responsibly is more important than anything else you're likely to do this year. It's a very serious business. **It's a matter of life and death.**

Are you the Best Coach for Your Teen?

Be honest. Do you have nerves of steel? Are you naturally patient and reassuring? Are you attentive, focused and a good communicator with excellent driving skills?

If you aren't, consider finding a friend or relative who can coach your teen—or hire a professional.

Preparing Your Teen to be a Passenger

Your teen may not be driving yet but they probably know other teens who are. You need to protect them from other teen drivers too.

Who is Your Teen Riding With?

You are committed to making sure your teens are safe when they drive (that's why you bought this book.) But what about their friends?

Is that boy your daughter's going out with on Friday as well prepared as your daughter will be—or is he an Eddie Haskell-type who will smile and nod and pull slowly away from the curb until he gets out of sight and then put the pedal to the metal and risk her life?

Will your son's best friend be talking on his cell phone and texting as he drives down the highway tonight?

Do you really want to take that chance?

Tip from Lauren, the Driving Instructor:

Note to Parents:

Remember—YOU are in control.

You have every right as a parent to take the keys away from your teen if they're abusing their driving privilege.

Make sure you have rules in place (*i.e. your driving contract*) about what your teen can and cannot do behind the wheel and have punishments in place for breaking the rules.

If you ever feel like your new driver is failing to be responsible behind the wheel DO NOT HESITATE to take away their privilege.

They may say they hate you for it today, but it could save their life, and it will help teach them about the responsibility of driving.

Remind your teen that driving is not a right, but a privilege, and that they are ***not entitled*** to drive.

(You'll find Lauren's Bio in the Resources section of TeensLearntoDrive.com)

This Can be Tricky ...

Other parents may not realize how dangerous it can be for their kids to be passengers in vehicles driven by other teens, so you could be on your own here.

Teens hate to be singled out and would prefer if their parents never question anything they want to do. But that's not what parenting is about. It's our job to help them make wise decisions and stay safe. Sometimes that's hard and we may ruffle a few feathers.

First, understand that you have the right—no, ***the obligation***—to say "no" when your teen asks if they can go out in someone else's car, if you think it could create an unsafe situation. Don't automatically say "yes."

If they really want to go somewhere and you're concerned about the skill-level or habits of the proposed driver, try to come to some acceptable compromise. Maybe your teen can drive (once they are licensed) or they can take the bus, etc. 'No' to the driver—doesn't necessarily mean 'no' to the activity.

Before your teen gets in the car with any other teen driver, consider the:

- Driver
- Vehicle
- Time of day
- Types of roads they'll be traveling
- Event they'll be attending
- Other passengers in the car.

The Driver:

- Do they have a valid driver's license? (*Are you sure?)*
- How long have they been driving? (Learner permits don't count!)
  NOTE: The first 6 months are the most dangerous for new drivers.
- It takes at least 3 years for drivers to develop reflexive driving skills.
- Have they ever ***been pulled*** over for a moving violation?

A lot of teens get pulled over but talk their way out of tickets.

- Have they had any speeding tickets or accidents? If you don't know—ask them or call their parents and ask. (While you're at it—find out whether their parents consider them good drivers.)
- The fact that they're nice kids doesn't mean they're good, responsible drivers.

The Vehicle:

- Sports cars and "hot" cars are out. They make speeding and showing off too tempting.
- You don't have to do a 50-point inspection but make sure the vehicle looks safe.
- If it's not the family car, is it fully insured?

The Time of Day:

- Remember that weekends after dark are the most dangerous—especially after midnight so set your curfew accordingly.

The Types of Roads They'll be Traveling:

- Highway driving is most dangerous due to the speed and unpredictability of other drivers.
- Country roads can be dangerous at night because they don't have streetlights and teens are often tempted to speed when there are no other cars around.

The Event They'll be Attending:

- Some events are more likely to involve drugs or alcohol.

Other Passengers in the Car:

- Who else will be in the car?
- Remember that the chance of a crash goes up significantly with each additional teen in the car.

The Teen Passenger Contract

In the Appendix at the back of this book, you'll find the "**Teen-Passenger Contract.**" Remove it from the book and complete it with your teens.

Change, add or delete items until you have a contract you are comfortable with.

Sign it and post it in a place where you'll see it often (like near the fridge.)

Periodically check in with your teens and make sure they're still abiding by the rules. Adjust the list of allowed drivers and situations, as necessary.

Note: The first year of driving is the most dangerous, so select drivers with a year or more of driving experience, if possible.

Chapter 2
Need-to-Know Info
Before Getting a Learner's Permit

Picture yourself behind the wheel of your dream vehicle:

You're cruising with your friends on the perfect day. The sun is shining and you're on top of the world! You're laughing at something your best friend just said when your favorite song comes on the radio and you lean over to-

Suddenly—in the blink of an eye—everything changes! Maybe the guy in the car ahead jams on his brakes or an animal dashes onto the road. Maybe a big truck swerves into your lane or you hit a patch of ice—but *now* that 2-ton metal can you're riding in could become a weapon of mass destruction! Your friends start screaming ...

This is the moment when all your training comes into play. If you were well prepared—your instincts will take over and save your lives. If you weren't—it's too late now!

Would this crash be your fault? No—*but you and your friends would be just as dead or broken.* The roads are unpredictable. You can't control the weather, the road conditions or what other drivers do. But you *can* control what *you* do, beginning right here by learning how to become a safe, responsible driver.

Isn't it worth it?

First—Are You Ready to Learn to Drive?

Driving is a privilege—not a rite of passage.

Not every teen is ready to drive when the government says they're eligible to start learning. Driving takes concentration, good judgment, and a willingness to listen and learn. It also requires the right attitude and personal habits.

Complete the quiz on the following page. Review the results with your parent.

• • • • •

Parents: Do you agree with your teen's answers? Do you feel they have what it takes to start driving?

Be honest. Teens mature at different rates and you don't want to make a decision now that you'll regret later.

If you don't think your teen is ready—tell them why. Create a plan together to help them strengthen the skills they lack. For example: if they're always late—talk about that. Come up with a plan together to help them manage their time better.

Agree to reassess the situation when they can demonstrate a pattern of improvement.

• • • • •

If—after the quiz—you agree that the time is now—you're ready to get started!

The "Are You Ready to Learn to Drive?" Quiz

Circle your answers to the questions below. Add up how many times you used each answer and enter the total in the box at the bottom of each column. Go to page 231 to find out how you did.

Are You Ready to Learn to Drive? A Self-Evaluation

1	I leave plenty of time to get somewhere so I don't have to rush.	Always	Usually	Rarely	Never
2	I'm punctual.	Always	Usually	Rarely	Never
3	People say I'm reliable.	Always	Usually	Rarely	Never
4	I focus on what I'm doing and am not easily distracted.	Always	Usually	Rarely	Never
5	I think things through and make good decisions.	Always	Usually	Rarely	Never
6	I do what I say I'll do.	Always	Usually	Rarely	Never
7	I plan ahead and make sure I'm prepared for unexpected problems.	Always	Usually	Rarely	Never
8	I have an even temperament and don't get angry or flustered easily.	Always	Usually	Rarely	Never
9	I have excellent hand-eye coordination.	Always	Usually	Rarely	Never
10	I listen well and follow instructions.	Always	Usually	Rarely	Never
11	I have good judgment and can make quick decisions when I need to.	Always	Usually	Rarely	Never
12	I'm not afraid to tell my friends when they're out of line.	Always	Usually	Rarely	Never
13	I'm alert and don't daydream excessively.	Always	Usually	Rarely	Never
14	I practice new skills until I get them right.	Always	Usually	Rarely	Never
15	I'm proud of what I accomplish.	Always	Usually	Rarely	Never
16	I like to do things well.	Always	Usually	Rarely	Never
17	I take care of my things.	Always	Usually	Rarely	Never
18	I am a problem solver.	Always	Usually	Rarely	Never
19	I take my responsibilities seriously.	Always	Usually	Rarely	Never
20	I ask questions when I don't understand something.	Always	Usually	Rarely	Never
21	I follow rules.	Always	Usually	Rarely	Never
22	I keep my word.	Always	Usually	Rarely	Never
	Totals				

Test Your Driving Knowledge QUIZ

Teens & Parents: Complete this quiz separately and compare your answers.

Circle your answers. (The answers are on page 232.)

1. The best hand-position for steering is:
   a) 10 o'clock and 2 o'clock
   b) 9 o'clock and 3 o'clock
   c) Wherever your hands are comfortable as long as you sit with the correct posture
2. **TRUE / FALSE:** Teens should not keep their cell phones in the car when they are driving.
3. **TRUE / FALSE:** Driving while impaired by drugs or alcohol is the biggest risk to young teen drivers.
4. **TRUE / FALSE:** You aren't really speeding if you drive at the same speed as the other traffic.
5. **TRUE / FALSE:** Pregnant women shouldn't wear seatbelts.
6. Drivers are driving impaired if:
   a) They've been drinking alcohol
   b) They've taken illegal drugs
   c) They are extremely tired
   d) All of the above.
7. **TRUE / FALSE:** Cruise control provides a safe way to maintain a constant speed in any weather.
8. **TRUE / FALSE:** Airbags protect drivers, whether or not they wear seatbelts.
9. **TRUE / FALSE:** A seatbelt will not protect you if you recline your seat.
10. Most car crashes involving teen drivers happen:
   a) On the way to school
   b) On the way home from school
   c) Late at night
   d) All of the above
11. **TRUE / FALSE**: When a teen is driving—the more teen passengers there are, the more likely they will be involved in a crash.
12. **TRUE / FALSE:** The most important driving skill is to be able to handle the car.
13. **TRUE / FALSE:** Teens who attend Driver's Training Courses have fewer crashes than those who don't.
14. If you're involved in a crash and aren't wearing your seatbelt, you are:

a) twice as likely to die
b) 4 times as likely to die
c) 8 times as likely to die
d) 16 times as likely to die

15. **TRUE / FALSE:** It doesn't matter what kind of motor oil you put in your car.

16. **TRUE / FALSE:** Static electricity can cause a fire when you're pumping gas.

17. **TRUE / FALSE:** When you're driving and very tired these things will keep you awake:
a) Caffeine—coffee, Red Bull, etc.
b) Opening the window to let fresh air in
c) Talking or singing
d) All of the above
e) None of the above

18. **TRUE / FALSE:** A tire gauge checks the tread on your tires.

19. **TRUE / FALSE:** If a passenger in your car refuses to wear a seatbelt—that's their problem.

20. **TRUE or FALSE**: If you're driving in the left (fast) lane and the car ahead of you is going too slow, you should flash your headlights to signal them to pull into the slow lane and let you pass

21. **TRUE or FALSE:** Legally—if your car has a "wheelchair" sign or plate, you can park in a handicapped spot—whether or not the person with the disability is riding with you.

22. **TRUE or FALSE:** Video games are good training for teen drivers because they teach quick reflexes.

23. **TRUE or FALSE:** When you call 911, the operator automatically knows where you are.

Bonus Question:

TEST YOUR MATH SKILLS
If you're driving your car at 60 miles per hour (97 kilometers per hour), how fast is your body traveling?
Answer: __________ miles per hour

True or FOAF QUIZ

Everyone's heard strange stories about cars and safety. Some are true and others are false. The false ones are often told as "this really happened to the Friend Of A Friend (FOAF) of mine." That makes them more believable but they still aren't true.

There are a lot of FOAF stories circulating on the Internet. I'll receive one email with information about something from a friend who swears it happened to someone they know. *Three years* later, I'll get the same information from another friend whose 'cousin' just experienced the exact same thing.

Coincidence? I think not!

This kind of thing happens so frequently that websites like Snopes.com exist just to separate fact from fiction. So if you've been duped, don't feel bad. You're certainly not alone.

The emails or stories always come with lots of details that sound realistic. The following quiz gives you the themes from many of them. If you want to read the whole stories, you'll find most of them on snopes.com.

(The answers on page 233 may surprise you!)

Can you separate fact from fiction? Test your knowledge:

1. True or FOAF Seatbelts are dangerous because they can decapitate the wearer.
2. True or FOAF Airbags can burst into flames and burn the driver or the passenger.
3. True or FOAF Sometimes passengers who don't wear seatbelts get saved because they're ejected from the vehicle.
4. True or FOAF It's safe to ride in the backseat without a seatbelt because the front seat protects you.
5. True or FOAF '#77' immediately connects you to the local highway patrol.
6. True or FOAF Don't flash your headlights when you see an oncoming car driving (at night) without headlights. This is a gang initiation ploy. Gang members shoot the drivers who flash their lights.
7. True or FOAF Using a cell phone while pumping gas can start a fire or set off an explosion.
8. True or FOAF Static electricity can start a fire or set off an explosion while you're pumping gas.
9. True or FOAF Police officers have been killed when they try to help motorists get into their cars with slimjims. The slimjim triggers the side airbag to explode, causing the slimjim to stab the officer.
10. True or FOAF You can do this to avoid losing points with your speeding ticket: Pay a little more than the ticket (e.g. $79 instead of $75) and you'll get a refund for the difference. Don't cash the refund check. This will disrupt the system so they can't process the points against your license.
11. True or FOAF You can beat a Breathalyzer by shoving a penny in your mouth just before you take it.
12. True or FOAF You can beat a speed trap by hanging a CD from your mirror. It confuses the radar gun so it can't get a proper reading.

13. True or FOAF — Seatbelts ***CAUSE*** as many injuries as they prevent—especially in fires or under water.
14. True or FOAF — It's dangerous to use cruise control when it's raining or the roads are wet.
15. True or FOAF — Thieves can electronically duplicate your remote code when you lock your car and use it to break into it after you leave.
16. True or FOAF — Ironically—one of the biggest opponents of seatbelt laws died because he wasn't wearing one.

Check your answers in the Answers section at the back of the book.

My # of correct answers is _______ out of 16

How did you do?

Graduated Driver Licensing GDL 101

Overview of Graduated Driver Licensing

Graduated Driver Licensing (GDL) programs are more complicated than the old systems but worth every ounce of effort that went into putting them together—***and then some!*** They really do save lives.

Some are better than others. The best ones are the most restrictive. You'll find a link to the rules in your area on our website at TeensLearntoDrive.com. Click on Resources and from the drop-down menu select Local GDL Laws. Print them so you can become familiar with them. You'll also use them to build your Family Driving Rules and Teen-Parent Driving Contracts.

16 Year-old drivers have:

- ***3 times*** more crashes than 17 year-olds
- ***5 times*** more crashes than 18 year-olds

Background

Since the fifties, cars have become a lot safer. Thousands of crash-test dummies have given their lives to help automakers cushion and support vehicles where they need it most. They've added seatbelts with shoulder harnesses and airbags—but still—teens were dying in crashes at catastrophic rates!

So the folks who control and maintain our transportation systems took a closer look at what was causing the crashes involving teen drivers. They found several things that contributed to crashes over and over again. Then they changed the rules for driver licensing to incorporate what they learned.

They added restrictions in those areas, to protect new drivers and give them time to gain experience before they added some of the more difficult challenges of driving.

In the UNITED STATES in 1 year:

- 3,490 teen drivers (15-20) died
- 272,000 teen drivers were seriously injured
- 64% of teens who died in crashes were not wearing seat belts
- 39% of teen-driver deaths involved speeding

NTHSA data for 2006

In CANADA in 1 year:

- 353 teens (15-19) died in crashes
- 24,594 teens (15-19) were seriously injured in crashes
- 360 young adults (20-24) died in crashes
- 26,730 young adults (20-24) were seriously injured in crashes

Traffic Injury Research Foundation 2006

GDL Levels and Restrictions

Most states and provinces have some form of GDL program. The best programs have 3 levels and are most restrictive. The section below provides a sample of what a GDL program might look like.

Level 1 License (Learner's Permit)

Qualifications: Prospective drivers must pass a written test, meet an age requirement and have a parent's permission to qualify for their Level 1 license.

They must have a parent/coach accompanying them in the front passenger seat of the car every time they drive. The coach must be a sober, fully licensed driver.

Level 2 License (Provisional / Restricted License)

Once teens master enough skills to complete the requirements at Level 1 and pass a road test, they graduate to Level 2. Level 2 allows new drivers to drive without an adult under some circumstances. However, restrictions regarding time of day, number of passengers and speed may apply. The restrictions are different in different places so make sure you know the rules in your area.

Level 3 License

This is the full license that most people have. It doesn't include any special restrictions and provides full privileges for driving standard vehicles.

Typical Restrictions

The driving restrictions addressed by GDL programs relate to these areas:

- Night-time driving
- Number of teen passengers allowed in the vehicle
- Speed
- Alcohol and drug use
- Seatbelt use

IMPORTANT: Not wearing a seatbelt continues to be the #1 thing that turns a teen-driver crash into a FATAL teen-driver crash.

You can see from the following charts, the large number of crashes that are influenced by the factors covered in GDL programs.

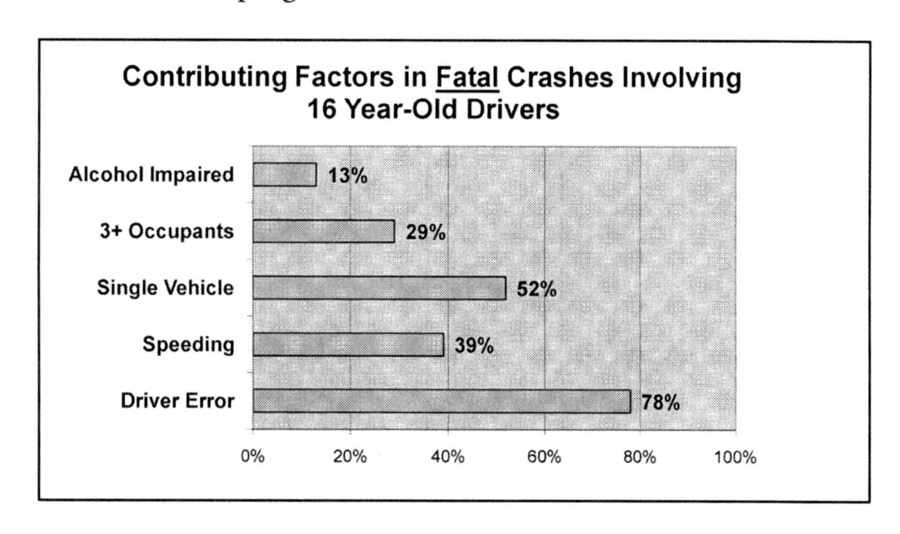

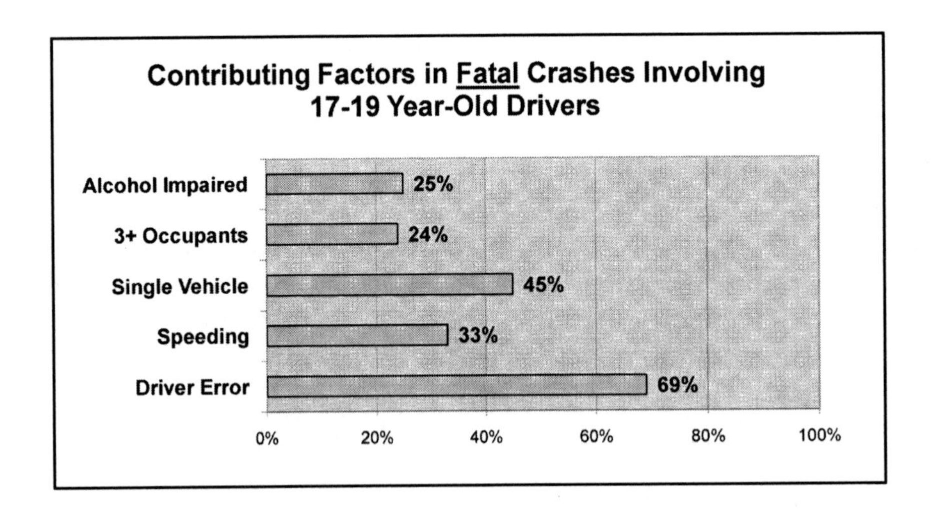

But It Will Never Happen to You, Right?

FACTS—

- Teen drivers are involved in more than 1 million crashes each year!
- 6,000+ teens in the U.S. and Canada die in teen-driver crashes every year!
- More than 300,000 more teens are crippled, burned and mangled!

So let's put that into perspective. How many students are at your high school? 500? 1200? Let's say there are 1,000 to make it easy.

Your High School—1,000 students

What if something horrible and catastrophic, like an earthquake, killed every one of those students! Wouldn't that be beyond devastating? It's unimaginable!

But—what if all the students in 5 surrounding high schools died too?

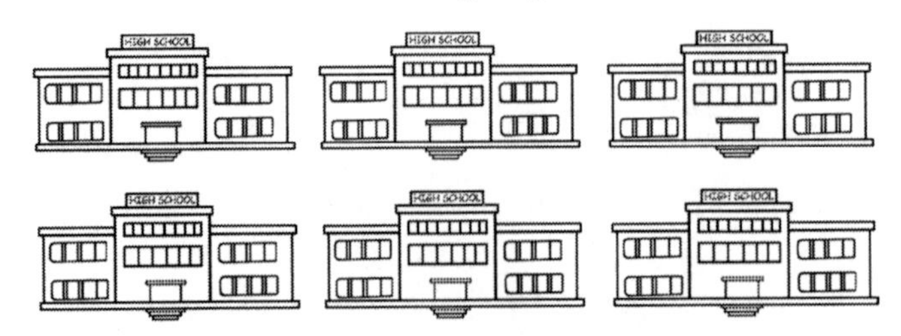

6,000 young lives lost!

That's how many teen drivers die in car crashes every year. Think about their families and all the people who love them. Those lives would be shattered too.

But there's MORE!

There are 300 high schools below. Each of them represents 1,000 teens. That totals 300,000 teens—the number of teens who get seriously injured in teen-driver car crashes every year.

Since there are 4 years of high school, take that final number and **MULTIPLY IT BY 4**. **That's how many teens will be severely injured in teen-driver crashes WHILE YOU'RE IN HIGH SCHOOL! 1,200,000 severe injuries!**

Injuries

When we're talking about the injuries teens sustain in teen-driver crashes each year, we're not talking about scratches and sprained ankles. We're talking about devastating, long-term injuries.

Go to TeensLearntoDrive.com. Select the link to the "Free Video Library" from your "Favorites" (per instructions on page 3). Under "Driving Lesson 2" select "Need-to-Know Info." Click on the video icon with the caption "The Other Breakfast Club" to get a feel for how difficult recovery can really be.

Responsibilities of the Passenger

Pretty soon you're going to be sitting in the driver's seat. Then you'll begin to understand how focused drivers need to be. If they're distracted for just a few moments, bad things can happen.

But for now you're still a passenger, so here's a question for you:

Would you ever tickle the driver or cover their eyes?

Some teens think doing stuff like that is funny but it's really scary and can cause a crash.

You may not do that—but if you were riding in the same car, would you have the guts to tell friends to quit distracting the driver?

- Almost 70% of teens admit they've felt unsafe when someone else was driving.
- Less than half of them would speak up—even though they were scared.

2005 Allstate Foundation study

Passengers have responsibilities too. They need to respect the driver and make sure the environment is calm and safe so the driver can concentrate on driving. This may sound like a no-brainer but sometimes friends do foolish things like encouraging the driver to:

- Read texts or look at photos
- Speed or race other cars
- "Lay rubber" (take off very quickly or screech to a stop so rubber tire tracks are left on the pavement.) This is dangerous, stupid and really reduces the life of your tires.
- "Do donuts" (Skidding around in circles)—Also terrible for tires.
- Chase cars or people. This can be scary and disastrous.
- Jump curbs. (This is stupid, dangerous and causes damage to the car and misaligns the tires.)
- Bark sudden directions so the driver makes quick, dangerous turns. ("Turn right HERE!")

Would you have the courage to tell your friend to stop speeding or driving dangerously?

Some teens say their driving must be good because their friends would tell them if it wasn't.

- Overcrowd the car so some passengers don't have seatbelts and it's hard for the driver to see and hear.

Two out of three teens who die as passengers are in vehicles driven by other teenagers.

Passenger Problems

When you're driving in someone else's car, you can't completely control the environment and that can get you in trouble too. For example, what if you got in a friend's car and found out their cousin in the back seat had illegal drugs with him. What would you do?

Do you know that if police stopped the car, you and the driver could be charged for possession of the drugs too?

What if there was a weapon in the car (like a gun) or an open bottle of alcohol? How would you handle that?

Your parents love you and want to help you make good decisions. They also want you to know that they will make sure you have a safe way to get home, no matter what happens.

Talk about what you should do in situations like these. Then complete the Teen-Passenger Contract. It's on page 250.

Getting Your Local Driver Training Manual

In order to get your Level 1 license, you'll need to pass a written test. Your local vehicle licensing office should have an inexpensive manual you can purchase to help you prepare. Their website should give you details. The manual contains all the information you'll need to know to pass the test.

The test is about basic information you need to know before you sit in the driver's seat. There are road signs you need to be able to identify. There are basic rules so you'll know how to handle common situations and there's information to help you drive safely.

Study the manual and have your co-pilot (parent) quiz you. If you don't understand something, make sure you ask.

This is not a test you can cram for, pass and forget about. You really need to know this stuff so you'll know what to do when you start your driving practices.

While you're in the vehicle licensing office to pick up your manual, find out:

- When you'll be eligible to take the test
- How and when to schedule your test
- Where it's held
- How much it costs
- What you need to bring with you to the test facility
- Any other tips they recommend to help you prepare

When you're ready—book your test and 'Good Luck'!

While you're waiting to take your test, continue preparing to drive by working through the rest of this section with your parent/coach.

Chapter 3
Structured Practice
Before Getting a Learner's Permit

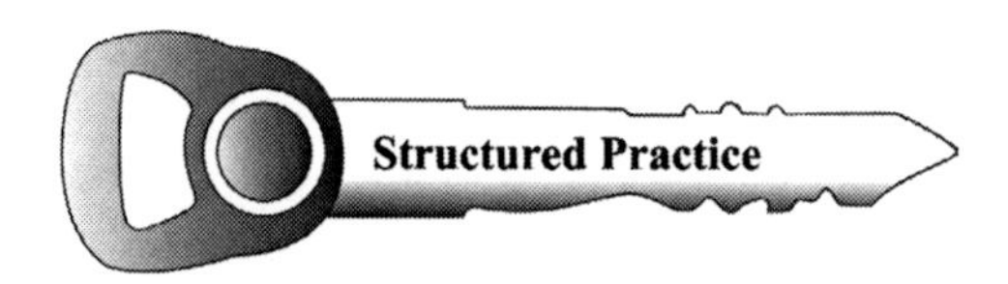

You can't begin your in-car practice sessions until you have your Level 1 License (Learner's Permit) in hand, but there's still a lot you can do to get ready to learn to drive.

This section will help you learn about your vehicle so you can care for it properly and deal with some emergencies. Read through it with your driving coach, then complete the "Saturday Morning with Dad" checklist on page 36.

Maintenance Basics Everyone Needs to Know

You don't have to get down and greasy but you should know some basic things about your vehicle. Your car will run better and you'll save a lot of money on repairs in the long run. Basic maintenance includes knowing about your:

- Tires
- Oil and Fluid Levels
- Battery

You'll find a lot of the information you need to know in your Owner's Manual. Most people keep it in the glove compartment of their vehicle. If you don't have the Owner's Manual, you should get one. Contact your local dealership or check the manufacturer's website to find out where you can purchase one.

Your Car's Fluids

The Importance of Motor Oil

Remember the Tin Man in the Wizard of Oz? He couldn't reach his oilcan so he rusted so badly he couldn't move. In the story, Dorothy squirted a little oil in the right spots and he was as good as new.

Your car needs oil as badly as the Tin Man but you need to be more proactive about taking care of it. If you ignore it, your engine will seize up like the Tin Man, but no amount of oil will be able to help it then!

The oil in your car:

1. Lubricates the moving parts of your engine
2. Cleans the engine
3. Seals tiny holes on piston rings and cylinder walls
4. Protects the engine from rust and corrosion
5. Cools parts of the engine.

> If you ignore the oil in your car, you will:
>
> 1. Wreck your engine (which costs thousands of dollars!)
> 2. Lose power
> 3. Spend a lot more on gas than you need to because your car will waste fuel

Check the oil level once a month. Pick a day. Any day. (Maybe the first Saturday of the month?) Then mark your calendar and make sure you check the oil level in your car on that day every month.

If your car is leaking oil, you'll have to check it much more frequently.

Get the Oil Changed according to the car manufacturer's recommendation. (Check your Owner's Manual)

> **Rule of Thumb:**
>
> Change the oil every 3,000 miles (5,000 km) or 3 months (whichever comes first.)

How to Check the Oil

It's ideal to check the oil at the service station when you stop to get gas. Most stations provide paper towels you can use.

1. The car engine must be turned OFF. It should be warm—which just means that it's been running. (You don't have to touch it.). If you drove it to the gas station, that's perfect.

   TIP: Make sure the car is parked on a level surface so you don't get a false reading.
2. Pull the hood release lever under the dashboard. Feel for the latch under the hood. Release the lever and raise the hood. Set the metal prop in place so the hood doesn't close while you're working.
3. Have a paper towel or rag handy. Locate the dipstick. You'll probably see a small loop sticking up near the spark plugs. If you pull it gently you'll see a long, skinny metal rod. That's your dipstick. Pull it all the way out.
4. Use the rag or paper towel to wipe off the dipstick so there's no more oil on it. Locate the mark on the dipstick that says "FULL". (It's near the pointy end—not the end you're holding.)

> ***Mineral or Synthetic?***
>
> There are 2 types of oil: Mineral and Synthetic.
>
> **Mineral** oil comes from the ground and is refined. It's less expensive and most cars use it.
>
> **Synthetic** oil is manufactured.
>
> Stick with one or the other. It's not a good idea to mix them.
>
> Motor oils also come in lots of grades. Check your Owner's Manual for the manufacturer's recommendation on what will work best in your car.

Note: Some dipsticks have 2 lines with a pattern between them. In this case, the oil is full when it is halfway between the 2 lines (in the middle of the pattern)

5. Push the dipstick back into the receptacle. Make sure it goes all the way to the bottom.
6. Pull the dipstick out again and hold it in front of you.
7. If the oil level is below the "full" marker, you will need to add oil.

WATCH IT ON VIDEO—Go to TeensLearntoDrive.com and click on the title called "How-To". Scroll Down to the video "Check Your Oil".

How to Add Oil

Make sure you get the oil that the manufacturer recommends for your vehicle.

1. Unscrew the oil filter cap.
2. Place a funnel into the oil receptacle. Slowly pour the oil into the funnel.
3. After you add the oil, check the oil level again using the dipstick. Add more if necessary but don't overfill because it's hard to remove if you add too much.
4. Replace the oil filter cap. Make sure you screw it on tightly.

The Importance of Regular Oil Changes

Relax. You don't have to change the oil yourself. It's quick, easy and pretty cheap to have it done by the pros. They'll check your fluid levels and top up anything else that's low too.

But the point is—you need to have the oil changed regularly. Check your Owner's Manual for the manufacturer's recommendation.

Coolant (Antifreeze)

One of the other fluid levels to keep an eye on is COOLANT. It's a greenish or orange-ish liquid that's sometimes called antifreeze. Without it, your engine could seize and that's a VERY expensive repair.

If you see a pool of greenish or orange-ish fluid under your car, have it checked by a mechanic immediately. If you can't do that, check the coolant level. (Your Owner's Manual will show you how.) If it's low, add coolant and then take it to a mechanic right away.

Your Tires: Where the Rubber Meets the Road!

You've got four tires and they hold up the car.

That's good enough, right?

Wrong! If you don't look after your tires you'll spend way more money on gas because you won't go as far on each gallon (liter) you buy. You'll also have to replace them sooner.

But that's not all! Bald, under-inflated or over-inflated tires are dangerous! They don't hug the road the way they're supposed to. They cause accidents, injuries and even—deaths.

At the very least tire-related accidents mean expensive repairs and skyrocketing insurance premiums—but you could also face criminal charges if your unsafe vehicle causes a crash!

And that's sad when tires are so easy to maintain. Ten minutes a month is all it takes to inspect your tires and make sure they're safe and performing the way they should. You don't even have to get your hands dirty.

If you knew that 10 minutes per month could save you $150 on gas and $2,500 in car repairs, wouldn't you do it?

> Under-inflated tires contribute to 660 deaths and 33,000 injuries every year.
>
> The National Highway Traffic Safety Administration (US)

Maintaining Your Tires

There are 4 things to be on top of—to keep your tires healthy. You'll learn more about them in the coming pages but they are:

Pressure—When it comes to tire pressure, think "Goldilocks." Not too much. Not too little. Just right!

Alignment—Periodically, tires get bumped and jolted and they need to be re-aligned.

Rotation—This is like musical chairs for tires. Tires wear differently in different spots so they need to be moved around regularly.

Tread—If you think "As long as I can see the pattern, my tires are okay," you're dead wrong!

> What should the pressure in your tires be?
>
> You'll find the recommended tire pressure in your Owner's Manual, on the driver's side doorjamb, on the glove box door or inside the fuel door of your car.

Tire Pressure

Some tires look flat but are okay. Others look okay but they're under- inflated. It's impossible to eyeball your tires accurately so you need to get a tire gauge. They only cost about ten bucks and can save you a bundle because you'll get much better mileage from every gallon of gas you buy. (Some gas stations still have tire gauges you can use but they're often faulty.)

Checking your tire pressure is easy. It only takes a few minutes. You'll need a tire gauge.

How to Use a Tire Gauge

A tire gauge is metal and looks a little like something the dentist might put in your mouth. One end is rounded and fits onto the tire's valve. The other end has a scale in it that shoots out when you press the gauge onto the valve. That scale gives you the tire pressure reading.

1. Remove the cap from the tire valve.
2. Fit the rounded end of the gauge firmly onto the valve.
3. Read the tire pressure on the scale at the other end of the gauge.
4. Repeat until you get the same reading 3 times in a row.
5. Compare the reading with the recommended pressure for your vehicle. If your tire pressure is too high, let a little air out. If it's too low, add some air at the closest gas station with an air pump. (If you aren't sure how to do this, ask a parent or the station attendant to help you.)
6. Replace the cap on the valve.

WATCH IT ON VIDEO—Go to TeensLearntoDrive.com and click on the title called "How-To". Scroll Down to the video "Check Tire Pressure".

Visual Inspection

The sides of tires are not as strong as the surface that contacts the road, so it's important to inspect them each month when you check your tire pressure.

Look for nicks, cracks, tears and bulges. If you see any of these things, have the tires inspected right away by a professional. The damaged tire might need to be replaced.

Tire Alignment

Remember that curb you accidentally smacked into? Or the pothole that jolted you on the highway? Any big bump can alter the alignment of your tires. If you want a smooth ride and maximum wear from your tires, you'll need to have them aligned periodically too.

Check your Owner's Manual for Alignment recommendations.

Tire Rotation

Each of your tires carries a different weight so it's important to switch them around periodically. Sounds silly, doesn't it? But the fact is that tires are expensive and rotating them will make them last longer.

Your tire dealer can do this for you (Yes—there's a fee but it's a lot less than new tires!)

You should have them balanced at the same time.

> Check your Owner's Manual for how often to rotate your tires. It will recommend a pattern for where they should go too.
>
> (Rule of Thumb is every 5,000 miles.)

Tire Tread

The tread on your tires is the part that grips the road. Contrary to popular belief, worn out tires don't look bald (smooth). You can still see the pattern, but it's not deep enough to provide the traction you need.

Many tires have tread bars. They're little rubber bits that stick up in the tire. (They look like bits that should be removed, but they have an important purpose.) If the tread bars are even with the tread on your tires, you need new tires.

> If you don't have tread bars, it's hard to eyeball tread depth so you need another tool—a penny.
>
> **In the U. S.—use a Lincoln-head penny.**
>
> Hold the penny so Lincoln's head is up. Insert the penny into the tread on your tire and press it as far in as it will go. Now look closely. If you can see all of Lincoln's head, your tire needs to be replaced.
>
> **In Canada—use the Queen's head on your penny.** Insert the penny into the tread on your tire and press it as far in as it will go. Now look closely. If you can see her crown, you should replace your tires soon.
>
> Try this again in several places. You should see the same amount of the head/crown each time. If it varies, your tires are wearing unevenly which may mean you need an alignment. Have them checked by your local garage or tire seller.

Common Tire Problems and Solutions

SYMPTOM	POSSIBLE PROBLEM	WHAT TO DO
Steering wheel pulls to one side	Misaligned front wheels	Take to tire dealer or repair garage ASAP
Bumpy, bouncy ride	Unbalanced Tire	Take to tire dealer or repair garage ASAP
Vibration in the steering wheel at a certain speed	Unbalanced Wheel	Take to tire dealer or repair garage ASAP

How to Change a Tire

For tips about **how to change a tire** see page 198.

Deal Or No Deal?

Question: Your cousin has a set of tires he doesn't need and he'll let you have them for $50! Is this a bargain?

Answer: Maybe. But just because they look the same, doesn't mean they'll fit your car. You need the right diameter plus other dimensions must be right too.

You want to make sure your cousin's tires are in good shape and will suit the driving conditions in your climate.

There is also some evidence that tires degrade as they get older. This website will help you determine how old the tires are—http://www.tirerack.com/tires/tiretech/techpage.jsp?techid=11

So—before you pony up the fifty bucks, have them checked by a professional.

Saturday Morning with Dad* Checklist *

or Mom or another knowledgeable adult

Go through this checklist together while the car is safely parked in the driveway.

First things first—

- ☐ Get Dad a cup of coffee just the way he likes it.

Your Instrument Control Panel (Dashboard)

- ☐ Discuss what the warning lights mean.

Your Tires

- ☐ Locate the spare tire.
- ☐ Learn how to remove the spare tire.
- ☐ Locate the jack and demonstrate how to assemble it.
- ☐ Talk about where to place the jack to change a tire.
- ☐ Identify the lug wrench and know how to use it.
- ☐ Talk about how you would remove the lug nuts
- ☐ Understand the steps for changing a tire.
- ☐ Locate your 3-in-1 oil and discuss how you would use it to loosen a lug nut.
- ☐ Locate the tire pressure guide for your car.
- ☐ The tire pressure for my tires should be: ____________
- ☐ Identify your tire gauge and use it to check the pressure on all 5 tires (including the spare).
- ☐ Later—add air to the tires, if necessary. (You'll need to do that at a gas station.)
- ☐ Check the tread wear on your tires.
- ☐ Perform a visual inspection of your tires.

Checking Your Oil

- ☐ Know how to raise and prop the hood.
- ☐ Locate the oil dipstick.
- ☐ Demonstrate how to check the oil.
- ☐ The oil my car requires is ____________

Checking Your Windshield Washer Fluid Level

- ☐ Locate the windshield washer receptacle under the hood
- ☐ What do you fill it with? _________
- ☐ Demonstrate how to fill it
- ☐ Locate the rear windshield washer receptacle (if your car has one)
- ☐ Demonstrate how to fill it

Inspect Your Wiper Blades

- ☐ Replace them if necessary

Your Battery

- ☐ Locate the battery under the hood
- ☐ Locate the positive and negative terminals
- ☐ Locate your jumper cables
- ☐ Discuss how to use them (page 202)
- ☐ Identify a solid metal area you could use to ground a jumper cable

Your Gas Tank

- ☐ Which side of the car is your gas tank on?
- ☐ Is there an icon on the dashboard to show which side it's on?
- ☐ Is there a release lever in the car?
- ☐ My car uses this type of gas: _______________

Your Lights: Demonstrate how and when to use—

- ☐ Headlights
- ☐ High beams
- ☐ Fog Lights (if you have them)
- ☐ Brake lights
- ☐ Turn signals
- ☐ Emergency Flashers
- ☐ Interior Lights
- ☐ Replace any lights that aren't working.

Your Trunk

- ☐ Is there a release lever in the car to open the trunk?
- ☐ Is there a release lever to open the trunk on the remote?
- ☐ Is there a release lever in the trunk that opens the trunk? (this is a safety feature in some vehicles in case you were ever trapped in the trunk of the vehicle.)
- ☐ When the trunk is open, is there a warning light on the dashboard?

Your Brakes: My car has

- ☐ Front-wheel ABS
- ☐ All-wheel ABS
- ☐ A different braking system _______________________

My car has:

- ☐ Front –wheel Drive
- ☐ Rear-wheel Drive
- ☐ All-wheel Drive

Heating and Air Conditioning

- ☐ Demonstrate how to adjust the temperature and discuss when you should make adjustments

Front and Rear Windshield Defrosters

- ☐ Locate the front and rear window defrosters. Talk about when to use them and how to turn them on.

Radio

- ☐ Choose a button and set it for your favorite radio station. This is the button you will push to get your station before you start driving each time. (Note: You'll keep the radio off for your driving lessons.)
- ☐ Discuss the maximum volume you will be allowed to use for the radio or music system.

Important Papers—Discuss where to find them and when you might need them:

- ☐ Proof of Insurance (usually kept in your wallet—must be with you in the car)
- ☐ Proof of Ownership (usually kept in your wallet—must be with you in the car)
- ☐ Roadside Assistance Plan Information (usually kept in glove box)

Your Driver's License (in your wallet)

VIN

- ☐ Locate the Vehicle Identification Number in your car

Chapter 3 Review Crossword

Complete the crossword puzzle on the next page and check your answers on page 235.

ACROSS

3. ____________ is a factor in more than 50% of teen crashes.
5. Driving too close to the car ahead is called ____________________.
7. Your seatbelt will not protect you if you _________ your seat.
10. Your _________ is the most important thing to your parents.
11 Driver _________ contributes to most teen crashes.
12 This is also called antifreeze. __________
16. ______-hand turns are the most difficult because you have to cross a lane of traffic.
17. Never ______ your family vehicle without your parent's permission.
18. You should change your oil approximately every _________ months.
20. Your __________ travels at the same speed as your car.

DOWN

1. After you gas-up, don't forget to _________ the gas cap.
2. Running _______ traffic lights is very dangerous.
4. If you turn the key and nothing happens, the problem could be your ___________.
6. Most cars use this type of oil. _________
8. Don't forget to signal before you change ________.
9. This person is ultimately responsible for your safety. ________
13. After you jump your battery, make sure you run the engine for at least ______ minutes to recharge the battery.

14. If you're very tired, you can't make yourself stay __________.
15. Most teens don't get enough of this. ____________
19. Use caution—even when you have the ________-of-way.
21. If you go partying, always have a designated ____________.

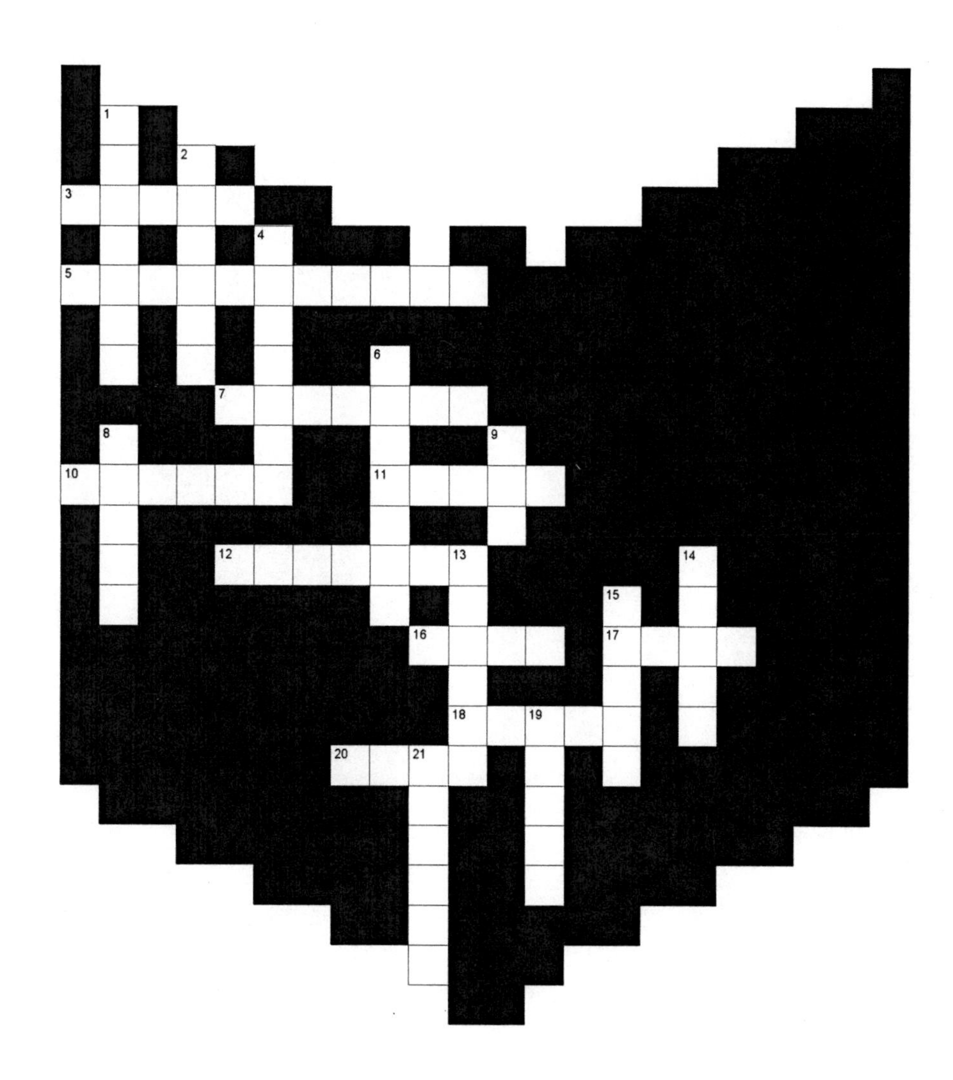

After Getting a Level 1 License (Learner's Permit)

In this Section:

- Information for Parent Coaches
- Reflexive Skills
- Purposeful vs. Recreational Driving
- How to Help Your Driver
- The Teen Brain
- Preparing the Car
- Coaching Tips for the Co-Pilot
- Stay the Course
- Developing a Seatbelt Habit
- Katie's Story
- Airbag Safety
- 8 Tips for Avoiding a Rollover Crash
- The Danger in Backing Up
- Dealing with Distractions
- Music
- Passengers
- Eating and Drinking
- Smoking
- Cell Phones and Texting
- Almost Home
- Lauren's Story
- Review Puzzles
- Basic Driving Skills and Tips
- In-Car Driving Sessions
- Recommended Lesson Plan
- First 20 Driving Lessons

Chapter 4

Actively Involved Parents

After Getting a Learner's Permit

Information for Parent Coaches

No Teen is Really a Safe Driver

Watch the news any evening and you'll quickly realize that driving is dangerous for **everyone.** Any 'typical' outing in a car can change in an instant. And when that happens, there's no time to think or weigh your options! That's when reflexive driving skills need to take over and experts agree they take at least 3 years to develop. So no matter how smart or coordinated or reliable 16 or 17 year-olds are—they are never really safe drivers.

They can know the rules and obey them, but they still don't have the reflexive driving skills they need to "take over" when they get into trouble. Reflexive driving skills take years of practice—not weeks or months.

Reflexive Skills

My daughter, Emily plays the piano. Many years ago, when her lessons began, she learned the basics—how to identify notes and find them on a keyboard. Then she learned all the rules concerning loudness, speed and dynamics.

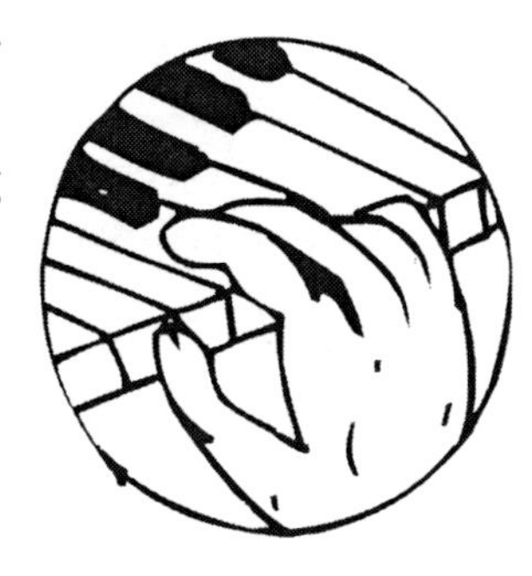

Now, when she learns to play a piece, she starts by reading the music, note by note, and finding each note on the keyboard. She memorizes how to play the right-hand first. Then she learns the left hand. She practices them separately for a long time.

Finally, she puts her hands together and labors through the piece. She makes a lot of mistakes but continues to practice until eventually her fingers know what to do. Then the magic happens! They find the keys on their own. She starts to play, and she finishes. In between her fingers find their marks—without her even realizing what they're doing! That's reflexive. When your body or brain knows what to do without you even having to think about it. And that comes from a lot of practice and experience. There is simply no shortcut.

Reflexive Driving Skills

Similarly—excellent reflexive driving skills take years of practice too. They are what helps you swerve safely around the crate that falls off the truck in front of you—without going into the ditch or oncoming traffic.

Teens don't have the maturity or experience to already possess these skills so they are automatically at risk every time they drive.

So—what can parents do to keep their teens safer?

You can get informed and understand the risks—then take advantage of every lesson, product and opportunity that reduces those risks. You can't make it **safe** but you can make it **safer.**

Be thoughtful every time your teen asks for the keys or asks to ride with another teen driver. Ask a lot of questions. Don't automatically say 'yes', and understand the difference between purposeful and recreational driving.

Purposeful vs. Recreational Driving

Some types of driving are riskier than others so it's important to know the difference. (I could leave this discussion until later since your teen won't be driving solo for a while, but I'm including it here because they might be passengers in cars driven by other teens and that puts them at risk too.)

Recreational Driving

When I was a kid, the family down the street used to go for Sunday afternoon drives in the country. Sometimes they'd stop for ice cream or sodas but the main activity was pure recreational driving. They didn't have a particular destination in mind or a fixed schedule. They just liked being together and enjoying the scenery.

Today, most families don't do a lot of recreational driving. Driving has a purpose. We drive to work, shopping and social activities. We look at cars as transportation rather than a means of recreation.

Except for teenagers with new drivers licenses. All of a sudden, just hanging out with friends or 'cruising' is recreation again—and that's a problem. When kids go joyriding, they are more likely to speed, take chances and drive dangerously—and that puts them at much higher risk for getting in a crash.

Purposeful Driving

When teens have a specific destination, a defined arrival time and an incentive to be on time, the risk of a crash is lower. They have a purpose and are focused **on the journey**—not socializing and having fun.

Of course, planning is a big part of purposeful driving too. They need to make sure they've left sufficient time to drive safely and arrive in plenty of time. They need to be familiar with their route and make allowances for bad weather or other factors that can cause delays.

How to Help Your Driver

Ask Questions

One way parents can reduce the risks is to understand where your teens are going and why. By asking lots of questions you can determine whether the trip is recreational or purposeful.

Who are they going with? (How many teens will be in the car?)
Where are they going?
Why?
What's their schedule?
When will they be home?
What route will they be taking?

You can use that information to decide if this outing is one you feel good about. Then weigh the risks before you hand over the keys or agree to allow your teen to go out with friends.

Help Them Plan

You can also help them plan their time and their route—especially in the beginning. Create a timeline together. For example, if your teen needs to be at school for a basketball game at 6:00 p.m. your timeline might look like this:

6:00 start of game
- 30 allow a 30-minute buffer for parking and to get seats
5:30

5:30
- 20 allow 20 minutes to drive there along a specified route
5:10

5:10
- 10 allow 10 minutes to pick-up a friend
5:00

So, in this situation the teen must leave home no later than 5:00 p.m. to get to the game. If he needs to stop for gas on the way or it's raining, that start time will need to be adjusted.

Return Trip

Make sure you work through the same process to determine what time they'll have to leave the school in order to get home before their curfew.

Plan the Route

Talk about which roads they're planning to take. Make sure your teens are familiar with them. If not, drive the route together first or suggest alternate roads your teen knows.

Before They Leave ...

Before they leave with the keys, remind your young drivers of speed limits, dangerous intersections or sharp curves—so they're fresh in their minds. And remind them to drive with care because you love them and want them to get home safely.

Reducing Other Risks

This book also helps you talk with your teens about distractions and behaviors that can cause crashes or create dangerous situations. You may be tempted to skip some of them because they're 'common sense.' You may think that some things are so obviously dangerous that your teen will automatically understand why and instinctively avoid them.

That would be a mistake.

Things that seem obvious to adults are not obvious to teenagers. Teens have limited experience so that's part of the problem but there's more. Scientific studies show that teenagers' brains are very different from adults'.

The Teen Brain

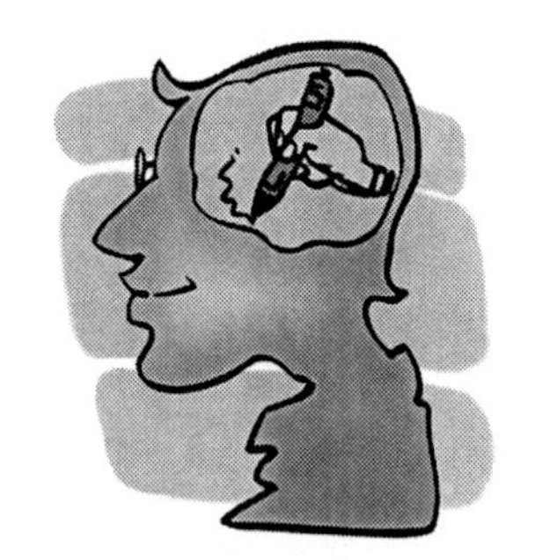

A five-year old is playing catch with a ball in the front yard. They miss and the ball bounces past them onto the road. They turn and run to get it—oblivious to the car that's approaching at 30 miles per hour!

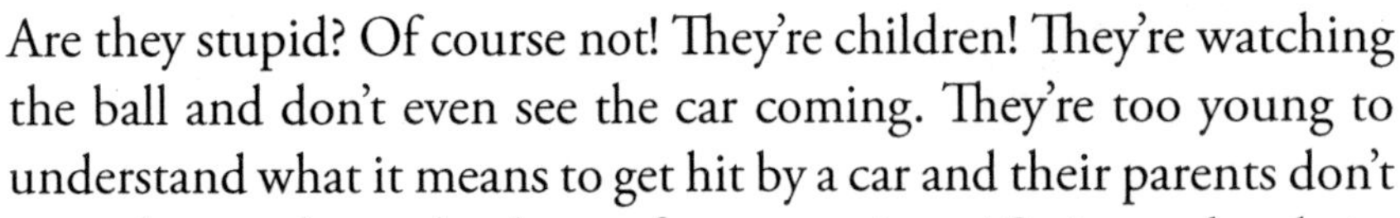

Are they stupid? Of course not! They're children! They're watching the ball and don't even see the car coming. They're too young to understand what it means to get hit by a car and their parents don't want them to learn that lesson from experience! So instead—their parents will watch closely and teach them not to run onto the road by imposing less dangerous—yet meaningful consequences. Maybe they'll get yelled at if they head for the road or the ball will be taken away for a while. But they'll learn to stay away from the road.

At 16 Teens May Look Like Adults, But ...

By the time they're 16, that boy or girl will look like an adult. Sometimes they'll even talk and act like adults. But it's important to remember they're not adults. Their ability to weigh risks and make decisions is not mature. Those functions are controlled by the frontal lobe of their brains and that part of the brain won't be fully developed until their mid twenties or later.

'Connect With Kids'* created a terrific video called "The Teenage Brain" that explains why teens take risks and do things adults think are stupid. Teens aren't trying to vex us. They aren't playing with death. Sometimes they really can't think things through far enough to realize an action could end badly. Their immature brains don't work that way yet. If it looks fun, and other kids are doing it—they want to do it too.

(The same part of the brain is responsible for sudden blasts of emotion like anger or sadness. That can be upsetting or embarrassing for teens but it's perfectly normal. Sometimes we blame it on hormones but it's really a brain thing. Teens can't help it.)

So what can parents do to help?

Just like they did with that 5 year old, parents can talk with teens about potential dangers and help them foresee the possible outcomes.

They can also remove the guesswork by making rules upfront and imposing consequences if the rules are broken. (This is not an area where "I thought you meant …" will do.)

This book helps parents accomplish both tasks. There are lots of stories here about teens who made bad choices with tragic consequences. It's important to read through them together and talk about them. This will help teens foresee problems in a very real way.

(* You'll find more information about 'Connect With Kids' and "The Teenage Brain" under the Resources tab at TeensLearntoDrive.com)

Preparing Your Teen to Think Like a Driver

"Talk" Your Drive

It's time to begin preparing your teen to sit in the driver's seat. You can start the process even before they get their learner's permit by talking to them about what you're seeing and doing while you drive. Read the section below.

Parents Make It Look So Easy

This is what your teen sees …

While Mom is driving to the mall she listens to what they say and responds intelligently. The radio is on. She remarks on the SALE sign at her favorite store and waves to the next-door neighbor. She never misses a turn and arrives safely at her destination every time.

Your teen figures, "No sweat! I can do that too!" But what they couldn't possibly know is—what's going on in her head while she's driving.

This is what's really happening ...

While Mom's talking or listening, she's continually looking around and checking her mirrors. She notices the cars in front, behind and beside her. She speeds up or slows down to leave a safe cushion of space around the car.

When cars or trucks try to "box her in" she maneuvers her car so she keeps an "escape route" available in case she needs it.

She's watching up ahead to see if there are obstacles. She notices the kids playing with the ball and is prepared to stop if necessary. She slows down as she enters curves and accelerates out of them. She notes road signs and adjusts her speed automatically.

Plus, in most places, she knows the streets, the speed limits, the almost-hidden stop signs and where the big potholes are located. If she misses a turn –she simply goes to the next block or next exit and finds her way back.

And even with years and years of experience—if she loses focus for one second—she could end up in a fender bender.

Thinking Out Loud

Parents—your teens aren't mind readers. They can't know what you're thinking while you're driving unless you tell them. It's important to let them know what you're seeing and how you're responding to it so they can start thinking and reacting the same way.

It's "stream of consciousness" talking but completely driving-focused.

You need to focus on your driving and start talking.

- What do you see? (Signs, obstacles, concerns, erratic drivers, etc.)
- What does that mean?
- What are your options?
- Where are the other cars? Are they driving appropriately? (speeding, changing lanes frequently, etc.)
- When do you check your mirrors?
- What obstructs your view and how do you compensate for that?
- Where is your "exit"? If you suddenly needed to avoid a collision, where would you go (shoulder of the road, lane change, etc.)?

For example:

- What do you see?

  "I see that red car ahead in the left lane slowing down. It isn't signaling but I think the driver may turn left into the mall."

- What does that mean?

  "The car behind the red car is going too fast and not watching. He may swerve into my lane to avoid the red car."

- What are you doing to react to that?

  "I'm going to slow down and move into the curb lane so he has room to get over if he needs to … I'm turning on my right turn indicator … I'm checking my mirrors and the lane is clear … I'm checking my blind spot. It's clear too … Now I'm making my lane change." etc.

It takes a little practice to start talking but this step is very important.

TIP: Before your teen begins driving, demonstrate this procedure several times. Then—while ***you're*** still at the wheel—get them to tell you what they see and how they'd deal with it—just the way you did. You'll be able to get a good sense of how much they're capturing and processing. You can coach them at this point—to help them develop their skills—without endangering life or limb.

Finally—when they get behind the wheel, they'll be more comfortable talking about what they see and how they're dealing with it.

Preparing the Car

What car will you use to teach your teen? It's best to use the same vehicle so they can become accustomed to how it feels and learn where things are. A car with an automatic transmission is easiest, especially at the beginning.

Before your teen gets behind the wheel, you'll want to make sure your vehicle is in peak condition and as safe as possible. If you haven't had it tuned up lately, this is a good time.

This also provides a terrific opportunity to run through "Maintenance Basics" (page 29) and the "Saturday Morning with Dad" checklist (page 36.)

This will help you check your tires so you'll know if they need rotating or even replacing. It will also help you top up all your fluid levels while you show your teen how to do it.

Cool Product

There may be some advantage to letting other drivers know your teen is learning to drive. Perhaps they'll be more patient and less likely to lay on the horn. Maybe they'll just allow your car a little extra space. Either would be a good thing.

StudentattheWheel.com offers car magnets and window clings you can put on your vehicle to warn other cars that your driver is learning. They're inexpensive and can be slapped on the car for your practice sessions and then packed away in the glove compartment until you need them next.

They're available in stores or through the website. Check the website for a list of stores that carry them.

Coaching Tips for the Co-Pilot

(That's you Mom and Dad!)

Before you begin your job as driving coach, think back to when ***you*** learned to drive. Remember how overwhelming it seemed the first time you sat in the driver's seat?

Did someone get annoyed at you because you didn't react quickly enough or understand what they meant when they gave an instruction? Use that experience to make sure you bring a positive, supportive attitude to your job as coach.

Plan each lesson using the tools provided and talk about the skills you'll be focusing on before you start each session. Lessons should become progressively more difficult.

TIP: Make sure you both take your driver's license with you when you're in the car.

Coaching requires active participation. Now is not the time to return phone calls. One of the toughest skills new drivers need to master is awareness of the other vehicles around them. That is—in front of them, on each side and behind them. Until they master that skill, it's your job to maintain that 360-degree awareness for them.

Tips for Your Driving Practice Sessions:

- Use a calm and respectful tone. Don't talk down to or belittle your teen. They really are trying their best.
- Turn off the radio and minimize other distractions.
- Speak clearly and give simple, clear instructions.
- As you're driving, give corrections, warnings and tips.
- Use questions to focus your teen's attention like "What's the speed limit here?" when they're going too fast or too slow.
- Anticipate turns and give lots of warning. "At the next light, turn left."
- Say, "That's correct" or simply "Yes" rather than "right" during your lessons. Reserve the word "right" for directions.
- Limit first lessons to 15 to 20 minutes. There's a lot for your teen to absorb. Increase lesson length as your teen's skill level grows.
- Summarize each lesson at the end.
- Give lots of encouragement and praise as your teen masters new skills.
- In the Driver's Log, note skills that are improving and ones that need more practice.
- Make this a time for the two of you—without backseat drivers.

Stay the Course

At some point, as you move through this program, you may begin to think, "driving is far too dangerous for teenagers. I don't want my son or daughter driving until they're twenty-five!"

Believe me—I understand! I have thought that many times. (And some teens are just not ready to learn to drive at a mere sixteen.) But for most teens, there is a trade-off. If you delay teaching your teen to drive until they turn 18—you'll lose most of your impact as coach and monitor. By that time, they will likely be going off to college or getting their first job. You won't be in a position to influence their driving habits much at all.

And in the meantime, they'll want to drive with friends who've received their licenses. So think about this: When will they be safer—

- when they're driving as passengers of friends who were trained by who-knows-who?
- or when they're driving themselves after they've been taught lovingly by you with the help of this program?

So—stay the course—but give it everything you've got and make sure your teen is the best prepared driver in the country!

Chapter 5
Need-to-Know Info
After Getting a Learner's Permit

If you want to create your own driving lesson plan, you can work through this chapter at your own pace. Alternately, if you plan to use the Lesson Plan we've provided, you can jump right to it in Chapter 6. Each of the 20 lessons in that plan has a 'classroom' segment that includes the material in this chapter.

Developing a Seatbelt Habit

Some teens think it's cool not to wear a seatbelt. Others think they don't need one when they're "just going down the block" or sitting in the back seat.

> Two-thirds of teen drivers and passengers killed in crashes were not wearing seat belts.

But 1 in 10 teens will be involved in a crash during their first year in the driver's seat. Many of the crashes will take place very close to home—and wearing your seatbelt could save your life.

Don't take foolish chances. Always buckle up; front seat and back. And wear your seatbelt properly—including the shoulder harness.

As the driver, you have POWER. You control what *you* do and where the car goes. You can also control your passengers by insisting they buckle-up too.

"Seatbelt Check!"

Before you put the car in gear, call out, "Seatbelt check!" Then have each person check that they are belted, and that the person next to them is belted too. In our family, we've caught two people in the last two weeks. In both cases they thought they'd buckled up, but were distracted by activity in the vehicle or a package on their laps.

> You're **16 times** more likely to be seriously injured if you're not wearing a seatbelt.
>
> NHTSA Data

Make 'Seatbelt Check!' a habit every time you get in the car. Even people who always wear their seatbelt sometimes make mistakes. And you know that can be deadly.

Seat belts dangerous? No—but people who don't wear them are!

If your friends refuse to wear their seatbelts because they say they're dangerous, set them straight. Seatbelts save lives and people who don't wear them are a danger to everyone else in the car. Unbelted people become torpedoes if the car crashes. They bounce around inside the car and can kill or severely injure other passengers!

Refuse to move the car until everyone buckles-up. Tell your friends the facts. If they still refuse, tell them about what happened to Katie Marchetti.

Katie's Story

Katie Marchetti was sixteen and had the world at her feet. She was pretty, smart and loved by family and friends. She wanted to make the world a better place and was doing something about it. She'd joined the Ophelia Project, where she mentored younger girls and helped them understand that beauty comes from within. She'd never missed a meeting.

Katie was fun and full of life but she was not a risk taker. She played by the rules and her parents did all the right things to try to keep her safe. Katie had a strict 11:00 pm curfew—which she tried, unsuccessfully, to extend from time to time.

Her parents had promised her a car for her sixteenth birthday. They found the safest one they could—with 5 airbags. And they waited until 6 months after her birthday, to get it—so she'd have that extra driving experience under her belt first.

On that fateful night, Katie went to a party with her boyfriend, A.J. It wasn't a rave. There were no drugs and they didn't drink any alcohol. In fact, they were probably the only teenagers there. It was an engagement party for a member of A.J.'s family. They went because family meant a lot to both of them.

The party was in a different city. Katie's parents agreed to let her go as long as A.J.'s parents drove them. Katie was not supposed to be driving that night. She'd driven to A.J.'s where she was supposed to leave her car, but something changed and she decided to drive the long distance to the event instead. Maybe she decided to drive because the car was new and fun. Maybe she knew A.J.'s parents would want to stay later than she and her boyfriend would want to stay. Either way, that day, Katie drove her car, even though she knew she was not supposed to.

When they arrived at the party, Katie called home to let her Mom know she'd arrived safely. She ended the call with, "I love you." That was the last time her Mom would ever talk to her.

Katie and A.J. left the party in plenty of time for her to make curfew. She started driving but quickly realized that high-speed highway driving is much scarier after dark. A.J. was nineteen and had a lot more experience. He agreed to drive the rest of the way home.

At some point on the long drive, Katie started feeling drowsy. She put her seat back and tried to sleep but the seat belt was bothering her. She shifted and squirmed but it was really uncomfortable. Finally—the girl who ***always wore her seat belt***—reached over and released the clip. She probably thought she was safe because they were almost home. She closed her eyes and drifted off to sleep.

It was 10:30 p.m. and it had been a long day for A.J. He'd been up since early morning and hadn't stopped. He was very tired. The road was long and dark. His eyelids started to feel heavy and sore. He rubbed them and yawned.

They must have closed for a moment and that's all it took to send the car careening into the guardrail. The horrific crunching brought A.J. back to consciousness and he struggled to hang on to the steering wheel. The car bounced off the rail and headed back across the highway into the cement wall on the other side.

A.J. watched in horror as Katie was thrown from the car onto the highway. She didn't have a chance. It happened too fast for the car behind them to stop or change direction. It ran over her.

Katie was rushed by helicopter to the closest trauma hospital. She fought hard to keep breathing and eight doctors worked frantically through the night to try to save her life.

She died early the next morning from massive internal injuries. She didn't even get a chance to say goodbye.

A.J. suffered a slight bruise to his shoulder—*probably from the seatbelt that held him safely in the car*—but the memory of that horrific night will be with him forever.

Crash Analysis

Using the details from the story, complete the chart below. (Answers are on page 236.)

Road Conditions	Visibility	Site of Crash
☐ Dry ☐ Wet or Icy	☐ Not a factor ☐ Poor - foggy, heavy rain, etc.	☐ City street ☐ Intersection ☐ High speed thruway or highway
Light Conditions	**# of Vehicles in Collision**	**Teen Passengers** (not including the driver)
☐ Daylight ☐ Dark: Late night or early morning	☐ 1 ☐ 2 or more	☐ None ☐ 1 only ☐ More than 1
Driver's Experience Level	**Driver's Physical Condition**	**Driving was:**
☐ Less than 1 year ☐ 2 to 3 years ☐ More than 3 years ☐ Unknown	☐ Alert ☐ Impaired by drugs ☐ Impaired by alcohol ☐ Extremely tired	☐ Purposeful ☐ Recreational
Was Driver Error a Factor?	**Wearing Seatbelts?**	**The Crash Happened:**
☐ Yes ☐ No ☐ Unknown	☐ Yes ☐ No ☐ Unknown	☐ Close to home ☐ Far from home

1. Based on your Crash Analysis what do you think caused this crash?

 ____

 ____

2. How could this crash have been avoided?

 ____

 ____

Did You Know?

> Katie made a big mistake by taking off her seatbelt—but she made another error too.
>
> Seatbelts **DO NOT** protect you when you recline your seat. You must **keep your seat upright** and use your seatbelt to be protected.

A Message to Parents from Katie's Mom, Laura:

Parents know there is no greater love than our love for our children. Katie was my only daughter. There are no words to describe her absence from all the lives she touched. Katie was my world. We loved to do things together like shopping, traveling, decorating for the holidays, cooking, mother and daughter dates, girl movies, girl talk and so much more.

She said so many times while growing up, "Mom, how are you going to be when I turn 18, or better yet, when I turn 21?" Katie knew she would always get the same reaction from me. I'd say, "Please stop growing. I want to keep you forever as you are at this moment." Never did I think that I would only have her for 16 ½ years.

Katie (in back) and Friends— Taken in a parked car

If Katie had only worn her seatbelt that fateful night, she would be here today and looking forward to celebrating that 21st birthday she talked about. Living our lives without her has been a tough journey. No family wants to experience our pain. We are not supposed to bury our children.

When the phone rang that night, it was thirty minutes before her 11 p.m. curfew, so I thought Katie was calling to ask if she could stay out later. I can still hear the voice at the other end of the phone screaming that something terrible had happened to my only daughter.

Now, my life has changed forever. Living without my daughter is a daily struggle. Some days are harder than others. I avoid all the places we used to go together. The memories are just too painful.

Talking to our children is so important. We must constantly remind them that every time they get into a car, they are at risk. They can do all the right things behind the wheel but there are always things they can't control. A tire can blow out or another car can cut them off. Wearing a seatbelt can mean the difference between life and death. Please talk to your teens today and remind them often that seatbelts save lives and their lives are so precious!

A Message to Teens from Katie's Mom:

"The most dangerous thing we do every day is get behind the wheel of a car. I held back letting my daughter, Katie, get her driver's license an extra six months so she would have more experience behind the wheel. I knew from research that the first six months after getting a driver's license were the most dangerous. We were a seatbelt-wearing family. Yet, my daughter chose one night to unfasten her seatbelt because she was tired. It cost my daughter her life at age sixteen.

I told Katie the day she got her license that the only thing I could not do to protect her, was to put my head on her shoulders. She would have to make her own decisions behind the wheel. She made one bad decision and now our family will spend the rest of our lives without her and the joy she brought us and everyone else who knew her.

Learn from her mistake. Your life can change in an instant. Your future can be changed forever. There are 5 critical reasons to wear a seat belt:

1. SEATBELTS prevent you from being ejected from the car
2. SEATBELTS shift the force of the crash to strongest parts of your body
3. SEATBELTS spread the force of the crash over a wide area of your body
4. SEATBELTS allow your body to slow down more gradually
5. SEATBELTS protect your head and spinal cord

Please give your family your greatest gift—the gift of your life. Make wearing a seat belt a habit. Lives will be saved. Serious injures will be prevented. I promise you, you are worth it."

Laura Marchetti

Families aren't the only people who suffer when a young life is lost. Here's a message from Katie's best friend, Lindsay:

Katie and I had a friendship unlike any other I have ever experienced. If there is such thing, she was my soul mate as a friend.

When we were together, there was not a care in the world other than having fun and living in that moment. We were known for telling our crazy stories of fun memories to all our friends, although we laughed so much while telling them it was hard to understand us.

BFFs—Lindsay and Katie

Very close friends sometimes tell each other "I don't know what I'd do if something happened to you". Katie and I exchanged those words many times.

All I can say is that you do survive when you lose someone like that but you look at life from a whole different perspective. You have to make the best out of any bad situation. I have cried many tears and have an indescribable pain inside, but I have learned a lot about life and try to prevent others from going through this heartache by telling her story. She will always be my best friend even if the memories are all I have.

Lyndsay Atkinson

Self-Reported Seat Belt Use among US Teens in Grades 9-12:

- 59% wear seat belts when driving
- 42% wear seat belts as passengers

(Briggs, Warren, Goldzweig, Levine, Warren. , Driver and Passenger Seat Belt Use Among US High School Students. Am J Prev Med 2008)

To learn more about Katie, and her family's campaign to protect other teens by promoting seatbelt use, visit: www.katiesstory.com

SEATBELTS: What Would You Do?

Five of your friends want to go to the movies with you. Your car has 5 seat belts. (Counting you, there would be 6 people in the car if you drive them all.)

The theater is a few blocks away.

Leslie says she'll sit on the floor in the back seat so no one will see her.

Max says Leslie can sit on his lap and he'll put the belt over both of them.

Connor says he'll ride in the trunk.

What would you do?

____

____

____

Answer is on page 236.

Groups LEAST Likely to Wear Seat Belts:

- Males
- Youths: Ages 16—24
- Occupants of Pickup Trucks
- Rural Occupants
- Rear Seat Passengers
- Residents of Secondary Law States
- People with Less than College Education
- Households with Income < $50,000
- Drivers Who Consume Large Amounts of Alcohol
- People Who Drive at High Speeds

NOPUS/VOSS Survey Data

Family Rules about Seatbelt Use

Seatbelt-use is required by law. As the driver, you have the ability to make sure you wear a seatbelt and that your passengers wear one too.

Decide on your family rules for wearing seatbelts in the car. Write them in the space below:

____

____

Airbag Safety

Seatbelts combined with airbags provide the best protection for drivers and front-seat passengers.

In every crash there are 3 collisions and they all happen at the same speed the vehicle is traveling. So if a car is driving 70 miles per hour (113 kph) and it hits a tree:

- The car hits the tree at 70 mph
- The driver hits the steering wheel at 70 mph
- The internal organs of the driver hit their ribs and outer shell at 70 mph

The last one is the most dangerous. Airbags help to absorb the blow so the driver will survive and there's no doubt that airbags save lives. The NHTSA estimates they've saved more than 25,000 lives in the last 10 years but they must be used properly.

Rules for Airbag Safety

1. You MUST wear your seatbelt to be protected
2. Children under 13 years MUST ride in the back seat (that includes babies in car seats.)
3. If your car's airbag has an on/off switch (on the passenger side), it must be ON when an adult is riding in that seat so you MUST check it every time you get in the car. (On/off switches are usually found in sports cars or pick-up trucks where there's no back seat.)
4. Front seat passengers MUST keep their feet on the floor. If they ride with their feet on the dashboard and the airbag deploys, their legs will be crushed!
5. Drivers MUST be at least 10 inches back from the steering wheel.
6. Passengers MUST be at least 10 inches away from the dashboard.
7. Seatbelts must be adjusted to fit snugly over your hips and upper thighs—not your belly.
8. The shoulder harness should fit snugly across your chest and collarbone—NEVER across your neck.
9. Don't hold anything in your lap that could impale you if your airbag deploys.
10. Never, never, never allow a child to sit on your lap in a car—front seat or back!

How Airbags Work

Bang!—Make that a BIG BANG!

When an airbag deploys it makes a deafening sound like a gunshot. In a fraction of a second, it inflates and deflates again, cushioning the blow of the body that's hurled into the steering wheel or dashboard.

A harmless gas is pumped into the airbag to inflate it. Then it quickly passes out through vents in the bag. It does not stay inflated like a pillow.

Are Airbags Harmful?

No—not if they're used properly. Sometimes a talcum powdery substance is released that might irritate the eyes or throat of the occupant, but that's a temporary thing. On occasion, occupants have also suffered abrasions from the coarse fabric the airbag is made from. Either of these discomforts is very minor compared to what can happen if you aren't protected by the airbag.

Types of Airbags

There are 4 basic types of airbags. Most vehicles come equipped with driver and passenger airbags. The others are optional.

<u>Driver</u>—located in the hub of the steering wheel.

<u>Passenger</u>—located in the dashboard in front of the passenger seat.

<u>Side-Impact</u>—located in the seat back, the door or the overhead roof rail.

<u>Rollover</u>—provide protection in rollovers so they stay inflated longer.

Used Airbags

Airbags are one-time use devices. Once an airbag has been deployed, it cannot be used again. A certified technician must replace it immediately. You can call your car dealer to find out where it should be done.

It will cost at least several hundred dollars to replace but it can save your life—(and if it's been deployed, it probably already has!)

Used Cars and Used Airbags

Because it costs a lot to reinstall airbags, people sometimes cheat when they resell the car. They make it look like the airbag is intact when it's actually been removed.

Make sure you have your mechanic verify that the airbag is in working condition before you buy the car.

Deactivated Airbags

On occasion, airbags are deactivated for safety reasons. This is very unusual and there's a lengthy government procedure that must be followed. Once the airbag is deactivated, the VIN (vehicle identification number) is entered into a government database.

Leading Causes of Fatalities by Vehicle-Type

- In SUVs : Rollover crashes are the leading cause of deaths
- In Passenger Cars: Frontal collisions are the leading cause of death

If you think the airbag in your used vehicle may have been legally deactivated, you can check the form at Safercar.gov. Simply enter your VIN and it will tell you if your vehicle is registered in the database.

Rollovers and Rollover Airbags

Rollover crashes are deadly. More than 10,000 people die in rollover crashes every year—most of them because they were ejected from the vehicle. (The people who are ejected but don't die, usually end up with debilitating head injuries that change their lives forever.) Seatbelts are absolutely key for surviving a vehicle rollover!

What causes rollover crashes?

Rollovers account for only 3% of crashes but 33% of deaths in crashes!

Most rollovers involve a single vehicle. There are two reasons why vehicles roll over:

1. Most often, they hit an obstruction or uneven surface that causes one side of the vehicle to be lower than the other. This sudden shift in balance causes the vehicle to roll over on its side. The force of that violent tipping movement causes the vehicle to continue rolling.
   The obstruction can be something as low as a curb or as high as a guardrail. A soft shoulder on a country road can be enough to put the vehicle off balance. A panicky driver who tries to jerk it back onto the road, could cause a rollover. (That's why it's important to practice the recovery maneuver in Driving Lesson 13.)
2. Rollovers can also happen when a driver swerves from side to side at a high speed. If the vehicle is carrying a load that shifts suddenly, the chances of a vehicle rollover go way up.

8 Tips for Avoiding a Rollover

1. Drive a vehicle that is less likely to roll over. (See list following and check NHTSA's ratings)
2. Use high-traction tires ("AA" is the highest traction rating) and make sure they are maintained in good condition.
3. Rollovers are often speed-related so remember to control your speed. Maintain the speed limit. Slow down in bad weather. Handle curves appropriately.

4. Don't drive impaired. Alcohol and drug-use often contribute to rollovers.
5. Load vehicles properly. Shifting loads are a big factor in rollover crashes. Your Owner's Manual will tell you the maximum load recommended for your vehicle, and the best way to distribute the load.
6. **If you're using a roof rack:** pay special attention to the manufacturer's instructions and weight limits. Any load placed on the roof will be raise the vehicle's center of gravity, and increase the chances of a rollover crash.
7. Practice the recovery techniques in Driving Lesson 13 so you can stay cool and safely recover from a situation where one set of wheels is lower than the other.
8. Use extra caution on rural roads.

Nearly 75% of all rollover crashes **occur in rural areas**

Three Tips for Minimizing Injuries in a Rollover

1. Always wear your seatbelt and do it up properly. Make sure all the other passengers are belted too so they don't injure you or other passengers.
2. Drive a vehicle equipped with rollover airbags.
3. Secure loose objects so they don't become projectiles in a rollover crash.

How Rollover Airbags Work

Vehicles that are equipped with rollover airbags also have very sophisticated rollover-sensing systems. In many cases, they can detect a rollover while the roll angle is very low and all 4 wheels are still on the ground.

When an impending rollover is detected, two things happen simultaneously. The seatbelts are cinched tighter so the occupants will stay firmly in their seats. At the same time, the side impact air bags are triggered so they protect the heads of the occupants from banging against the walls of the vehicle as it flips over. These airbags stay inflated longer than the dashboard ones, so they can continue to protect the occupants as the vehicle rolls over.

Note: All side airbags are not rollover airbags.

The Danger in Backing Up

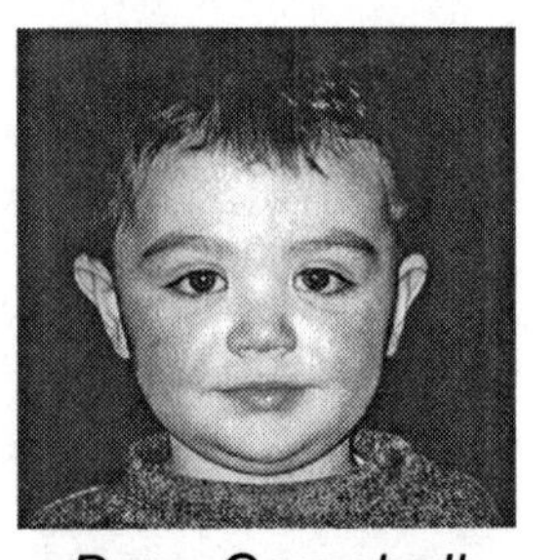

Drew Campbell

Every year, thousands of children are hurt or die because a driver who was backing up didn't see them.

Back-over accidents often happen because a toddler followed a parent into the driveway.

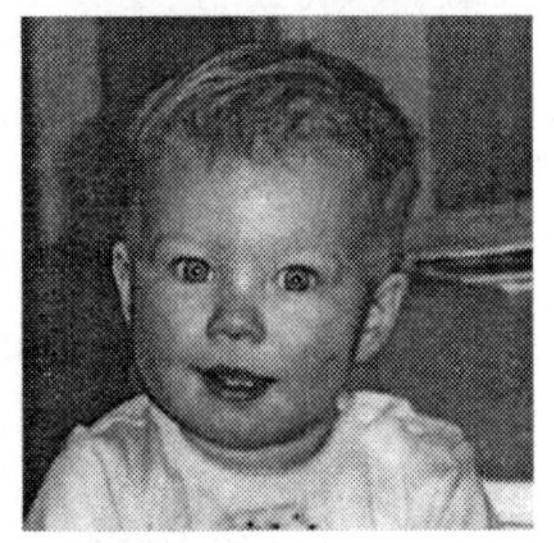

Madison Chatten

Little kids don't understand the danger. They can't protect themselves so you need to protect them. Before you jump in your vehicle and tear out of the driveway, remember these faces. They are 2 of the small children who were killed when vehicles backed over them. You'll find their stories on the following pages.

Drew's Story

Excitement was in the air. It was Easter Sunday and 2 year-old Drew was utterly delighted with the basket of goodies the Easter Bunny had left. He sampled several of the candies before heading outside with his dad to get things ready for the company. (The Campbells had moved into their brand new house 3 weeks ago and the whole family was coming for dinner tonight to celebrate the holiday and see their new home.)

Drew followed his dad, Steve, around 'helping' the way toddlers help but he kept thinking about that basket full of treats. Finally, his dad took him back into the house where his mom, Shannon, was putting the ham in the oven. He waited as patiently as he could until she finished. Then she held the basket of candies so he could choose the ones he wanted. (She still remembers exactly which pieces he picked.) When he finished his candy, she let him go back outside to help his dad.

Meanwhile, Steve decided to move his truck over to make room for the company. He backed part way out of the driveway and then pulled back in, closer to the side so another car would fit. He wasn't concerned when he hit a couple of bumps because the driveway wasn't paved yet and he figured they were just rocks.

He opened the door of the truck and jumped down. Then he started screaming so loudly that Shannon came running out of the house. Drew's little legs were sticking out in front of the truck and Steve suddenly realized that the bumps he felt were his own dear boy.

Drew was rushed to the hospital by helicopter. He died before his mom arrived in the police car. Other officers detained Steve so they could question him while they investigated the scene. They weren't familiar with this kind of accident and wanted to make sure Steve hadn't hurt his boy deliberately. Can you imagine how Steve felt?

As a father, Steve would have done anything to save his son. He would have run into a burning building to pull Drew out. He would have given his life for his boy—and now he was responsible for his death.

All Steve did was back out of his driveway. He didn't know Drew was there. Even though he was looking behind him when he backed up, he couldn't see Drew because the truck was high and the driveway had an incline. Drew was completely in his blind zone.

EVERY WEEK in the United States :

- 48 children are critically injured because they were backed over
- At least 2 children are ***killed*** because they were backed over
- Countless beloved pets, bicycles and other items are also destroyed

MOST:

- Victims are toddlers
- Vehicles are trucks, vans or SUVs
- Drivers are close relatives
- Incidents happen in family driveways or parking lots

Consider installing:

- Cross view mirrors
- Audible collision detectors
- A rear view video camera or some other type of back-up aid

DID YOU KNOW?

A 5'1" driver in a pickup truck can have a rear blind zone of 8 ft. by 50 ft.!

Every vehicle has a blind zone directly behind it. The area is larger on trucks and SUVs. Don't take chances.

- Before you get in your car to drive, walk all the way around it
- Back up slowly
- Look behind you and continually scan your mirrors while you're backing up

Madison's Story

Aaron Chatten got the call at work. Something terrible had happened to his daughter, Madison, at daycare! It would take several weeks, after the police investigation, for him to find out how his only child had died.

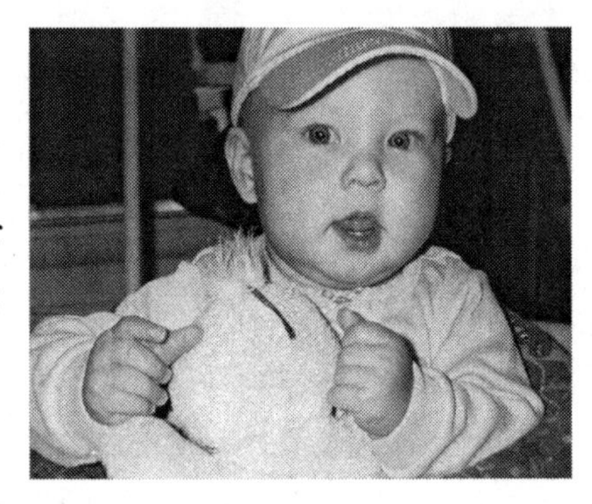

vMadison was a very active 14-month-old. She loved music and made her parents laugh when she bopped to the beat on the radio or the melodies from her favorite toys. She'd started walking at 7 months, so by the time she was a toddler, she was fast on her tiny feet. Both of her parents, Aaron and Sheena worked, so Madison went to a private daycare during the week. She was a sweet-natured girl and she'd made a special friend who she liked to play with.

On that day, the children had been playing in the yard when Madison's friend's mom arrived to pick up her daughter. The mom waved to the lady who was supervising the children to let her know she was taking her daughter. She was in a hurry because they were already late for a doctor's appointment. She whisked her daughter out to her waiting Suburban SUV. After buckling her daughter into the car seat, she'd backed out of the lot in a rush.

She'd backed over Madison who had followed her friend out of the backyard. Madison died before her parents were able to reach her.

Talk About It

1. What could the people in the above stories have done differently to prevent these accidents and save Drew and Madison's lives?
2. The Chattens live in Glasgow, Montana. It's a small community with a population of 3,500. Aaron is quick to point out that all the people involved in Madison's tragedy are good people. The sad truth is that terrible tragedies usually involve good people. (Only psychopaths set out to purposely ruin other people's lives.)

Tragedies happen for one of 2 reasons:

1. Good people don't understand the danger and they are rushed or careless so they make bad choices
2. Good people understand the danger and know what they should do but choose not to do it because they're so arrogant that they believe nothing terrible will ever happen to them

You know how dangerous backing up can be. What will you do to make sure this situation never happens to you or anyone you love?

FYI

Aaron Chatten talks to new teen drivers as often as he can. One of the things he talks about is how large the blind spot is, directly behind a large SUV. One time he got an entire class of 15 kids to crouch behind an SUV and the driver could not see them!

Check the Resources Section of our website for more information about The Madison Chatten Foundation.

Thanks to KidsandCars.org, for their help with this section. Don't take chances. If you need more reasons to back up safely, check out their website. They have far too many.

Additional tips for avoiding a back-over accident:

- Keep toys and other sports equipment off the driveway.
- Trim grass and bushes near the driveway so the driver can see pedestrians and they can see the driver too
- Never leave children alone in or around cars—not even for a second! They are faster than you think and have no fear of what could happen.
- Keep vehicles locked at all times—even when they're parked in the garage or driveway
- Most driveways have slight inclines. Use your parking brake to ensure the vehicle doesn't roll down the driveway accidentally.
- Make sure all child passengers leave the car after you park
- Take the hands of small passengers until they are safely away from all vehicles
- Keep your keys and remote device away from little ones. They aren't toys.
- Be especially vigilant during busy times, schedule changes and periods of crisis or holidays

Dealing with Distractions

I'm always amazed by the things people try to do while driving: putting on mascara, cuddling pets, reading books and studying maps. I even saw a man driving with a video camera pressed to his face one crowded holiday weekend. He was doing 60 mph on a 6-lane highway at the time!

Most adult drivers have sipped a coffee, downed a sandwich or changed a radio station at some point while they were behind the wheel. They've lived to tell the tale, so how bad could it be?

The fact is that each year, drivers who take their eyes off the road 'just for a moment', cause thousands of crashes. Spilled coffee, poked eyes and dropped CDs have caused thousands more.

Any distraction can be deadly, but novice drivers like you are particularly at risk because you don't have a lot of skill or experience yet.

Nearly 80% of crashes and 65% of near-crashes involved some form of driver inattention within three seconds before the event

HTSA Data 2006

Parents and Teens: This chapter deals with some of the most common driving distractions for teens. At the end of each section, there's a place to write

your Family Rule concerning that distraction. You'll use those Family Rules to modify Your Teen-Parent Contract before you both sign it.

Music

Teens love their tunes. Whether it's CDs, MP3s, or the radio—music is a big part of their lives.

There are 2 potential problems here:

1. Getting distracted while you change stations or CDs
2. Having the music so loud that it drowns out noises from outside the car including sirens, horns and even screams!

NOTE: Headphones and earbuds are illegal in many places. The driver of a car should **NEVER** wear them.

Are you the driver who sings your heart out every time your favorite songs come on?

> Many teens believe—
>
> **"If I'm sober, I'm safe."**
>
> In fact, alcohol is NOT a factor in more than 85% of crashes involving 16 year-old drivers.
>
> 2005 Allstate Foundation study

Singing is fun! You may get some funny looks from the drivers who pull up next to you at stoplights—but so what? It's okay to have some fun when you're driving.

Singing becomes a problem only if you close your eyes or take your focus off the road. Some teens (especially girls) get so carried away that they really crank the music and dance while they're driving. This can be disastrous if you accidentally hit the brake instead of the accelerator (or vice versa.)

Keep your hands on the wheel, your eyes on the road and your focus on driving—and singing to the music won't be a problem for you. (Oh—and keep the music at a level that rocks but still allows you to hear what's going on around you.)

Recommendations about Changing Stations or CDs

Ask your passenger to change the music for you. When you're alone, wait until the car is stopped before you make changes.

Family Rules about Music in the Car:

Decide on your family rules for music in the car. Write them in the space on the next page:

____

____

____

Passengers

Question: What do you get when you put 3 or more teens together?

Answer: A party!

Teens like to have fun and a car provides lots of opportunity for laughs. But some teens pressure each other to take risks and do things they wouldn't do on their own.

Research proves that the more teens are in the car, the more likely it is to be involved in a crash.

Some teens think it's funny to cover the driver's eyes or tickle them when they're driving.

Tip from Lauren, the Driving Instructor:

Know the risks.

A study done in 2008 by the AAA showed most parents know driving is dangerous for new drivers, but knowingly allow their teens to take part in dangerous driving habits—***especially driving with teen passengers.***

> 47% of teens admit that passengers sometimes distract them.
>
> 2005 Allstate Foundation Study

Make it your job to educate yourself on the things that increase your teen's crash risk and create policies for this behavior. To be effective these policies must be enforced.

(**Note:** That's what your Teen-Parent Driving Contract is all about!)

What are your family rules about interfering with the driver?

Family Rules about Passengers in the Car

Many states and provinces limit the number of teen passengers who are allowed in the car with a new driver. Start with those restrictions and then decide on your family rules for passengers in the car. Write them in the space below:

____

____

____

Eating and Drinking

You need two hands on the wheel. Eating and drinking are distractions that take your mind off driving and at least one hand off the wheel.

Pull over to eat or drink. You'll enjoy it more and you aren't as likely to spill ketchup on your shirt or hot coffee in your lap.

Are there some foods that you should never eat in cars? What about:

- Pasta
- Salads
- Meats that needs to be cut with a knife
- Foods that are dipped in something else

Family Rules on Eating and Drinking in the Car

Decide on your family rules for eating and drinking in the car. Write them in the space below:

____

____

____

Smoking

Smoking is smelly and unhealthy. Ashes fall and burn holes in your clothes and upholstery. Smoking lowers the resale value of your vehicle and leaves sticky yellow scum on your windshield. It's also a distraction that takes a hand off the wheel.

Fires have been started when drivers accidentally drop their cigarettes or flick their butts into the back seat. Passengers are exposed to second-hand-smoke.

There's simply no 'upside' to smoking in the car.

Family Rules about Smoking in the Car

Decide on your family rules for smoking in the car. Write them in the space below:

____

____

____

Cell Phones and Texting

Conversations in Cars

Can you imagine if people acted in cars, the way they act in elevators? It would be *so* uncomfortable. Everyone would be staring straight ahead and nobody would be talking.

Nobody thinks you should drive like that. Talking is sociable and it's part of what makes driving so much fun. But talking is a distraction too—and talking on a cell phone is very dangerous!

When You're in a Car: Talking on a Cell Phone is NOT the Same as Talking to Your Passenger.

It's More Like Driving Drunk!

> **When you're texting—the chances of getting in a crash go up to 8 times!**
>
> **46% of teens admit to texting while driving**
>
> www.underyourinfluence.org

It's a matter of brainpower and it doesn't matter how smart you are, how talented you are, or how mature you are. Talking on a cell phone makes you **4 times** more likely to get in a crash—even if you're using a hands-free device! That's the same as if you were legally impaired with a blood-alcohol level of 0.08!

Dr. David Strayer is a professor at the University of Utah and he's spent a lot of time studying how talking on cell phones affects drivers. "The brain doesn't work the way we want it to work," he says. "When drivers talk on cell phones, they have a sort of tunnel vision. It's partly because they fixate straight ahead and stop looking at their side mirrors. But it's more than that too. Talking on a cell phone requires multitasking and the fact is—less than 2% of people can multitask effectively."

Real science backs that up. Dr. Strayer and his team measured the brain activity of people involved in conversations. When they talked on cell phones while driving—their brain activity was cut in half. It seems that the frontal cortex of the brain which controls multitasking becomes overloaded and simply can't process all the information it receives—so it leaves things out. And when the info that gets left out involves obstacles you should be seeing—that's scary!

What You See When You're Distracted

What's Really There!

All of a sudden, the driver doesn't see what's happening in the periphery of their vision. That means they can't see pedestrians or cyclists to their sides—even though they're in plain view. Their brain blocks them out and there's nothing they can do to stop it. It's called 'inattention blindness.'

The driver concentrates straight ahead—but even there—their mind plays tricks! Details and objects can disappear completely. They don't see them because their overloaded brain just doesn't process them.

So why is it different when you're talking to the passenger next to you?

Your passenger provides a second set of eyes on the road. They automatically stop talking as you approach an intersection and wait until you're clear before they continue. They also point out obstacles you may not be aware of.

The person at the other end of the cell phone, however, doesn't know where you are or what you're doing so they continue to talk regardless of what's happening on the road. And you instinctively continue to listen—instead of giving that intersection ahead your full attention.

Even the most mundane conversations are dangerous.

It doesn't matter what you're talking about. All cell conversations are dangerous while you're driving.

> More than 56% of teens admit to using their cell phone while they drive.
>
> 2005 Allstate Foundation study

"What are you doing?"

" Nothing."

"How was school?"

"Fine."

Those conversations aren't very creative but they still overload your brain and quadruple your chances of getting in a crash. Angry, upsetting or sad conversations are even worse. And if you're negotiating, need to write down numbers or remember directions—yikes! You are a disaster waiting to happen!

And texting is even worse. Your brain will continue to play tricks on you, but now your eyes are off the road for several seconds at a time too.

When you're texting—the chances of getting in a crash go up to 8 times!

Dr. Strayer warns teens, "Every generation thinks they're different. We all think we're better drivers than our parents. Teens believe they're better texters and cell phone users too because they've grown up with the technology—and they probably are. But that doesn't mean they can talk on their cells and drive or text while they drive. No one can.

Technology is addictive like gambling. We use it all the time so we get lulled into a false sense of security. This is very dangerous for everyone, but teens are most at risk because they are the least experienced drivers."

Passengers can talk and text as much as they want, but drivers should NEVER send or receive texts. If you think ***you*** can handle it—check out the story below.

Almost Home

Leeza held her cell phone at arm's-length and her two best friends automatically leaned in and made faces. She snapped the photo and then burst into laughter when she saw the shot. Three goofy girls with their eyes wide and their tongues out! (*Even so—they were beautiful!*)

Annie waved at the waiter to get their bill and popped a final nacho in her mouth. She loved Leeza and Kate. When this evening started, she'd been down in the dumps about something that had happened at school. Leeza had insisted they get together to talk about it over food. Leeza did everything "over food." It was their joke.

Annie really hadn't wanted to come out tonight. It was late and she was into her pity party. But Leeza had a way of seeing the bright—or funny—side of everything. And she never gave up about anything so there was no point in saying no anyway. (That was probably why she had so many medals and trophies at home. Leeza could do anything! She ran track, made swim team, starred at lacrosse—you name it!)

And now Annie was glad she'd come. The world seemed brighter and everything seemed okay again. Whatever happened—she had her friends and they could make anything better.

The three of them linked arms and headed out to the parking lot—laughing and talking all the way. Leeza jumped into the driver's seat and started the car. She was still laughing at something Kate said as she tossed her purse into the backseat with Annie. In all the confusion and activity, she forgot to do up her seat belt.

She pulled out of the parking lot onto Eastside Drive and headed toward Kate's house. They were only a few blocks away. She inched into the intersection at Main Street and waited for the light to change so she could complete her left turn.

• • • • •

Andrew was supposed to meet some friends at a new restaurant on Eastside Drive for a late night snack. He was having trouble finding it so he grabbed his cell phone and did a quick search. He was scrolling down to the address when the light ahead turned red. He didn't see it.

• • • • •

A witness said Andrew was doing 50 to 55 miles per hour (the speed limit was 30) when he rammed into the driver's side of Leeza's car—crushing her on impact. A paramedic was in the car behind her and rushed to help. There was nothing he could do. Annie and Kate survived the crash but Leeza died at the scene. She was seventeen years old.

Think About It

1. 19 year-old Andrew wasn't seriously injured in the crash and he wasn't charged with murder even though he was impaired. (Tests showed he had marijuana in his system). Instead, he was allowed to plead guilty to negligent homicide, which carries a sentence of up to one year in prison.
2. If you were on Andrew's jury, what do you think a fair sentence would be?

3. Leeza was an innocent victim in this story, but she made two mistakes. Did you catch them?

   a) ______________________________

   b) ______________________________

Answer to #3 is on page 237.

Lauren's Story:

"Almost Home" is based on the true story of Lauren Mulkey. She was seventeen years old when she died on March 18, 2007. Like Leeza, she was smart, pretty and athletic. She loved life. She was a good friend and daughter. Her future was bright and she could have accomplished anything.

That night her mom, Linda, warned her about drunk drivers. It was St. Paddy's Day and people would be drinking. But Lauren wanted to visit her girlfriends. She was a safe and sober driver and she promised to be careful.

Neither mother nor daughter worried about a driver armed with a cell phone.

So Many Changed Lives...

A sudden, tragic death changes the lives of all the people left behind. No one who knew and loved Lauren will ever be the same.

Her mom is Linda Mulkey. Linda's alone now. More than two years have passed and you can still hear the pride—and sadness—in her voice when she talks about her only child.

Being Lauren's mom was the most important thing in the world to her and now Lauren's gone. Sometimes Linda goes to lacrosse games and sporting events that Lauren's friends participate in. If the sadness overwhelms her, she has to leave because she can't stop crying.

Linda's mission is to warn other teens about the danger of cell phones and texting while driving. She hopes they'll listen to Lauren's story so no other family will be destroyed as hers was. She talks to student groups when she can and runs a website called hangupsavealife.com.

The Driver and His Family

Theodore Jorgensen, the driver who crashed into Lauren, was devastated. One minute he was happily looking forward to a meal with friends, and the next minute he was responsible for the death of a beautiful young woman, injuries to her friends and countless thousands of dollars in damage.

He hadn't used a gun or a knife. He hadn't intended to hurt anyone at all—but the damage was done just the same, and he could never undo it.

His family was grief-stricken for the victims and terrified of what could happen to their son and brother in prison. But they were lucky. They received an incredible blessing. Lauren's mother, Linda, had been in the courtroom every day. She'd watched Theodore and had seen how young and frightened he looked. Even though her heart was broken, she didn't want his life to be destroyed in prison. Linda asked the court to show mercy on him. As a result, he was sentenced to probation and 500 hours of community service.

Theodore hadn't known how dangerous it could be to use a cell phone while driving, but now **you** do. How much are you willing to give up to use your cell phone while you drive?

TIP: Check the Resources section of TeensLearntoDrive.com for information about new technologies that restrict cell phones and texting while driving.

Crash Analysis

Using the details from the story, complete the chart below. (Answers are on page 237).

Road Conditions	Visibility	Site of Crash
☐ Dry ☐ Wet or icy	☐ Not a factor ☐ Poor - foggy, heavy rain, etc.	☐ City street ☐ Intersection ☐ High speed thruway or highway
Light Conditions	**# of Vehicles in Collision**	**Teen Passengers** (not including the driver)
☐ Daylight ☐ Dark: Late night or early morning	☐ 1 ☐ 2 or more	☐ None ☐ 1 only ☐ More than 1
Driver's Experience Level	**Driver's Physical Condition**	**Driver's Mental Condition**
☐ Less than 1 year ☐ 2 to 3 years ☐ More than 3 years ☐ Unknown	☐ Alert ☐ Impaired by drugs ☐ Impaired by alcohol ☐ Extremely tired	☐ Focused on Driving ☐ Distracted ☐ Other
Was Driver Error a Factor?	**Wearing Seatbelts?**	**The Crash Happened:**
☐ Yes ☐ No ☐ Unknown	☐ Yes ☐ No ☐ Unknown	☐ Close to home ☐ Far from home

1. Based on your analysis (above) what do you think caused this crash?

____

____

2. How could this crash have been avoided?

____

____

Recommendation:

Leave the phone on if you need to—but don't answer it. Have a signal for emergency calls like "Ring once. Hang up and call right back." Then, if you're driving and hear that signal, pull off the road in a safe place and respond to the message the caller left you.

But if the temptation to talk or text while you're driving is too great—turn the phone off completely.

Go to TeensLearntoDrive.com for links to videos about cell phones and texting.

Family Rules about Talking and Texting in the Car

Decide on your family rules for cell phone use (talking and texting) in the car. Write them in the space below:

____

____

Word Search Puzzle: Distractions

```
              N O Q R E
          Z N Y I X D T G
        A T J I K     L N B
      W W U Q N S       S E L
    G L D Z K S R         X M V
    J S A F M E C         W P U E K A M
  E C A L O S C H E E S E B U R G E R K D
  G N I K L A T L X L K S D N E I R F M B O
N A J I K K Q S X O Y L S C A D X J A F H L
V E N J U F C E R E C A P H D N O P O D O E
N G V I D T L A P F T Y G H A Q C N F L I C
V D K R T X P T O B J V R X O M G E J Q M O
Z V I Z X U Z D W I K B W Q R N E E U K V
    C C Z R                 R E R L
      N E                     C W
```

Read the questions below and fill in your answers. Then find your answers in the word search puzzle above. (The Answers are on page 238.)

HINT: The answers can be in any direction—including backwards.

1. This kind of heated conversation can be very distracting. ____________
2. Talking on this takes your mind off the road. ____________
3. You'll enjoy this more in a restaurant. _________

4. You don't want to spill this in your lap! ___________
5. Some kids like to _______ to the music but not when you're driving. (You could confuse the accelerator with the brake!)
6. When you're the driver, you're responsible for their safety. _____________
7. This can help you find your way. ______
8. Swatting these when you're driving can be more dangerous than getting stung! ________
9. Girls—put this on before you leave home—not in the car.
10. If you don't have a GPS, read this _______
11. Changing this to your station can be a distraction.
12. Distractions are dangerous because they take your eyes (and your mind) off the ___________.
13. Adjust this before you start the car or you could slide too far forward. __________
14. Doing this makes your car smelly and leaves yellow scum inside your windshield. ___________
15. ___________ with friends takes your mind off the road.
16. Reading these messages, takes your eyes off the road. ______________

Driver Distractions Crossword Puzzle

How much do you remember about distractions that can cause crashes? Try the crossword puzzle below to test your memory. (Answers are on page 239.)

ACROSS

2. When you're really, really sleepy, you're too ________ to drive.
3. Don't drive without this because accidents are very expensive. ______________
4. This will keep you safely inside your car. _______________
8. Drivers should always be ___________ the road ahead for obstructions or hazards.
9. Don't use ________ control when it's raining.
11. This person loves you and wants you to stay safe. ___________
13. Don't let your car run out of this or you could get stranded. _________
15. If you get into trouble, ________ your parents for help.
16. Never do this and drive. _____________
18. Speeders often run through _________ lights.
21. Teens drive a lot during the summer and on the ______________.

DOWN

1. Every driver should know how to read a ________.
2. The ____________ driver must stay sober.
5. Doing this takes your eyes off the road. _____________
6. Every new driver and their parents should sign one of these. ______________
7. Cutting off another driver can lead to road ____________.
10. A spark from ___________ electricity can ignite gas fumes.
12. You do this 3 times a day—but not while you're driving please!
14. This kills—so slow down! __________
17. Let your parents _________ where you're going is case you need help.
19. If you play your music too ______ . you can't hear sirens and other important noises outside the car.
20. Driving a car is a lot more complicated than riding a ________________.

Basic Driving Skills and Tips

Dress for Success

Drivers need to dress for success. You don't have to wear a racing jumpsuit but you should dress comfortably with footwear that allows you to move freely.

Here are some tips:

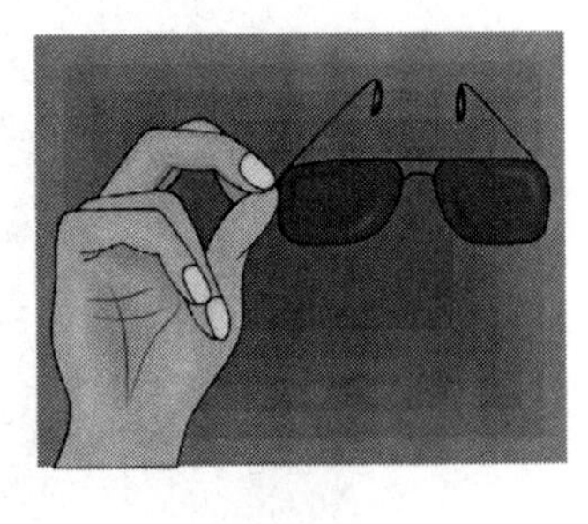

- You NEED good polarized sunglasses with a protective case. Reserve them for driving and keep them in the car.
- Hats are okay as long as they don't impair your vision or restrict your movement.
- No bare feet because your feet will sweat and could slip off the pedals
- No rubber flip-flops because they can get tangled in the pedals
- No heavy boots that make it difficult to swivel your foot between the accelerator and the brake
- No bulky jackets that make it difficult to move around
- If you wear gloves make sure they're leather or have palm grips
- Mittens are not advisable for driving

About Steering

When I learned to drive (in the Dark Ages), I learned hand-over-hand steering. My hands were in the 10 o'clock—2 o'clock positions, which provided a firm grip on the wheel. Turns were smooth and I had control of the car.

But—guess what? That's not the preferred steering method any more. Airbags have changed that. The problem with hand-over-hand steering is that your hands cross over the airbag. If the airbag activates it could break your arms.

Micro-Steering

New drivers often make a big mistake by trying to stay in the middle of their lane by micro-steering the car. They watch the lines on the road and try to stay within them. You can't do it and it's dangerous to drive that way. You need to be looking much further down the road. The car will go where your eyes are looking.

Try the following experiment.

A Steering Experiment

Fill a glass with water—to 1" from the top. Walk across the room, trying to keep the water from spilling by watching the glass and keeping it steady.

Now—refill the glass and walk across the room again. This time—don't watch the glass. Focus on the other side of the room.

Conclusion: It's much easier to keep the water in the glass if you don't watch it. Your body will automatically do the job if you just focus on where you're going.

Steering a car works the same way. Keep your eyes on the road ahead. Watch where you're going and you'll stay within your lane.

Tips from Lauren, the Driving Instructor:

Steering:

"10 and 2 is actually not the proper place for hands on the steering wheel. This out of date placement doesn't take airbags, or steering ability into account. When the hands are at 10 and 2, the driver's arms are in front of the steering wheel's airbag. If the airbag goes off with hands in this position (or at the top of the steering wheel) the arms can be broken.

Proper hand placement is at 3 and 9. This puts the arms **to the side of the airbag;** not in front of it. The driver also has **more control** of the car at 3 and 9 than at 10 and 2. With this hand position, the steering wheel can be turned further without binding the arms, or being forced to remove the arms from the steering wheel to complete a turn. Keeping both hands on the steering wheel as much as possible is very important to maintaining control. 3 and 9 makes this possible.

Also, if you ever lose control of the car, it may be difficult to reorient yourself with the steering wheel if you're looking for 10 and 2.

It is far **easier to locate 3 and 9**, because this is where practically every steering wheel spoke starts. If you're in a spin and need to "find straight", you have a better chance doing so with 3 and 9."

Chapter 6
Structured Practice
After Getting a Learner's Permit

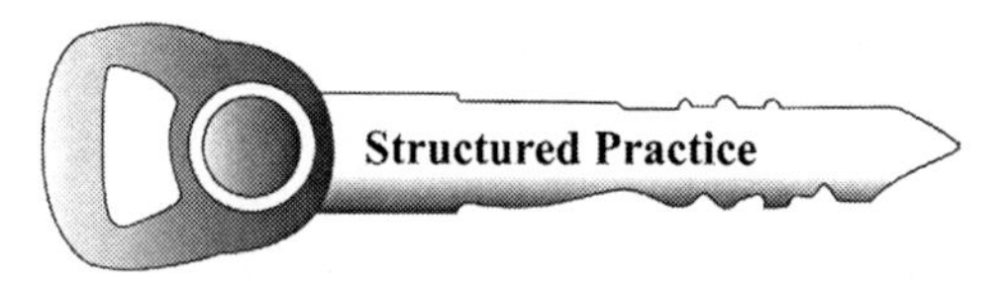

In-Car Driving Sessions

Once your teen has earned their Level 1 License (Learner's Permit), they can begin learning to drive. You can then:

- Sign them up for a professional driver training course (recommended) and use the following lesson plan to supplement that course. These lessons will help your teen develop the reflexive driving skills they need and ensure you cover all the bases. *(You'll find tips on how to choose the right driver training program in the Resources section at the back of this book.)*
- Or you can begin teaching them to drive using the lesson plan that follows.

Tip from Lauren, the Driving Instructor:

"Start out right. Before you let your teen drive an inch, make sure seating, hand, and mirror positions are correct."

Recommended Lesson Plan

Overview:

In this plan, each lesson takes about one week. You can move ahead on some lessons faster if you achieve mastery more quickly, but don't move on to the next lesson until you've mastered the current one. (Your coach will determine when you're ready to move ahead).

You've scheduled 2 or 3 sessions with your coach each week, so break down the activities into manageable chunks.

2-Part Lessons

This lesson plan was developed to make sure you cover all the material. It has 2 essential parts:

1. **Need-to-Know Info**—This "classroom" portion includes critical safety and maintenance information for drivers. It should be done at home. Access to a computer with Internet is required.
   Written Tips, Stories and Activities—Go to the specified page numbers in this book to find great information about each topic.

Related Videos—Go to TeensLearntoDrive.com. Select the link to the "Free Video Library" from your "Favorites" (per instructions on page 3). Scroll down to the correct lesson number. Select "Need-to-Know Info" to see the videos that relate to that lesson. Click on each video to watch it.
TIP: Rainy days and evenings are good times to do the "Need-to-Know Info" which is "classroom" work.

2. **Structured Practice**—
This is where you 'take it to the street' (or the parking lot!) You'll find helpful checklists here and information about when and where the driving sessions should be held.
Written Tips and Instructions—You'll find expert tips about proper form and how to execute maneuvers right in the lesson plan. Read them in the car, while you're parked in a safe place *before* you start the lesson. Never read instructions while you're driving.
Video Tips—Go to TeensLearntoDrive.com immediately before your driving lesson, to watch expert videos on driving techniques. Then they'll be fresh in your mind when you try to duplicate them while you're driving in the car.
To see the instructional videos, Select the link to the "Free Video Library" from your "Favorites" (per instructions on page 3). Scroll down to the correct lesson number. Select "Structured Practice" to see the videos that relate to that lesson.
Click on each video to watch it.

In-Car Practice TIPS:

You may wish to limit your first in-car lessons to half an hour or less because there's a lot to absorb and remember. Extend the lesson length as your skills develop. Review each previous session until it's mastered before moving on.

At the end of each session, complete an entry in the Driving Practice Log on page 267.

Parent/Coach: Take a few minutes to plan each in-car session. Read through the skills you'll be practicing and decide on a location to suit those activities.

Lesson Checklist

Check off the lessons below as you complete them.

- ☐ LESSON 1: Preparing to Drive, Starting & Stopping
- ☐ LESSON 2: Turning
- ☐ LESSON 3: Backing Up
- ☐ LESSON 4: Basic Parking Skills
- ☐ LESSON 5: Emergency Stops
- ☐ LESSON 6: Emergency Stops with Steering
- ☐ LESSON 7: Space Management and Scanning
- ☐ LESSON 8: Right Turns on Residential Streets
- ☐ LESSON 9: Left Turns on Residential Streets

- ☐ LESSON 10: Navigating the Neighborhood
- ☐ LESSON 11: Turns on Busier Roads
- ☐ LESSON 12: Interacting with Other Vehicles
- ☐ LESSON 13: Driving on Country Roads
- ☐ LESSON 14: Other Parking (Parallel, Underground, etc.)
- ☐ LESSON 15: Rain & Wet Ground
- ☐ LESSON 16: Night Driving
- ☐ LESSON 17: 2-Lane Highways
- ☐ LESSON 18: Pulling Over
- ☐ LESSON 19: Snow and Ice
- ☐ LESSON 20: Following Directions and Finding Your Way

Note: There are 5 additional lessons on advanced skills in Chapter 9.

LESSON 1: Preparing to Drive, Starting & Stopping

Coaches: This week make sure you get off to a good start. Your teen will want to get in the car and start driving, but don't cut corners. Make sure they understand and practice all the steps they need to take every time they get behind the wheel.

Don't forget to review the coaching tips on page 50.

This week work through the following sections. Check them off as you complete them:

- ☐ Developing a Seatbelt Habit (page 53)
- ☐ Airbag Safety (page 59)
- ☐ Dress for Success (page 76)
- ☐ About Steering (page 77)

Related Videos:

Go to TeensLearntoDrive.com. Select the link to the "Free Video Library" from your "Favorites" (per instructions on page 3). Under Driving Lesson 1" select:

- ☐ "Structured Practice" to watch videos related to your in-car session.
- ☐ "Need-to-Know Info" to watch videos that relate to the "Need-to-Know Info" sections listed above.

Check them off when you complete them.

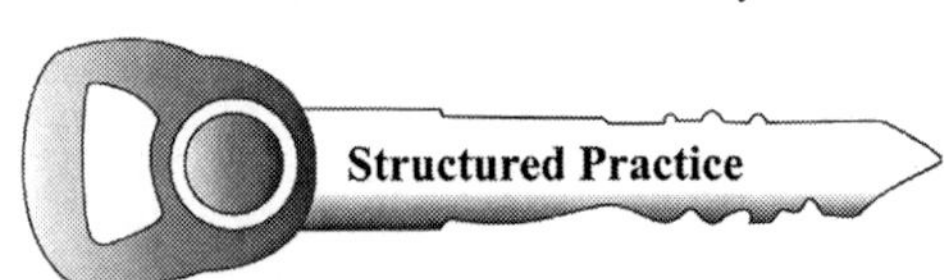

Location: An empty parking lot (The parent/coach should drive to and from the practice lot.)

Conditions: Clear, dry, daylight

Lesson Length: 30 Minutes

Materials Required: A tape measure, the Owner's Manual for your vehicle, this workbook

Goals:

- ☐ Review your vehicle
- ☐ Learn the 7 things you need to do <u>every time</u> you drive
- ☐ Start and stop smoothly

Start by Reviewing Your Vehicle

You don't need the car keys yet.

Using your "Saturday with Dad Checklist", make sure you remember where everything is located. Review the dashboard and what all the dials and symbols mean.

NOTES:

- Turn the **<u>radio off</u>** for all driving lessons. It's a distraction and you need to focus your complete attention on the road and on your coach.
- Turn your **<u>headlights on</u>** for all driving lessons. It will help other cars see you—even on sunny days.

7 Things to Do Before You Start the Car:

1. ***Walk Around the Car***
   a) Get in the habit of walking around the car before you get in. Then you'll see if there are any obstacles in front or behind you. There have been many tragic accidents when children were hidden behind cars that backed out of driveways.
   b) You'll also notice if there is any damage to your car. If someone scratched your car in a parking lot, you want to know before you drive away.
2. ***Adjust your Seat***
   You need to be high enough to see clearly and close enough to use the accelerator and brake. You also need to be <u>at least 10 inches</u> back from the airbag so if it explodes, you won't get hurt.
   Tip: Use your measuring tape to make sure you're at least 10 inches from the steering wheel.

Lauren's Tip for Proper Seat Adjustment

"Parents: Have your teens sit with their backs against the seat and their hands over the top of the steering wheel. Their wrists should 'break' at the top of the wheel and drape over the side.
If they have to lean forward to do this, they are sitting too far back. If the steering wheel hits further up their arm, they are too far forward.
Now, everyone's body proportions are different. Some people have longer arms than others. Some modifications may be necessary to ensure safety.
If your teen's knees hit the dash when their arms are at proper distance, try these adjustments:

- Move the seat down
- Change the position of the steering wheel
- Put the seat back and/or up"

3. ***Adjust Your Mirrors***
   On most modern cars, blind spots can be minimized or eliminated by setting the driver-side and passenger-side mirrors correctly.
   Simply follow Lauren's instructions below.

Lauren, the Driving Instructor on Understanding Your (Side) Blind Spots

"Cars have blind spots because we adjust our mirrors improperly. When you look at your side mirrors you can probably see the side of your car.
Why do you want to see that? It's going where the front of the car is going, and no one is going to steal your gas cap at 65 mph.
As drivers we have this notion that we need to see how our car is positioned in the lane through our rear view mirrors. (Just look out the windshield for that.) Your mirrors may also overlap with the rear view mirror. (Meaning, when you look in both your side mirrors and your rear view mirror, you see the same objects.) This isn't taking full advantage of the visual possibilities of side mirrors."

Lauren's Tips for How to Properly Adjust Your Mirrors:

Parents- Stand an arm's length away from the rear quarter panel of the car.
Have your teen adjust the side view mirror so they can see your body. (Often—they'll want to adjust it to see your face. That's incorrect. Make sure they understand they should look at your body. That's the height where another car would be.) Do the same for the other side.
Slowly walk around the car at arm's length, stopping every so often to ask if your teen can see you. *They should be able to.* You will start to disappear when you get toward the front door, but a car is much longer than you are. *When the front of a car is where the front door is, the rear of the car will still be visible in the mirror, thus eliminating the blind spot.*

> When I learned to drive, I knew I had blind spots that weren't covered by my mirrors. I learned to use peripheral vision and quick glances over my shoulders to ensure there were no cars nearby that I couldn't see in my mirrors.
>
> So when Lauren told me I could eliminate the blind spots by setting my mirrors correctly, I was skeptical. But I have to tell you—it worked. I was able to eliminate my side blind spots.
>
> Try it out in the driveway first. Set your mirrors as she recommends and have your parent walk around the car. Can you see them everywhere? If not—try readjusting your mirrors.

NOTE: There is also a blind spot below the rear window on your vehicle. This spot cannot be removed without technology like back up cameras and parking sensors. That's why it's always best to walk around your car before you get in and drive.

4. ***Adjust Your Headrest***
   The headrest has a purpose beyond comfort. If you get in a crash, the headrest will support your head and could keep you from getting whiplash. You need to make sure you position it properly.
   Position the headrest so it's squarely behind your head. When you're sitting upright (ready to drive) your head should be within a couple of inches of the headrest.
5. ***Adjust the steering wheel***
   Adjust the steering wheel so it's comfortable. Slightly tilted is best.
6. ***Do your "Seatbelt Check!"***
7. ***Lock the doors***
   (If they don't automatically lock when you put the car in gear.)

Starting and Stopping Smoothly

Now you're almost ready to move the car. Read through this entire section before you get started.

Moving the Car Forward Smoothly

You don't have to touch the gas pedal to make the car move. Really!

Before you start the car: Locate the gas pedal and the brake pedal. Put your foot in position with your heel on the floor so you can swivel back and forth between the gas and the brake comfortably.

Make sure the car is in PARK. Now start the car. With your foot on the brake, put the car in 'Drive'. Slowly lift your foot off the brake. Do not give the car any gas. The car will move forward slowly.

> ***The Parking Brake***
>
> Most people rarely use their parking brake. They reserve it for when they're parked on steep inclines or need extra stopping power. However, it's still a good idea to check that the brake isn't on before you try to move the car—especially if you weren't the last one who drove it.

This will be all the speed you need for some maneuvers. Hover your foot over the brake in case you need to stop suddenly. Lift it slowly off the brake to start moving again.

Repeat the same maneuver in 'Reverse.' This slow speed is all the speed you'll need for backing up in many cases. Don't forget to walk around behind the vehicle before you back up.

Braking Smoothly

It's important to be able to stop smoothly. When you brake, you use your right foot. That's the same foot you use for the gas. Your heel should be on the floor so you can swivel your foot easily between the gas and the brake.

Continue Practicing

Practice starting and stopping until you get the feel for the gas and brake pedals and can apply pressure evenly. Then give the car a little gas and watch the speedometer to see how fast you're moving.

When you're driving, your eyes will be moving constantly between your mirrors and the road ahead. You'll also need to keep an eye on how fast you are going so get in the habit of glancing at your speedometer often.

Continue to increase your speed until you can stop and start smoothly at low speeds. This is the kind of starting and stopping you'll be doing most of the time—smooth and controlled. But sometimes you'll need to stop suddenly and that takes additional skill. (You'll cover sudden stops in Lesson 5.)

Practice these skills:

- ☐ 11- Point start-up checklist
    - ☐ Before you get in the car, open the hood. Check your windshield washer fluid level. If it's low, fill it up.
    - ☐ Walk around the car
    - ☐ Check your gas gauge
    - ☐ Adjust your seat
    - ☐ Adjust your mirrors
    - ☐ Adjust your headrest
    - ☐ Adjust your steering wheel
    - ☐ Turn off your cell phone during your driving lessons. Once you have your license, you might decide to leave it on but not answer or let your passenger answer.
    - ☐ Secure any loose objects
    - ☐ Seatbelt check
    - ☐ Lock the doors
- ☐ 9 o'clock/ 3 o'clock hand position
- ☐ Smooth starts
- ☐ Smooth stops
- ☐ Smooth acceleration (Keep it to low speeds)

LESSON 2: Turning

Parents/Coaches: Be sure to cover the "Need-to-Know Info" sessions by watching the videos and completing the lessons with your teen. This week's videos are all about distractions. New drivers need to focus on the road. Distractions can be deadly. These topics will also be used later to build your Teen-Parent Driving Contract.

In the driving practice, you'll be working on turns. Turning is an important driving skill that's best practiced without the interference of traffic and pedestrians, so stay in the parking lot this week. Take as much time as you need, to make sure their turns are smooth and controlled.

Did you know there are 3 parts to every turn? Watch the "Structured Practice" videos with your student, to find out what they are and how to execute safe turns.

Don't forget to have your driver complete a Driving Practice Log entry at the end of the lesson.

This week work through the following topics. Check them off as you complete them:

- ☐ Dealing with Distractions (page 65)
- ☐ Music (page 66)
- ☐ Passengers (page 67)
- ☐ Eating and Drinking (page 68)
- ☐ Smoking (page 68)

Related Videos:

Go to TeensLearntoDrive.com. Select the link to the "Free Video Library" from your "Favorites" (per instructions on page 3). Under Driving Lesson 2" select:

- ☐ "Structured Practice" to watch videos related to your in-car session.
- ☐ "Need-to-Know Info" to watch videos that relate to the "Need-to-Know Info" sections listed above.

Check them off when you complete them.

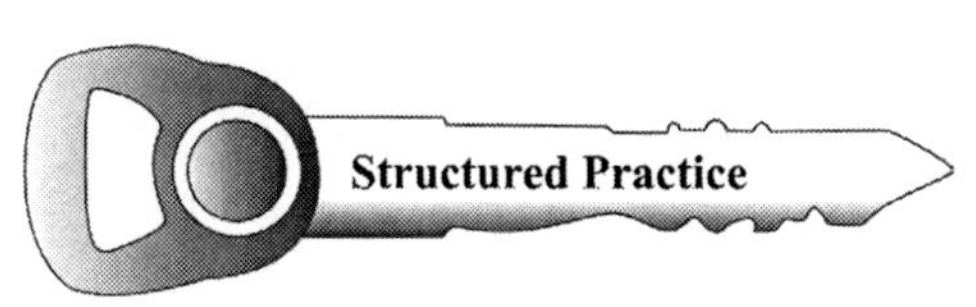

Location:	An empty parking lot. (The parent/coach should drive to and from the practice space.)
Conditions:	Clear, dry, daylight
Lesson Length:	30 minutes

START-UP CHECKLIST			
1	Check your windshield washer fluid.	7	Adjust your steering wheel.
2	Walk around your vehicle.	8	Turn off your cell phone.
3	Check your gas gauge.	9	Secure any loose objects.
4	Adjust your seat.	10	Buckle your seatbelt and make sure your passengers buckle-up too.
5	Adjust your mirrors.		
6	Adjust your headrest.	11	Lock the doors.

Right and Left Turns

You'll need to be able to make wide turns and tight turns, so choose an empty parking lot that gives you lots of space.

Drivers need to be able to make tight, controlled turns. These are the kinds of turns you'll be making when you turn right and when you park.

You'll also need to be able to make smooth wider turns. You'll make wider turns when you turn left or when you're driving on a curved ramp to enter a highway.

All turns and curves must be controlled. Driving too fast into any curve can cause you to lose control.

Practice Basic Turning

Practice these exercises to make sure you understand how your vehicle responds at different speeds.

1. Make a large circle around a light standard or signpost. Circle it several times at a constant, slow speed.
2. Increase your speed slightly and tighten your circle.
3. Make a figure-8 pattern to practice slow, controlled turns in both directions.
4. Increase your speed slightly and tighten your turns to get the feel of how the car responds at different speeds

Turning at Intersections

Now that you have a feel for how the car reacts, it's time to add the other things you need to do when you turn on busy streets.

You're still practicing in an empty parking lot so you won't have to worry about other traffic, but it's still important to practice all the steps so you'll know what to do when you take it to the street.

Now that you have the feel of turning, practice approaching an intersection and making a turn.

9 Steps to Making a Safe Turn at an Intersection

Use these 9 steps every time you make a turn at an intersection;

1. As you approach the turn, check your rearview mirror so you know who's behind you and how close they are. You need to do this well in advance so you don't get rear-ended by someone who's following too closely. If they aren't giving you enough room—gently (and briefly) touch your brakes to let them know you'll be slowing down soon.
2. Check your side mirrors, so you know where the other vehicles are.
3. Make sure you're in the correct turning lane.
4. Signal your intent to turn.
5. Start slowing down.
6. Double-check your mirrors.
7. Check right and left into the intersection and assess what other vehicles are doing. (Remember—just because someone else is signaling a turn, it doesn't mean they're going to turn and vice-versa!)
8. When making a left turn—come to a full stop before you enter the intersection. When the way is clear, ease into the intersection slowly.
   For right turns slow down to a slow speed that allows you to turn safely and view any pedestrians or obstacles that might be in your path. Be prepared to stop.
9. Complete your turn when the way is clear.

Practice Turning at "Intersections"

Pretend you're driving neighborhood streets and practice turning using the 9 steps listed above:

- Drive the perimeter of the parking lot practicing your right-hand turns.
- Drive the perimeter of the parking lot practicing your left-hand turns.

Practice these skills:

- ☐ 11- Point start-up checklist
- ☐ 9 o'clock/ 3 o'clock hand position
- ☐ Smooth starts
- ☐ Smooth stops
- ☐ Smooth acceleration (Keep it to low speeds)
- ☐ Correct right-hand turns
- ☐ Correct left-hand turns

LESSON 3: Backing Up

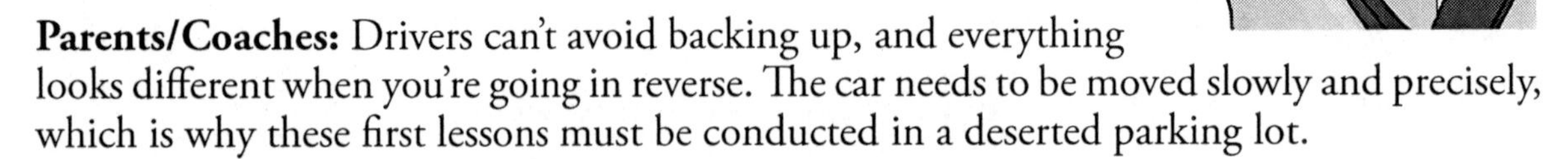

Parents/Coaches: Drivers can't avoid backing up, and everything looks different when you're going in reverse. The car needs to be moved slowly and precisely, which is why these first lessons must be conducted in a deserted parking lot.

When you start the lesson, make sure your driver goes through all the start-up steps they learned in Lesson 1. If they miss something, provide a gentle reminder. It's important for them to build good habits.

Keep an eye on your driver's feet. Make sure they don't use the gas pedal while they're backing up. Their foot should hover over the brake so they can stop suddenly if they need to.

Be sure to give lots of encouragement. Your driver will be doing their best but there's a lot to remember and this is new territory for them.

This week work through the following topics. Check them off as you complete them:

- ☐ The Danger in Backing Up (page 62)
- ☐ Cell Phones, PDAs and Other Handheld Devices (page 69)
- ☐ Chapter Review Puzzles (pages 74 and 75)

Related Videos:

Go to TeensLearntoDrive.com. Select the link to the "Free Video Library" from your "Favorites" (per instructions on page 3). Under Driving Lesson 3" select:

- ☐ "Structured Practice" to watch videos related to your in-car session.
- ☐ "Need-to-Know Info" to watch videos that relate to the "Need-to-Know Info" sections listed above.

Check them off when you complete them.

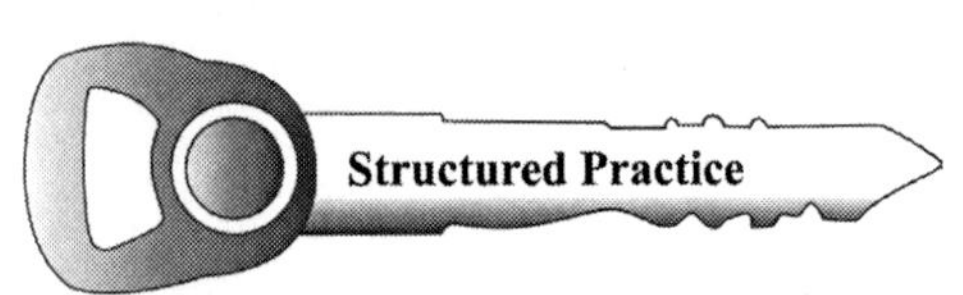

Location:	An empty parking lot (The parent/coach should drive to and from the practice space.)
Conditions:	Clear, dry, daylight
Lesson Length:	30–45 Minutes

START-UP CHECKLIST			
1	Check your windshield washer fluid.	7	Adjust your steering wheel.
2	Walk around your vehicle.	8	Turn off your cell phone.
3	Check your gas gauge.	9	Secure any loose objects.
4	Adjust your seat.	10	Buckle your seatbelt and make sure your passengers buckle-up too.
5	Adjust your mirrors.		
6	Adjust your headrest.	11	Lock the doors.

Backing up is easy once you get the hang of it. Make sure you practice this until you're very comfortable because it's a lot easier here than in a crowded parking lot with lots of distractions.

Practice going straight back first. Slowly (no gas) and in control. If your car doesn't move, touch the gas pedal very lightly.

When you're an expert at that, practice turning while backing up.

Tips for Backing Up:

- Steer in the direction you want the back of the car to go
- Turn your head so you're looking where you want to go (over your right shoulder to see the back of the car)
- Hover your foot over the brake so you can stop quickly
- Most cars will move without gas, so try that first. If your car doesn't move, touch the gas pedal lightly with your foot. Be prepared to swivel your foot to the brake to stop.

Practice these skills:

☐ 9 o'clock/ 3 o'clock hand position

☐ Back up—straight back

☐ Back up while turning right

☐ Back up while turning left

LESSON 4: Basic Parking Skills

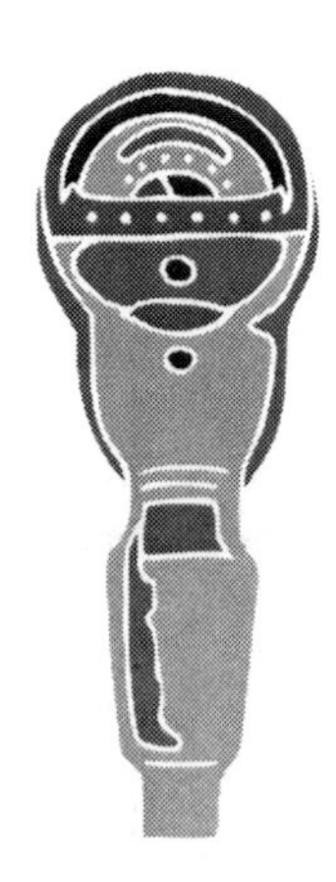

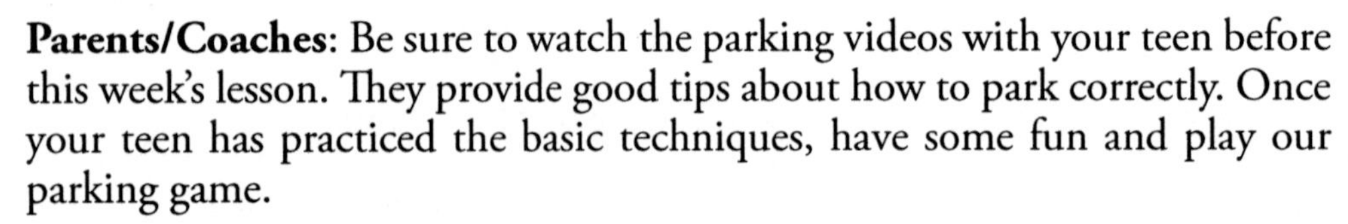

Parents/Coaches: Be sure to watch the parking videos with your teen before this week's lesson. They provide good tips about how to park correctly. Once your teen has practiced the basic techniques, have some fun and play our parking game.

Choose a reward for when they hit the targeted number of points—like go for ice cream or a soda. Then de-brief the lesson while you enjoy your treat!

This week work through the following topics. Check them off as you complete them.

- ☐ Parking Lot Safety, Responsibility and Etiquette (page 191)

Related Videos:

Go to TeensLearntoDrive.com. Select the link to the "Free Video Library" from your "Favorites" (per instructions on page 3). Under Driving Lesson 4" select:

- ☐ "Structured Practice" to watch videos related to your in-car session.
- ☐ "Need-to-Know Info" to watch videos that relate to the "Need-to-Know Info" sections listed above.

Check them off when you complete them.

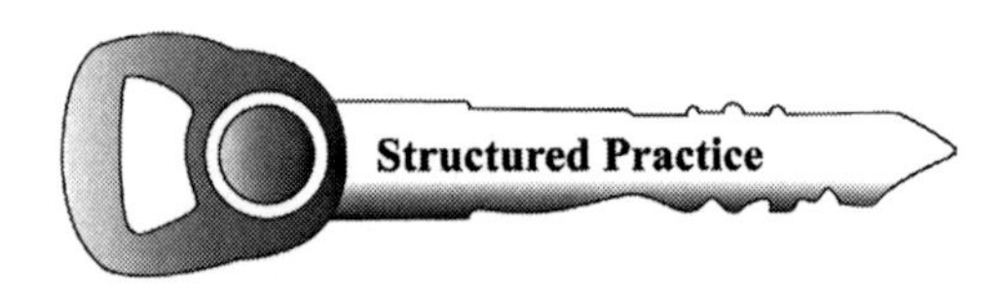

Location: An empty parking lot (The parent/coach should drive to and from the practice space.)

Conditions: Clear, dry, daylight

Lesson Length: 45 Minutes

START-UP CHECKLIST			
1	Check your windshield washer fluid.	7	Adjust your steering wheel.
2	Walk around your vehicle.	8	Turn off your cell phone.
3	Check your gas gauge.	9	Secure any loose objects.
4	Adjust your seat.	10	Buckle your seatbelt and make sure your passengers buckle-up too.
5	Adjust your mirrors.		
6	Adjust your headrest.	11	Lock the doors.

Practice these skills for 90⁰ (Perpendicular) Parking:

- ☐ Driving forward into the parking spot correctly
- ☐ Backing out of the parking spot correctly
- ☐ Backing into the parking spot correctly
- ☐ Driving out of the parking spot correctly

There are lots of different ways to park cars. Ninety-degree (90^0) or perpendicular parking is the most common. It's the kind of parking you'll do in most parking lots. You need to be able to drive your vehicle into the painted space without hitting anything.

Learning to park is important plus it helps you perfect your maneuvering skills and backing up skills.

When you park your car in a defined parking space it's important to stay within the painted lines with an equal amount of space on both sides of the car. This way you and your passenger can get in and out of the vehicle easily. It will also help protect your car from the car doors of the vehicles parked on either side of you.

It's important to pull fully into the spot so your car doesn't stick out further than other vehicles. The front bumper should be close to the end line of the space. When you're finished, you should be perfectly within the painted lines.

Remember:

- The radio should be off.
- Try moving without using your gas pedal. You can probably move slowly and stay in control by just lifting your foot off the brake. If that doesn't work, give your car a little gas.
- Hover your foot over the brake so you can stop quickly when you need to.

Practice until you're comfortable. When you're ready, play the parking game.

The Parking Game

You can make parking practice fun by assigning points as follows:

> 10 POINTS for equal distance on both sides of the vehicle
> 5 POINTS for slightly right or left, but within the lines
> 0 points for on or over the sidelines

plus

> 5 BONUS POINTS for being within the lines (front to back)

Decide how many points you will play to: 50, 75 or 100.

Talk about:

- ☐ How to use parking meters
- ☐ How to use parking lots with prepaid ticket machines
- ☐ How to use parking lots with attendants (where you must leave your key)
- ☐ Where to park on city streets
- ☐ Where not to park on city streets
- ☐ How to deal with parking tickets

LESSON 5: Emergency Stops

Parents/Coaches: Prepare to be shaken—not stirred! This lesson will have lots of sudden stops and could be uncomfortable. Remember to stay calm. It's important for your teen to get the "feel" of the brakes on the car, so they don't panic when they need to stop suddenly.

Read through the driving lesson together before you get started. Talk about the braking system on your vehicle. Tell your teen exactly what to do, and explain what they should expect to happen. Start very slow and increase your speed gradually.

You'll need a very large, empty parking lot for this one.

This week work through the following topic.

Check it off when you complete it.

- ☐ Speeding and Speed Management (page 163)

Related Videos:

Go to TeensLearntoDrive.com. Select the link to the "Free Video Library" from your "Favorites" (per instructions on page 3). Under Driving Lesson 5" select:

- ☐ "Structured Practice" to watch videos related to your in-car session.
- ☐ "Need-to-Know Info" to watch videos that relate to the "Need-to-Know Info" sections listed above.

Check them off when you complete them.

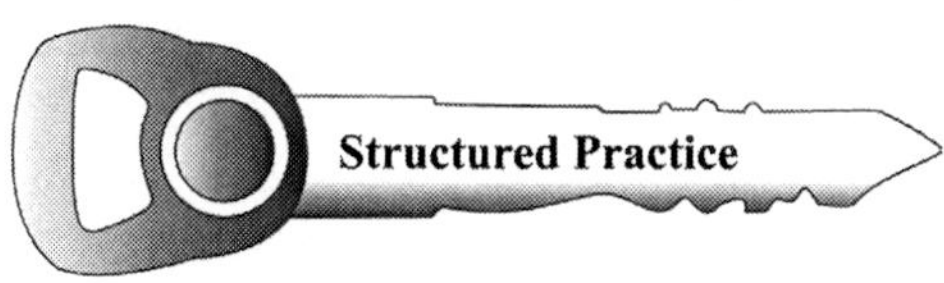

Location:	A large empty parking lot (The parent/coach should drive to and from the practice space.) You need room to accelerate and practice sudden braking techniques.
Conditions:	Clear, dry, daylight
Lesson Length:	45 Minutes

START-UP CHECKLIST			
1	Check your windshield washer fluid.	7	Adjust your steering wheel.
2	Walk around your vehicle.	8	Turn off your cell phone.
3	Check your gas gauge.	9	Secure any loose objects.
4	Adjust your seat.	10	Buckle your seatbelt and make sure your passengers buckle-up too.
5	Adjust your mirrors.		
6	Adjust your headrest.	11	Lock the doors.

Controlling Sudden Stops

The following exercise will help you learn how much pressure to apply to the brakes in order to stay in control for sudden, abrupt stops. It will also help you understand how much room you need to stop (without crashing into the car ahead of you.)

What Kind of Braking System Do You Have?

But first—What kind of braking system do you have? After "Saturday Morning with Dad" you should be able to answer that question and it matters here because ABS work differently than traditional braking systems.

ABS Background

In the old days, in an emergency situation where you needed to stop suddenly, you jammed on the brakes! Sometimes they'd lock and that would be disastrous! The tires would stop turning which put the car into a skid and you couldn't steer anymore! (You can just hear the crash!)

So, drivers learned to 'pump' the brakes. They'd apply pressure then ease up, many times. This would keep the brakes from locking so they could maintain control of the car. That was better.

Then someone invented ABS systems (Anti-lock Braking Systems). Basically they do the 'pumping' for you—but faster and more efficiently than you could. This keeps the brakes from locking and helps you maintain control of the car. ABS are great.

How to Use Your Brakes

During normal stopping, ABS work the same as other types of brakes, but in emergency stopping situations you need to operate them differently.

With ABS:

There are 2 kinds of ABS and they operate differently so you need to use them differently. If you aren't sure which kind you have, check your Owner's Manual.

Rear-wheel ABS—(on some light trucks, vans and SUVs) prevent wheel lock of the rear wheels only. Since the front wheels can still lock up, drivers should stomp on the brake, then ease up with just enough pressure to allow the front wheels to start rolling again, so the driver can steer.

Four-wheel ABS—(on most cars) Maintain firm and continuous pressure on the brake while steering to enable four-wheel ABS to work properly. Avoid pumping the brake, even if the brake pedal is pulsating.

Practice with your ABS

When you apply that firm, pressure you'll feel the brakes grabbing and letting go and you may hear some strange noises. That can be scary but it's normal. Practicing now will help you know what to expect so you don't panic in a real emergency braking situation.

Without ABS:

In emergency stopping situations, if your car doesn't have ABS, you'll still need to pump the brakes to maintain control and keep them from locking.

Lesson for smooth emergency stops at various distances

After you figure out what kind of brakes you have and determine the best procedure for using your brakes, try this exercise:

At one end of the LARGE, EMPTY parking lot, start the car and increase the speed to 15 mph (25 kph). Using the proper technique for your braking system, stop sharply.

Try this several times until you know what to expect and can brake smoothly.

Then try it again at:

- 20 mph (30 kph). Practice until controlled.
- 25 mph (40 kph). Practice until controlled.
- 30 mph (50 kph). Practice until controlled.

What have you noticed about how far it takes you to stop?

The faster you're going, the longer it takes you to stop. So the faster you drive, the more stopping distance you need to leave between you and the car ahead of you.

NOTE: It takes even longer to stop when you're carrying a car full of people or a heavy load!

LESSON 6: Emergency Stops with Steering

Parents/Coaches: If you haven't checked your tires lately, now's the time to do it. The "Need-to-Know Info" session this week will help you assess their health. Correct any inflation problems or replace them if necessary. Worn-out or improperly inflated tires are dangerous and can put your young driver in a situation they aren't capable of dealing with. Take them along when you do your inspections so they know what to look for too.

The Driving Session: New drivers tend to panic when something unexpected happens. Use this lesson, to make your driver understand they must stay in control and keep steering, no matter what happens.

This lesson may take many in-car sessions to master. Don't rush it. These skills are critical.

Don't forget to make an entry in your Driver's Log.

This week work through the following topic. Check it off when you complete it.

- ☐ Your Tires (page 32)

Related Videos:

Go to TeensLearntoDrive.com. Select the link to the "Free Video Library" from your "Favorites" (per instructions on page 3). Under Driving Lesson 6" select:

- ☐ "Structured Practice" to watch videos related to your in-car session.
- ☐ "Need-to-Know Info" to watch videos that relate to the "Need-to-Know Info" sections listed above.

Check them off when you complete them.

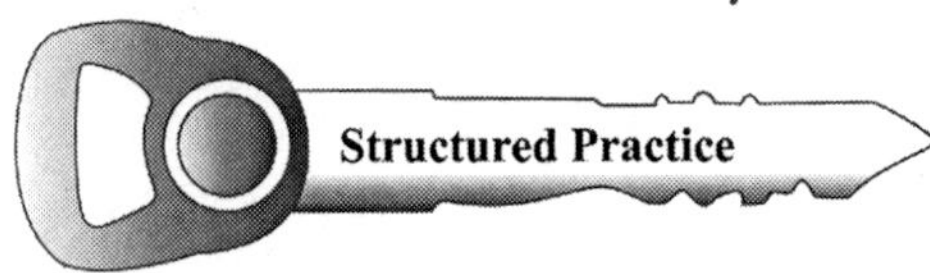

Location:	A large, empty parking lot (The parent/coach should drive to and from the practice space.)
Conditions:	Clear, dry, daylight
Lesson Length:	45 Minutes—1 hour
Materials Required:	A traffic cone or an empty cardboard box

START-UP CHECKLIST			
1	Check your windshield washer fluid.	7	Adjust your steering wheel.
2	Walk around your vehicle.	8	Turn off your cell phone.
3	Check your gas gauge.	9	Secure any loose objects.
4	Adjust your seat.	10	Buckle your seatbelt and make sure your passengers buckle-up too.
5	Adjust your mirrors.		
6	Adjust your headrest.	11	Lock the doors.

You've practiced emergency stops ... now add steering

Once you have the stopping part pretty well under control, it's time to learn to steer while you're stopping. It's easy but it takes some practice. Whatever happens—it's important that you always maintain control of the vehicle.

Don't give up!

Go back to your parking lot. This time take with you a plastic parking cone if you have one or something large like a box that you can see from a distance but don't mind running over.

Place your cone ¾ of the way to the other end of the parking lot. Start the car and get the speed up to 15 mph (25 kph). Brake hard when you are about 20 to 30 feet (6 to 10 meters) from the cone. Try to stop in front of the cone. If you can't stop, steer around the cone.

Repeat at various speeds (like the previous exercise) with this steering component.

LESSON 7: Space Management and Scanning

Parents/Coaches: One of the toughest skills for new drivers to master is 360-degree awareness. Drivers need to know what's in front of them, behind them and on both sides of them—at all times. They also need to ensure there's always a safe "cushion" of space around their vehicle, so they can stop or change lanes safely in an emergency situation. Those skills take time to develop, so you'll have to maintain that 360-degree awareness and "cushion" awareness for them for a long time.

You'll be "taking it to the road" this week and there will be lots going on around the car. Make sure you are watching out for other vehicles, bicycles and pedestrians.

Don't forget to put the masking tape across the windshield and look at your driver's eyes periodically. Make sure they are looking above the tape. (See Lauren's tip in this lesson.)

EXPERT TIP from Lauren: To get your teen looking further down the road, instruct them to look through the top half of the windshield. *Put a thin piece of painters tape across the center of the windshield* (lengthwise) *to help them lift their eyes.*

It will take a while to retrain them to look far ahead, so make sure you look at their eyes from time to time, or ask them what they are looking at.

NOTE: Use the thinnest tape you can find. You don't want to obstruct their vision.

Ask your driver to tell you what they see. Gently point out other things they should be seeing.

Make sure your teen continues to start each lesson by completing their Start-up Checklist.

Coaching TIPS:

- As you drive, talk about what you see and possible obstacles ahead.
- The Coach should always be watching ahead and pointing out potential hazards as necessary.

This week work through the following topics. Check them off as you complete them.

- ☐ Road Racing (page 166)
- ☐ High Emotion (page 167)

Related Videos:

Go to TeensLearntoDrive.com. Select the link to the "Free Video Library" from your "Favorites" (per instructions on page 3). Under Driving Lesson 7" select:

- ☐ "Structured Practice" to watch videos related to your in-car session.
- ☐ "Need-to-Know Info" to watch videos that relate to the "Need-to-Know Info" sections listed above.

Check them off when you complete them.

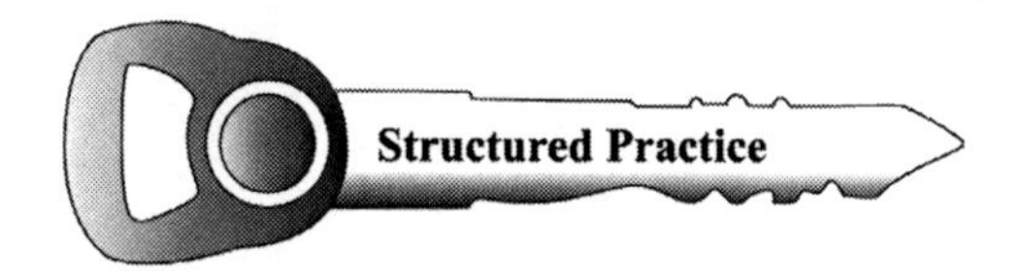

Location: Quiet residential streets with long stretches of straight roads. (The parent/coach should drive to and from the selected neighborhood.)

No left-hand turns at this point and a minimum number of right-hand turns. (You'll be practicing those in the next lessons).

Conditions: Clear, dry, daylight

Lesson Length: 60 Minutes

Materials Required: A roll of narrow masking tape, this workbook

START-UP CHECKLIST			
1	Check your windshield washer fluid.	7	Adjust your steering wheel.
2	Walk around your vehicle.	8	Turn off your cell phone.
3	Check your gas gauge.	9	Secure any loose objects.
4	Adjust your seat.	10	Buckle your seatbelt and make sure your passengers buckle-up too.
5	Adjust your mirrors.		
6	Adjust your headrest.	11	Lock the doors.

Scanning

It's important to watch as far down the road as you can see—so you'll spot any potential problems before you actually reach them.

But your job doesn't end there. You need to keep your eyes moving. Watching your rear-view mirror. Watching your side mirrors. You need to know who else is on the road and where they are—all the time.

You also need to plan an "exit" if you need it.

Lauren, the Driving Instructor, says:

"It's easier to avoid a hazard ***if you see it***, and it's easier to see a hazard ***if you are looking.***

This seems like common sense, but in this world of texting, computers, and video games, teens are used to looking a few inches in front of their faces. They need to be retrained to look further ahead when driving.

If you see a hazard sooner, you have more time to avoid it.

And if, you are constantly scanning your mirrors, you know where your exit is before you hit the hazard.

Use Your Mirrors to Scan

Constant scanning of mirrors is necessary to ensure the highest level of safety on the road.

Mirrors aren't just used when changing lanes. They are important tools to assess what is going on around you at all times.

If someone suddenly comes into your lane, or a mattress drops off the truck in front of you, you need to know what your options are to avoid the crash.

By setting your mirrors correctly, you'll minimize your blind spots and give yourself a better view of what's going on around you. That makes checking mirrors for avoidance maneuvers much faster—***saving precious seconds*** that could mean the difference between avoiding a collision or being involved in one."

LESSON 8: Right Turns on Residential Streets

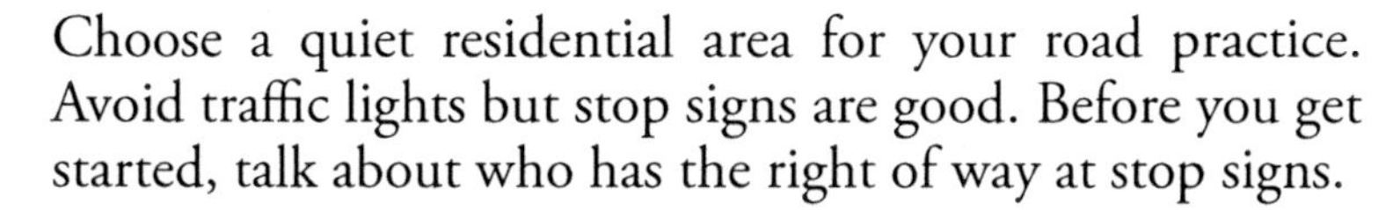

Choose a quiet residential area for your road practice. Avoid traffic lights but stop signs are good. Before you get started, talk about who has the right of way at stop signs.

As you're driving, ask your driver to tell you what they see. Don't forget the masking tape and make sure your driver's eyes are focused down the road so they can see what's happening up ahead.

If you purchased "Student at the Wheel" or similar decals/magnets, don't forget to affix them to the vehicle before you go.

This week work through the following topics. Check them off as you complete them.

- ☐ Stuff You Should Have in Your Car (page 195)
- ☐ Stuff You Should NOT Have in Your Car (page 196)
- ☐ Great Gifts for New Drivers (page 196)

Related Videos:

Go to TeensLearntoDrive.com. Select the link to the "Free Video Library" from your "Favorites" (per instructions on page 3). Under Driving Lesson 8" select:

- ☐ "Structured Practice" to watch videos related to your in-car session.
- ☐ "Need-to-Know Info" to watch videos that relate to the "Need-to-Know Info" sections listed above.

Check them off when you complete them.

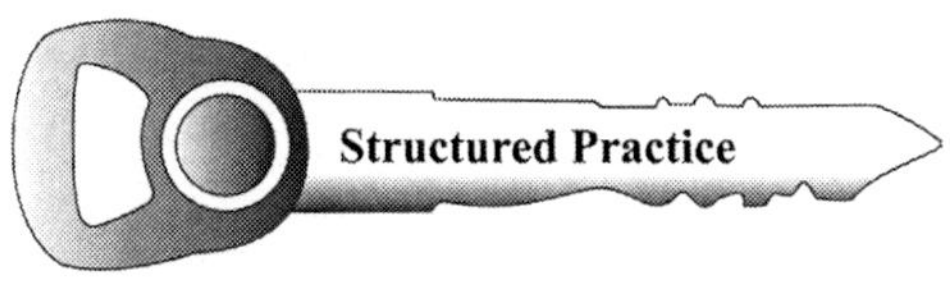

Location: A quiet residential neighborhood.

Conditions: Clear, dry, daylight

Lesson Length: 60 Minutes

Materials Required: This workbook, masking tape.

START-UP CHECKLIST			
1	Check your windshield washer fluid.	7	Adjust your steering wheel.
2	Walk around your vehicle.	8	Turn off your cell phone.
3	Check your gas gauge.	9	Secure any loose objects.
4	Adjust your seat.	10	Buckle your seatbelt and make sure your passengers buckle-up too.
5	Adjust your mirrors.		
6	Adjust your headrest.	11	Lock the doors.

Traffic Lights

Your route won't include traffic lights this week, but it's important to become aware of how they work so you'll know what to do in future lessons.

You know that a red light means 'stop', and a green one means 'go.' So dealing with stoplights should be easy, but it's not because people don't always obey the rules.

A distracted driver may miss the changing red light. Another driver in a hurry may speed up to get through the yellow one.

And green may mean you have the right-of way but that will be little consolation if you cross paths with those other two guys!

'Stale' Yellow Lights

Yellow traffic lights caution drivers that the light is about to turn red.

As each driver approaches a yellow light, they need to make a decision whether or not they can stop safely or they should continue through the intersection.

In order to make a good decision, you need to know how much time you have. A good indicator is, 'how long has the light been yellow?' If the light just turned yellow as you reached the intersection—it's 'fresh' so you have plenty of time. If it's already 'stale' (it's been yellow for a while), you should stop.

> 25% of crashes happen at intersections.
>
> **All teens are at risk in intersections.**
>
> The risk is slightly higher for girls.

Before you hit the brakes, make sure you've checked your mirrors and you know how close the car behind you is. If he's too close and going too fast to stop, you may need to proceed through the intersection to avoid being hit from behind. Your coach will help you understand when you should go and when you should stop.

So when you're scanning ahead, make sure you're aware of the traffic lights ahead of you. You need to determine which ones are fresh and which ones are stale.

Practice these skills:

- ☐ Spotting 'stale' yellow traffic lights
- ☐ Correct 9-step turning procedure (from Lesson 2)

LESSON 9: Left Turns on Residential Streets

Parents/Coaches: Left turns are one of the most dangerous maneuvers on the road because when you turn left, you need to cross in front of a moving stream of traffic.

New drivers have difficulty judging how quickly traffic is coming toward them. Some vehicles are moving slowly. Others are speeding.

They also have to decide whether or not the approaching vehicles will stop. As a seasoned driver, you know that drivers are unpredictable. They signal without turning; they turn without signaling and they run red lights. You cannot depend on them to "tell" you what they intend to do.

Your driver needs to learn to do the right things—without expecting other drivers to do the right thing.

Some of the exercises in this session are not done in the car. Don't skip them. They'll help your teen understand how intersections work and how dangerous they can be. They'll also provide some useful tools that can help your teen make those critical GO/NO GO decisions.

Remember—that above all—the most important message to get through to your teen about intersection is this:

If you aren't sure that it's safe—WAIT! No matter what anyone else says. Even if your friends are yelling "Go!" Even if the guy in the car on the other side of the lane motions for you to go. Even if the guy behind you is honking for you to go.

Wait until YOU are sure it's safe to go.

This week work through the following topic. Check it off when you complete it.

- ☐ Intersections (page 88)

Related Videos:

Go to TeensLearntoDrive.com. Select the link to the "Free Video Library" from your "Favorites" (per instructions on page 3). Under Driving Lesson 9" select:

- ☐ "Structured Practice" to watch videos related to your in-car session.

- ☐ "Need-to-Know Info" to watch videos that relate to the "Need-to-Know Info" sections listed above.

Check them off when you complete them.

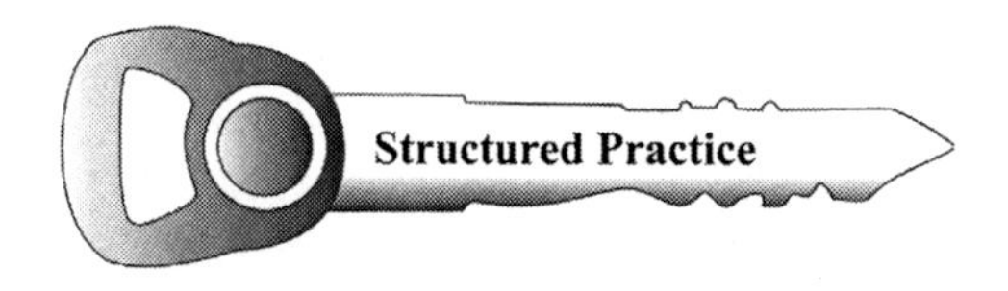

Location: **Activities ONLY**—Busy intersection where you can observe turning cars.

Driving Practice—Quiet residential streets

Conditions: Clear, dry, daylight

Lesson Length: Activities—60 Minutes

Driving Practice—60 Minutes

Materials Required: This workbook, masking tape

START-UP CHECKLIST			
1	Check your windshield washer fluid.	7	Adjust your steering wheel.
2	Walk around your vehicle.	8	Turn off your cell phone.
3	Check your gas gauge.	9	Secure any loose objects.
4	Adjust your seat.	10	Buckle your seatbelt and make sure your passengers buckle-up too.
5	Adjust your mirrors.		
6	Adjust your headrest.	11	Lock the doors.

Intersections

Have you ever noticed how often you see debris (like broken headlights and chunks of fender) in the middle of intersections? That's because intersections are dangerous places—and the ones where you see the most rubble—are the most dangerous!

Tips for Dealing with Intersections:

- If the light ahead has been yellow for a while, start slowing down as you approach it. While you do, check your mirrors to make sure the guy behind you has time to stop too.
- When your light turns green, don't race off the mark Pause for 2 to 3 seconds. Look left- then right—then left again. Proceed across the intersection when you're certain it's safe.
- Don't enter an intersection unless you're certain there's room to make it through completely before the light changes to red. Sometimes when traffic is snarled, cars get stuck in the middle after the light changes. You definitely don't want to be there. At the very least, you'll cause a gridlock situation that will make all the drivers around you very angry.
- Sometimes the driver behind you will honk if he thinks you're moving through the intersection too slowly. Don't let him rush you. NEVER proceed until you're certain you can do so safely.
- NEVER cross lanes of traffic when you can't see what's coming—even though other drivers may beckon you that the way is clear. If you can't see for yourself, wait until you can.

Turning Left

In order to turn left, you need to cross the line of traffic coming from the other direction. While you're sitting in the middle of the intersection waiting to make your turn—you are very vulnerable to being hit by oncoming traffic.

Part of the problem is that it's difficult to determine how quickly oncoming cars are approaching. Sometimes it might look like you have enough time to turn but the approaching car is going faster than you think.

Or the light might turn yellow and you think it's your turn to go, but the approaching car decides he's going to speed up to get through the yellow light instead. Or sometimes drivers get distracted so they don't notice the light changing, and go through the intersection anyway.

Important Note:

Establishing "Markers" will help you determine when NOT to try to complete your turn.

It will <u>NOT tell you when you DO have enough time</u> to turn because cars travel at different speeds. You'll still need to use judgment to determine if it's safe to turn.

WHEN IN DOUBT—WAIT!

It's important to remember that you never have the right-of-way when you are turning left. You must wait for all approaching vehicles to come to a stop or clear the intersection before you complete your turn.

Activities for the Driver and Coach:

Before you start left-hand turns on busy streets, stake out a nearby intersection for an hour or so—without your car. If there's one with a bench you can sit on (like near a bus stop) that would be great.

Exercise 1—How to determine if cars will stop at an intersection

Watch what cars do when they approach the intersection. Try to predict which ones will go through, and which ones will stop.

What do you notice about the ones that stop? Do they slam on their brakes at the last second or can you see them slowing down?

What do you notice about the ones who run the intersection? Do they drive through at a constant speed or speed up to make it through before the light turns red?

Or—are they completely unpredictable because they don't all act the same way?

Never enter an intersection until the oncoming traffic has **stopped**. Cars may look like they're going to stop but you can't really be sure, until they stop.

Exercise 2—How to create 'markers' for intersections you'll use frequently

Many crashes have occurred because someone making a left turn thought they had enough time to complete the turn, but misjudged how quickly an oncoming car was approaching. Judging the speed of oncoming traffic is especially hard for new drivers.

This exercise will help you create markers at intersections you'll be frequenting, so you can better judge when you don't have enough time to make your turn.

Part 1—Determine how much time you'll need to turn

In most cases, people making left turns, do it in two stages. First, they pull carefully into the intersection, to a position where they can see the oncoming traffic. They stay in that position until the traffic has stopped or there is a large enough gap in traffic for them to cross the traffic stream safely.

The first thing you need to do is figure out how long it takes a car to complete a turn from that 'standing' position in the intersection. The easiest way to do this is to "time" other drivers as they complete their turns.

From your position on the bench, figure out how long it takes cars to clear the intersection when they turn. Watch a car pull into the intersection. Start counting 'steamboats' (1 steamboat, 2 steamboats, etc.) when the way is clear and they start moving to complete their turn.

Now watch several more cars and count how many steamboats it takes them to complete the same maneuver. Now take the **longest** time. (It is probably around 5 steamboats—but it will depend on how fast you count—among other things.)

Part 2—Determine how long it takes cars to reach the intersection

Now—pick a landmark down the block. It should be something permanent like a sign or lamppost (not a parked car).

When an oncoming car reaches that landmark, start counting 'steamboats' again. How many 'steamboats' does it take for them to reach the intersection from your landmark? Watch several more cars at various speeds and 'time' them as well. Take the **longest** time.

Now do the math. If it takes that car 6 steamboats to reach the entrance to the intersection and you calculated you will need 4 steamboats to clear the intersection—that's a good landmark for this intersection. You know that if an approaching car has passed the landmark, you DO NOT have time to complete your turn before it enters the intersection.

If the landmark you chose is too close to the intersection (say 3 steamboats away) simply choose another one that's further away.

Repeat until you have a landmark you can use to gauge the intersection every time you visit.

Repeat this exercise at other intersections you'll be visiting frequently.

Left-Turn Practice

Now move to your quiet, residential neighborhood and practice your left turns, using the 9-step turn procedure.

Start on streets with 4-way stops. When you're comfortable, include quiet streets with stoplights.

Left-Turn Safety Tips:

1. Always make sure you have a clear view of oncoming traffic. Sometimes cars that are turning the other way can block your view. Don't proceed until you are certain there's no oncoming traffic.
2. It's important to stay in your lane when you turn. If you're in the left lane, you must turn into the left lane on the other road. This is especially important when there is more than one left-turn lane.
3. When you pull into an intersection, keep your wheels straight. (Don't turn them in the direction you want to go.) This way, if your car gets hit from behind, you won't be pushed into oncoming traffic.
4. Be aware of pedestrians and bicyclists who may be ignoring the traffic lights.
5. Be wary of oncoming cars with their turn signals on. They may not turn.

Practice these skills:

- ☐ 9 o'clock—3 o'clock hand position
- ☐ Correct 9-step turning procedure (from Lesson 2)
- ☐ Awareness of speed limit in changing areas
- ☐ Maintaining a protective "cushion" around the car
- ☐ Correct 4-way stop etiquette
- ☐ Identifying stale yellow lights

LESSON 10: Navigating the Neighborhood

Parents/Coaches: You may have lived in the same place for the last 16 years, but don't expect your new driver to know how to negotiate the neighborhood in a car. Everything looks different from the driver's seat and the chances are, that they haven't really been watching while you chauffeured them around for all those years.

So while you're practicing these lessons, it's a good idea to use the street names so they start learning them. "We're approaching Colonial Avenue. When we get to the corner, I want you to turn right onto Colonial Avenue."

> **Tip:** Remember that when you're coaching:
>
> - Use 'right' for directions.
> - Use 'correct' to agree with something your teen says.

This week work through the following topic in Chapter 5. Check it off when you complete it.

- ☐ Dealing with Your Passengers (page 67)

Related Videos:

Go to TeensLearntoDrive.com. Select the link to the "Free Video Library" from your "Favorites" (per instructions on page 3). Under Driving Lesson 10" select:

- ☐ "Structured Practice" to watch videos related to your in-car session.
- ☐ "Need-to-Know Info" to watch videos that relate to the "Need-to-Know Info" sections listed above.

Check them off when you complete them.

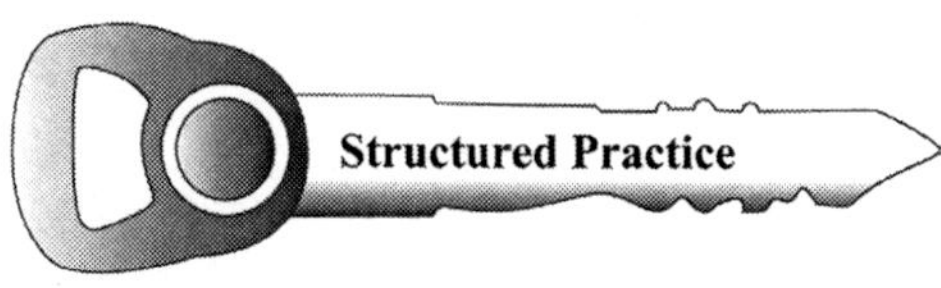

Location:	Your neighborhood. Familiar streets that you'll be driving often. The coach should point out difficult areas and how to deal with them. For example, hidden driveways, busy intersections, etc.
Conditions:	Clear, dry, daylight
Lesson Length:	60 Minutes

Materials Required: This workbook

START-UP CHECKLIST			
1	Check your windshield washer fluid.	7	Adjust your steering wheel.
2	Walk around your vehicle.	8	Turn off your cell phone.
3	Check your gas gauge.	9	Secure any loose objects.
4	Adjust your seat.	10	Buckle your seatbelt and make sure your passengers buckle-up too.
5	Adjust your mirrors.		
6	Adjust your headrest.	11	Lock the doors.

Practice these skills:

- ☐ 9 o'clock—3 o'clock hand position
- ☐ Right turns
- ☐ Left turns
- ☐ Stoplights
- ☐ 4-Way stops
- ☐ Maintaining a protective "cushion" around the car

LESSON 11: Turns on Busier Roads

Parents/Coaches: Take some time to think about the route you'll drive before you jump in the car for this lesson. You want to include busier roads but avoid any tricky spots like double-turn lanes, merging lanes or construction areas where lanes can appear or disappear unexpectedly.

Remember to keep using street names and give plenty of warning before you want them to turn. If they miss a turn, simply instruct them to continue to the next street and turn there. You want them to get into the habit of making good decisions.

Don't forget your masking tape. Maintain that 360 degree awareness and encourage your driver to keep talking about what they see ahead and where they believe their "exits" would be.

This week work through the following topics. Check them off when you complete them.

- ☐ Alcohol and Driving (page 167)

Related Videos:

Go to TeensLearntoDrive.com. Select the link to the "Free Video Library" from your "Favorites" (per instructions on page 3). Under Driving Lesson 11" select:

- ☐ "Structured Practice" to watch videos related to your in-car session.
- ☐ "Need-to-Know Info" to watch videos that relate to the "Need-to-Know Info" sections listed above.

Check them off when you complete them.

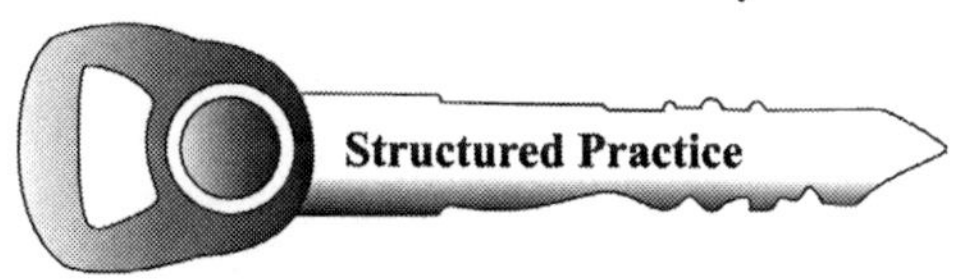

Location:	Busier streets. Downtown or shopping area is good. Include a parking area to practice parking skills too.
Conditions:	Clear, dry, daylight
Lesson Length:	60 Minutes
Materials Required:	This workbook, masking tape.

START-UP CHECKLIST			
1	Check your windshield washer fluid.	7	Adjust your steering wheel.
2	Walk around your vehicle.	8	Turn off your cell phone.
3	Check your gas gauge.	9	Secure any loose objects.
4	Adjust your seat.	10	Buckle your seatbelt and make sure your passengers buckle-up too.
5	Adjust your mirrors.		
6	Adjust your headrest.	11	Lock the doors.

Practice these skills:

- ☐ 9 o'clock—3 o'clock hand position
- ☐ Right and left turns
- ☐ Awareness of speed limit in changing areas
- ☐ Maintaining a protective "cushion" around the car

LESSON 12: Interacting with Other Vehicles

Parents/Coaches: Your teenager probably hasn't noticed all the things you do when you're driving, so now is the time to talk about how to interact safely with other kinds of vehicles and drivers.

Make sure that your route this week includes a school zone and a hospital zone. The speed limit should also vary.

If your teen starts driving too slow or too fast, remember to ask, "What's the speed limit here?" rather than just telling them what the speed limit is. That will help them become accustomed to looking for the speed limit signs as they drive.

This week work through the following topics. Check them off as you complete them:

- ☐ Road Rage (page 181)
- ☐ Blame Your Parents (page 181)
- ☐ Daydreaming (page 183)
- ☐ Tailgating (page 183)
- ☐ Right-of-Way (page 184)
- ☐ Motorcycles (page 184)
- ☐ Railway Crossings (page 185)

Related Videos:

Go to TeensLearntoDrive.com. Select the link to the "Free Video Library" from your "Favorites" (per instructions on page 3). Under Driving Lesson 12" select:

- ☐ "Structured Practice" to watch videos related to your in-car session.
- ☐ "Need-to-Know Info" to watch videos that relate to the "Need-to-Know Info" sections listed above.

Check them off when you complete them.

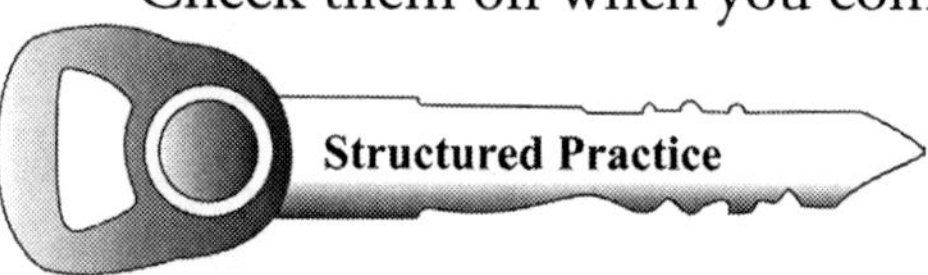

Location: Mix it up with busier streets, a shopping area, a parking lot, and a residential neighborhood. Include one-way streets, a school zone, a hospital zone and other unusual features of your area.

Your Mission: You're practicing driving appropriately for the environment today. Adjust your speed accordingly. Don't forget to keep talking about what you see and how you would deal with hazards.

Conditions: Clear, dry, daylight

Lesson Length: 60 Minutes

Materials Required: This workbook

START-UP CHECKLIST			
1	Check your windshield washer fluid.	7	Adjust your steering wheel.
2	Walk around your vehicle.	8	Turn off your cell phone.
3	Check your gas gauge.	9	Secure any loose objects.
4	Adjust your seat.	10	Buckle your seatbelt and make sure your passengers buckle-up too.
5	Adjust your mirrors.		
6	Adjust your headrest.	11	Lock the doors.

Talk about what to do when you encounter:

- ☐ Ambulances on city streets or country roads
- ☐ Ambulances on thruways and high-speed highways
- ☐ Police Cars on city streets or country roads
- ☐ Police Cars on thruways and high-speed highways
- ☐ Fire Trucks on city streets or country roads
- ☐ Fire Trucks on thruways and high-speed highways
- ☐ School Buses

Practice these skills:

- ☐ Right and left turns
- ☐ Awareness of speed limit in different areas
- ☐ Adjusting speed limit in different areas
- ☐ Maintaining a protective "cushion" around the car

Driving Etiquette—When someone stops to let you in, don't forget to smile and wave to them to say "thanks" for the consideration.

LESSON 13: Driving on Country Roads

Parents/Coaches: **Don't skip this lesson.** If you live in a city, it might be difficult to make your way into the country to do this lesson. If that's the case, postpone this lesson until a weekend when you can take that purposeful drive in the country, but don't cancel it.

Driving in the country may sound serene and peaceful, but the combination of higher speeds and soft shoulders on the roads make rollovers a higher risk in the country. Rollovers are deadly and a particular concern for young drivers.

This week work through the following topics. Check them off when you complete them.

- ☐ Rollovers (page 61)
- ☐ Best Cars for Teens (page 147)

Related Videos:

Go to TeensLearntoDrive.com. Select the link to the "Free Video Library" from your "Favorites" (per instructions on page 3). Under Driving Lesson 13" select:

- ☐ "Structured Practice" to watch videos related to your in-car session.
- ☐ "Need-to-Know Info" to watch videos that relate to the "Need-to-Know Info" sections listed above.

Check them off when you complete them.

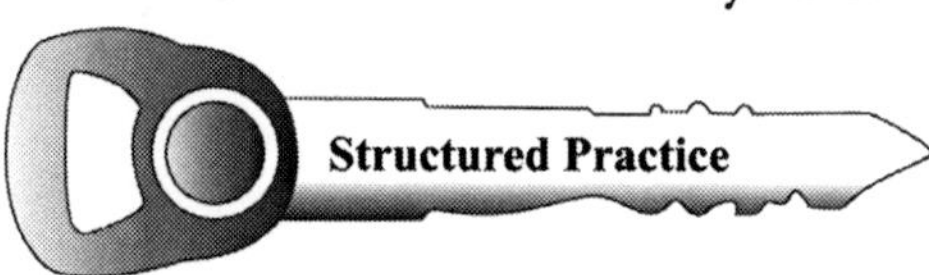

Location: Driving country roads requires new skills. There are fewer cars and often higher speeds. You're also more likely to encounter slow-moving vehicles like tractors, or animals that dart onto the road out of nowhere. The roads might be dirt rather than asphalt and there is likely a gravel shoulder.

Conditions: Clear, dry, daylight

Lesson Length: 60 Minutes

Materials Required: This workbook

START-UP CHECKLIST			
1	Check your windshield washer fluid.	7	Adjust your steering wheel.
2	Walk around your vehicle.	8	Turn off your cell phone.
3	Check your gas gauge.	9	Secure any loose objects.
4	Adjust your seat.	10	Buckle your seatbelt and make sure your passengers buckle-up too.
5	Adjust your mirrors.		
6	Adjust your headrest.	11	Lock the doors.

Take Extreme Care When Passing Tractors

Tractors are large slow-moving vehicles, that weren't intended to be driven on major roadways. But sometimes farmers need to get from one field to another, and the only way to do that is to use the same road you're driving on.

Be patient. Don't crowd them. Remember that the tractor is a very top-heavy vehicle that's already prone to rollovers and the shoulder of the road is soft or gravel. The driver has no seatbelt or roll bar.

Beware of the phantom shoulder!

Most country roads have deep ditches on both sides. Weeds grow high in the ditches and tractors come along periodically to cut them. They cut the weeds to the level of the road so it looks like the road extends out further than it does. Be very careful when you're turning around or pulling to the side of the road. It might be much narrower than you think.

Highway-Induced Driver Conditioning

Country roads are long and don't end with stop signs and traffic lights as frequently as city roads. As a result, you can drive a long way without having to slow down. You become "conditioned" to cruising at that constant speed and can lose your focus on driving.

It's important to stay alert! Many tragedies have occurred when drivers 'missed' stop signs in-the-middle-of -nowhere!

"Driver-Conditioning—The Unexpected Killer" is a workbook designed for both new and experienced drivers. You'll find more information at: sandyjohnsonfoundation.org

Many deaths or serious injuries have occurred when city slickers, in a hurry, passed a turning tractor too closely and forced it onto the soft shoulder, causing a rollover crash.

Wait until you have sufficient time to pass and you can do so safely—without putting the tractor driver at risk.

Practice these skills:

- ☐ Driving on the dirt road
- ☐ Recovering from being forced onto the gravel shoulder. (watch video demonstration)
- ☐ Talk about how to avoid a head-on collision.
- ☐ Recognizing hazards

LESSON 14: Other Parking (Parallel, Underground, etc.)

Parents/Coaches:

Parallel Parking—Parallel parking is tricky. If you live in the city, there will come a day when your driver can't avoid it—so it's better to practice now and get their technique down-pat. This practice will help fine-tune their vehicle handling skills as well.

Begin your parallel parking practice on a quiet street, in an open stretch where they won't need to squeeze between 2 cars. Find a car with a lot of space behind it and practice parking there until they get the hang of it.

Once your driver is comfortable there, you can move to a more challenging location and try parking between two cars. Be sure to view this week's videos for some great tips and instruction on proper technique.

Underground Parking—Underground parking is difficult because the spaces are tight, the lanes are narrow and there are pillars in places you don't want them and can't see them. All you have to do is look at the damage on the pillars to know that underground parking is very tricky.

Finding where you parked your car can also be frustrating. Up until now, your teen has probably just followed you back to the car. Soon they'll have to locate it themselves. Finding the right row and spot can be challenging, but underground parking is even tougher because you add different levels to the mix.

Share all your tips and tricks and be sure to review the tips on page 192.

This week work through the following topic. Check it off when you complete it.

- ☐ Insurance Tips (page 221)

Related Videos:

Go to TeensLearntoDrive.com. Select the link to the "Free Video Library" from your "Favorites" (per instructions on page 3). Under Driving Lesson 14" select:

- ☐ "Structured Practice" to watch videos related to your in-car session.
- ☐ "Need-to-Know Info" to watch videos that relate to the "Need-to-Know Info" sections listed above.

Check them off when you complete them.

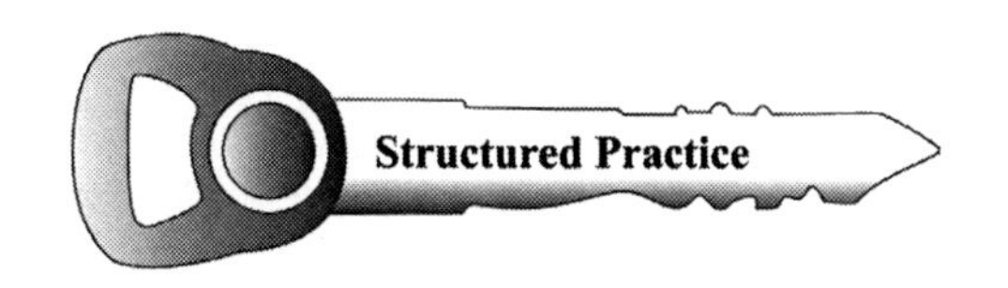

Location: Choose a quiet residential neighborhood where you have lots of room to practice parallel parking. Also choose an underground parking lot on a day and time that it isn't too busy.

Conditions: Clear, dry, daylight

Lesson Length: 60 Minutes

Materials Required: This workbook

START-UP CHECKLIST			
1	Check your windshield washer fluid.	7	Adjust your steering wheel.
2	Walk around your vehicle.	8	Turn off your cell phone.
3	Check your gas gauge.	9	Secure any loose objects.
4	Adjust your seat.	10	Buckle your seatbelt and make sure your passengers buckle-up too.
5	Adjust your mirrors.		
6	Adjust your headrest.	11	Lock the doors.

LESSON 15: Rain & Wet Ground

Parents/Coaches: Heavy rain makes it hard to see. You should instruct your driver to pull over in a safe place whenever their visibility is impaired by heavy rain or fog.

Stress that when it's hard for them to see, it's hard for other drivers to see them too, so whenever possible they should take the closest exit and pull off the roadway completely. They should park in a safe place (like a parking lot) and wait until the rain lets up before they continue.

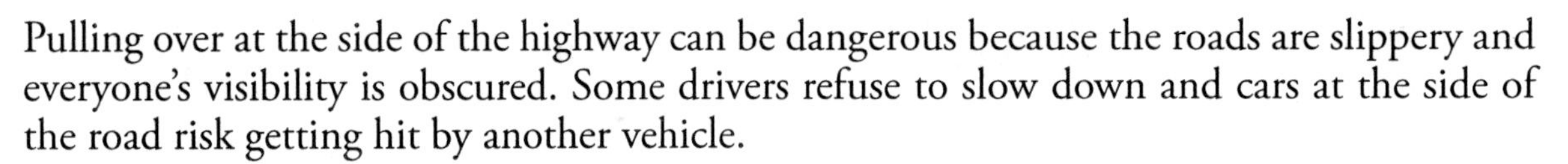

Pulling over at the side of the highway can be dangerous because the roads are slippery and everyone's visibility is obscured. Some drivers refuse to slow down and cars at the side of the road risk getting hit by another vehicle.

The big lessons here are:

- How to use the windshield wipers effectively (make sure they're in good shape and work properly)
- SLOW DOWN on wet roads
- Leave extra space between them and the car ahead of them
- How to identify when the cars ahead are slowing down

This week work through the following topic in Chapter 5. Check it off when you complete it.

☐ Plan, Share and Update (page 187)

Related Videos:

Go to TeensLearntoDrive.com. Select the link to the "Free Video Library" from your "Favorites" (per instructions on page 3). Under Driving Lesson 15" select:

☐ "Structured Practice" to watch videos related to your in-car session.
☐ "Need-to-Know Info" to watch videos that relate to the "Need-to-Know Info" sections listed above.

Check them off when you complete them.

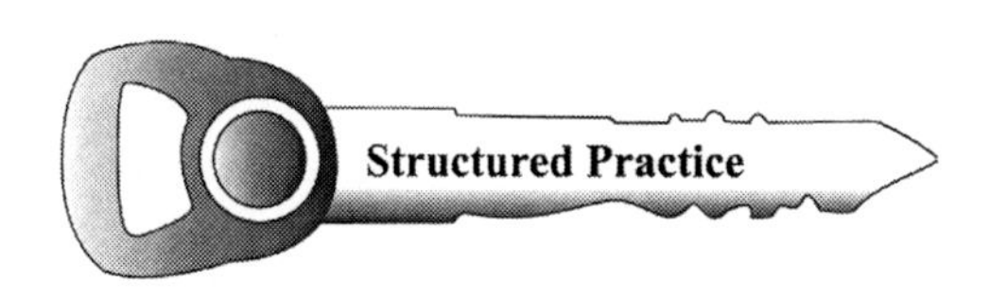

Location: Your neighborhood. Start on quiet streets. Move to a busier area when you are confident.

Conditions: Wet and/or rainy, daylight

Lesson Length: 60 Minutes

Materials Required: This workbook

START-UP CHECKLIST			
1	Check your windshield washer fluid.	7	Adjust your steering wheel.
2	Walk around your vehicle.	8	Turn off your cell phone.
3	Check your gas gauge.	9	Secure any loose objects.
4	Adjust your seat.	10	Buckle your seatbelt and make sure your passengers buckle-up too.
5	Adjust your mirrors.		
6	Adjust your headrest.	11	Lock the doors.

Practice these skills:

- ☐ Operating the windshield wipers
- ☐ Leaving a safe "cushion" around the vehicle
- ☐ Adjusting speed for the conditions
- ☐ Stopping safely on wet roads
- ☐ Making safe Go/No Go decisions at intersections
- ☐ Using the headlights in bad weather so other cars can see you

LESSON 16: Night Driving

Parents/Coaches: Everything looks different at night. Landmarks and street signs aren't as visible and neon lights show up in places you didn't notice before. Things seem to move slower at night too.

Drowsy driving is a particular danger for teens and young adults so make sure you review the related materials in the Need-to-Know Info section.

This week work through the following topic. Check it off as you complete it.

- ☐ Drowsy Driving (page 158)

Related Videos:

Go to TeensLearntoDrive.com. Select the link to the "Free Video Library" from your "Favorites" (per instructions on page 3). Under Driving Lesson 16" select:

- ☐ "Structured Practice" to watch videos related to your in-car session.
- ☐ "Need-to-Know Info" to watch videos that relate to the "Need-to-Know Info" sections listed above.

Check them off when you complete them.

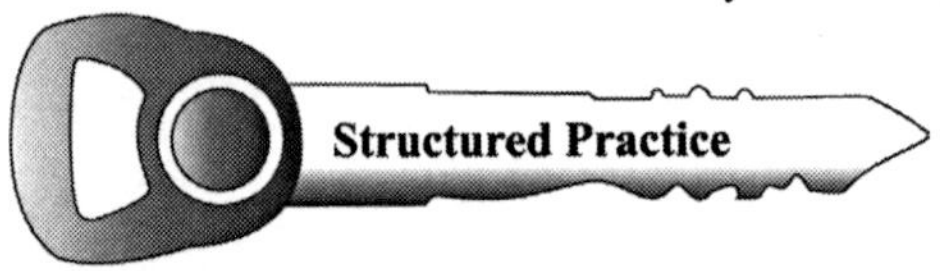

Location: Familiar neighborhood streets

Conditions: Clear, dry, after dark

Lesson Length: 60 Minutes

Materials Required: This workbook

START-UP CHECKLIST			
1	Check your windshield washer fluid.	7	Adjust your steering wheel.
2	Walk around your vehicle.	8	Turn off your cell phone.
3	Check your gas gauge.	9	Secure any loose objects.
4	Adjust your seat.	10	Buckle your seatbelt and make sure your passengers buckle-up too.
5	Adjust your mirrors.		
6	Adjust your headrest.	11	Lock the doors.

Practice these skills:

- ☐ Turn on Headlights
    - ☐ Low beams
    - ☐ High beams
- ☐ Adjust mirrors for night driving (if necessary)
- ☐ Adjust brightness of control panel
- ☐ How to avert your eyes from oncoming vehicle using high beams

Talk about:

- ☐ How things look different at night
- ☐ When to turn on your headlights
- ☐ How to signal oncoming cars that they have no headlights on
- ☐ What to do if someone flashes their lights at you
- ☐ When to use high beams
- ☐ When to use low beams

LESSON 17: 2-Lane Highways

Parents/Coaches: The first time you take your student onto a two-lane (one lane in each direction) highway, don't let them pass any other vehicles. They need to get the feel of how the car moves at this higher speed.

When you are confident they're ready to learn to pass, demonstrate this skill for them first. Explain beforehand, exactly what you're going to do. Then repeat each step as you do it.

Thousands of people are killed every year when they attempt to pass unsafely. Make sure your teen knows what to do and what NOT to do.

This week work through the following topics. Check them off as you complete them.

- ☐ Dealing with Emergencies Part 1 (page 197).
  - ☐ Roadside Assistance Plans
  - ☐ How to Change a Tire
  - ☐ What to Do if You Run Out of Gas

Related Videos:

Go to TeensLearntoDrive.com. Select the link to the "Free Video Library" from your "Favorites" (per instructions on page 3). Under Driving Lesson 17" select:

- ☐ "Structured Practice" to watch videos related to your in-car session.
- ☐ "Need-to-Know Info" to watch videos that relate to the "Need-to-Know Info" sections listed above.

Check them off when you complete them.

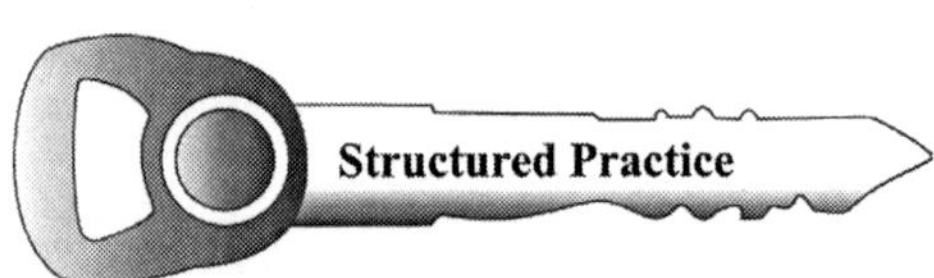

Location: A 2-lane (one lane in each direction) highway where the speed limit is higher than residential streets but there are no merging lanes. Make sure that the speed limit on the highway is within the range allowed with a Learner's Permit in your area.

Conditions: Clear, dry, daylight

Lesson Length: 60 Minutes

Materials Required: This workbook

START-UP CHECKLIST			
1	Check your windshield washer fluid.	7	Adjust your steering wheel.
2	Walk around your vehicle.	8	Turn off your cell phone.
3	Check your gas gauge.	9	Secure any loose objects.
4	Adjust your seat.	10	Buckle your seatbelt and make sure your passengers buckle-up too.
5	Adjust your mirrors.		
6	Adjust your headrest.	11	Lock the doors.

Two-lane highways have one lane in each direction. They are high speed roadways.

If there is a slow-moving vehicle ahead of you, it is sometimes necessary to pass it. To do that, you need to move into the lane of the oncoming traffic, accelerate past the slow vehicle and move safely back into your lane.

Passing Other Vehicles

This is a tricky maneuver. NEVER attempt to pass if you aren't certain you have sufficent time. Have patience. Wait for the right time when:

- You can see the other lane clearly and there are no approaching vehicles
- You are sure you have time to complete this manuever safely
- The lines on the road indicate that it's okay to pass in this area
- You are not approaching a hill or a curve in the road

Practice these skills:

- ☐ Steering at high speeds
- ☐ Maintaining a safe cushion around the vehicle
- ☐ Passing other vehicles
- ☐ Watching road signs and understanding where you are
- ☐ Entering and exiting the highway
- ☐ Maintaining a safe, consistent speed

LESSON 18: Pulling Over

Parents/Coaches: Sometimes drivers need to pull off the road. This lesson is about how to handle those situations safely.

Is your driver continuing to do everything on the Start-Up Checklist? It's important to make sure they do it all—every time they drive.

This week work through the following topics. Check them off as you complete them.

- ☐ Police Stops and Pulling Over (page 194)
- ☐ Tips for Girls (page 206)

Related Videos:

Go to TeensLearntoDrive.com. Select the link to the "Free Video Library" from your "Favorites" (per instructions on page 3). Under Driving Lesson 18" select:

- ☐ "Structured Practice" to watch videos related to your in-car session.
- ☐ "Need-to-Know Info" to watch videos that relate to the "Need-to-Know Info" sections listed above.

Check them off when you complete them.

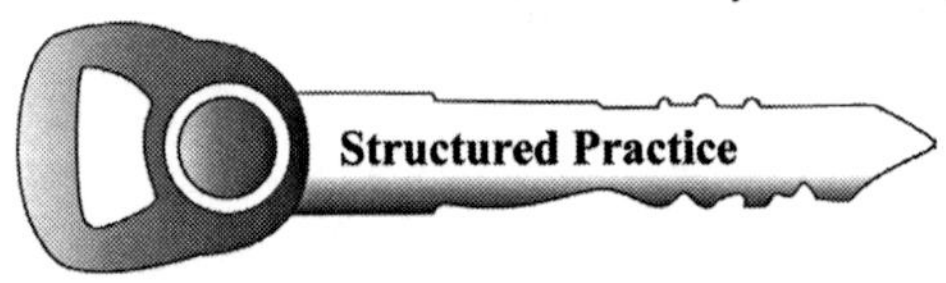

Location: Various roads including a stretch of 2-lane highway

Conditions: Clear, daylight for first lessons. Later, practice again after dark.

Lesson Length: 60 Minutes

Materials Required: This workbook

START-UP CHECKLIST			
1	Check your windshield washer fluid.	7	Adjust your steering wheel.
2	Walk around your vehicle.	8	Turn off your cell phone.
3	Check your gas gauge.	9	Secure any loose objects.
4	Adjust your seat.	10	Buckle your seatbelt and make sure your passengers buckle-up too.
5	Adjust your mirrors.		
6	Adjust your headrest.	11	Lock the doors.

Sometimes you have to pull over to the side of the road. Maybe your car has a problem like a flat tire or you ran out of gas. Maybe you're lost and need to get your bearings or make a cell phone call. Maybe it's raining hard and you can't see the road clearly.

Whenever you can, it's always best to move away from the road completely. A nearby parking lot is much safer than the shoulder of the road.

Practice these skills:

- ☐ Pulling over to the side of the road
- ☐ Re-entering traffic
- ☐ Using your 4-way flashers

Be sure to watch the videos at TeensLearntoDrive.com for more tips on how to pull over safely. Then talk about:

- ☐ When you should pull to the side of the road vs. when you should find a different place to stop
- ☐ Safe places to stop vs. unsafe places to stop
- ☐ When to stay in the car vs. when to find a safer place to wait for help
- ☐ When to use emergency flares and how to light them
- ☐ What information to provide and how to act if you're pulled over by police

Important—If you must pull over to the side of the road, never stand near the car or between two cars.

LESSON 19: Snow and Ice

Parents/Coaches: This lesson is important because snow and ice are different hazards than rain—and most drivers will experience these conditions at some point in their driving career.

If you live in a perpetually warm climate, at least talk about how to handle snow and icy road conditions.

This week work through the following topic. Check it off when you complete it.

- ☐ Winter Driving (page 204)

Related Videos:

Go to TeensLearntoDrive.com. Select the link to the "Free Video Library" from your "Favorites" (per instructions on page 3). Under Driving Lesson 19" select:

- ☐ "Structured Practice" to watch videos related to your in-car session.
- ☐ "Need-to-Know Info" to watch videos that relate to the "Need-to-Know Info" sections listed above.

Check them off when you complete them.

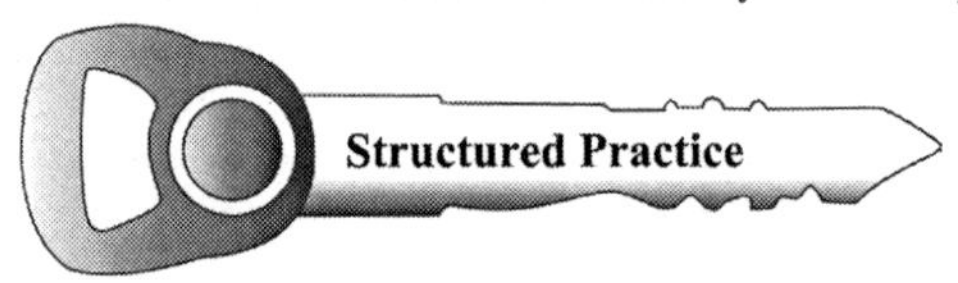

Location: Go back to the parking lot initially to practice braking and steering. Then move to quiet streets until you have built up a lot of confidence.

Conditions: Snowy or icy conditions during daylight

Lesson Length: 60 Minutes

Materials Required: This workbook

START-UP CHECKLIST			
1	Check your windshield washer fluid.	7	Adjust your steering wheel.
2	Walk around your vehicle.	8	Turn off your cell phone.
3	Check your gas gauge.	9	Secure any loose objects.
4	Adjust your seat.	10	Buckle your seatbelt and make sure your passengers buckle-up too.
5	Adjust your mirrors.		
6	Adjust your headrest.	11	Lock the doors.

Thanks to The Bridgestone Winter Driving School in Colorado for providing the information for this section. You'll find more information about them in the Resources section at the back of this book.

Essential Winter Driving Tips from the Pros

A lot of teens believe that quick reactions make a good driver, but they're wrong. The world's best drivers are trained to anticipate problems early and direct the vehicle appropriately before they become involved in a problem.

Reacting too quickly can be dangerous if the driver's response is inappropriate. Remember to:

- Anticipate problems
- Respond to them early
- Avoid panic
- Maintain your calm

The driver and vehicle are equally important to success on ice and snow. Winter driving can, and should, be an enjoyable, hazard-free experience for everyone.

While Driving in Winter ...

- Know your car and know your brakes.
  In everyday driving situations, cars with both ABS (Anti Lock Brakes) and traditional braking systems are basically identical. In an emergency stopping situation, two distinctly different techniques are required.

Anticipate Difficult Situations

Studies have shown that 80% of all crashes could be prevented with only 1 additional second to react. In many situations, this 1-second can be gained by looking far enough down the road to identify problems.

Vehicle Spacing on the Road

Allow plenty of space between yourself and other vehicles. It takes from four to ten times more distance to stop on ice and snow than on dry pavement. Following distances should be adjusted accordingly.

Braking on Icy Roads

Icy roads make traction difficult and sometimes when you try to brake you could start skidding.

If Your Wheels Start to Skid ...

- DO remain calm and in control. (Don't panic.)
- DO keep your eyes on where you WANT to go—(NOT where your skidding car is headed!)
- DON'T stomp on the brake (that will only make the situation worse!)
- DO steer into the skid (point the wheels in the direction that you would rather be going)
- Once the car is under control, DO accelerate smoothly. Smooth acceleration will cause a weight transfer to the rear wheels and help regain grip.

If Your Vehicle Refuses to Turn and the Front Wheels are Skidding ...

- DON'T panic.
- DON'T hit the brake or jerk the steering wheel
- DO lift off the accelerator
- DO turn back toward straight a slight amount (this will allow the front wheel to regain grip and start rolling again)
- Once grip and steering effectiveness are restored, you can smoothly steer back in to the curve.

This correction goes against natural instinct and takes considerable room to perform but is the only way to correct this situation.

Use Grip (Traction) Efficiently—When roads are slippery, use all of the grip (traction) available for one action at a time. Brake only in a straight line prior to the curve when the car is traveling straight. Taking your foot off the brake before you steer into the curve allows you to use all of the grip available just for steering. Accelerate only when you are able to straighten the steering wheel at the exit of the turn. This technique will allow you to be 100% effective at each maneuver- braking, steering and acceleration.

A Few Words about Snow Plows

Snow plows move at a slower speed than other traffic and it can be very frustrating to get caught behind them, especially when you're in a hurry.

If you get stuck behind a plow, take a deep breath and calm yourself. Passing snow plows is extremely dangerous and you really are better off behind the plow than in front of it. And forget about being in a hurry. If the roads are so bad that the snow plows are out, you'd be risking your life if you try to rush. Take it slow, stay behind the plow and you'll arrive safely at your destination.

4 Reasons You Should Never Pass a Snow Plow:

1. The road surface is clearer behind the plow than in front of it.
2. The plow is wider than the lane it's travelling in so it needs a lot of extra room. It's hard to judge how much extra room you need to leave when you pass.
3. Plows are wider at the front than they look from the back because of their blades. This makes it even more difficult to figure out how much room you need to leave when you pass.
4. Visibility near the plow is severely impaired by spraying snow.

Snow Plow Safety Tips

1. Most snow plows have flashing blue lights. When you see them, you know that the vehicle ahead is moving slowly so slow down accordingly.
2. Leave extra room between your car and the plow.
3. When you approach a snow plow from the opposite direction, move as far from the center line as safely possible to lessen the affect of the blowing snow on your visibility. Remember, however, that there could be a "phantom shoulder" so don't pull too far over onto the side of the road either.
   (Note: A "phantom shoulder" is created when a plow levels the area beside the road. This makes it look like the road is wide but the snow could actually be hiding a ditch.
4. **NEVER pass a snow plow on the right!**

LESSON 20: Following Directions and Finding Your Way

Parents/Coaches: Up until now, your driver has depended on you to tell them where to go and how to get there. Soon they'll need to find their way on their own. That will mean asking for directions and following them—without help.

This week your job is to help them learn to follow a map and follow directions. If you have a GPS, don't use it now. Make sure they know how to use it too, but it may not always be available.

TIP: If you don't have a map of your area, print one off Google Maps or Mapquest.com.

Drivers should never be studying maps while they're driving. Have them look at the map and tell you which route they'll take—before they start the car. You can help by repeating the directions they identified, while they drive. If they get lost or are unsure which way to go, ask them to pull over in a safe place and take another look at the map.

Your job is to stay calm and coach them through mistakes. If they miss a street, ask them to pull over and find another route or to turn around in a safe place.

> **Cool Fact:**
>
> If you ask a man for directions, he'll probably draw you a map or tell you which streets to take.
>
> Women are more likely to drive by landmarks—"Turn right at the corner with the 7-Eleven on it and the big sign that says …."

This week work through the following topic. Check it off as you complete it.

- ☐ Giving and Getting Directions (below)

Related Videos:

Go to TeensLearntoDrive.com. Select the link to the "Free Video Library" from your "Favorites" (per instructions on page 3). Under Driving Lesson 20" select:

- ☐ "Structured Practice" to watch videos related to your in-car session.
- ☐ "Need-to-Know Info" to watch videos that relate to the "Need-to-Know Info" sections listed above.

Check them off when you complete them.

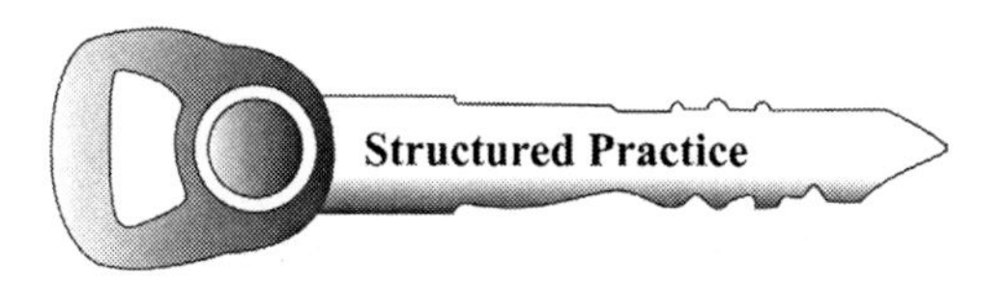

Location: Coach—Choose a mystery location and a start position that are several miles apart.

Tip: It would be nice if the mystery location is someplace fun—like a movie theater or an ice cream shop.

Conditions: Clear, dry, daylight.

Lesson Length: 60 Minutes

Materials Required: This workbook

START-UP CHECKLIST			
1	Check your windshield washer fluid.	7	Adjust your steering wheel.
2	Walk around your vehicle.	8	Turn off your cell phone.
3	Check your gas gauge.	9	Secure any loose objects.
4	Adjust your seat.	10	Buckle your seatbelt and make sure your passengers buckle-up too.
5	Adjust your mirrors.		
6	Adjust your headrest.	11	Lock the doors.

Activity

1. Have teen drive to the START position. You can give them step-by-step directions.
2. Show them where the MYSTERY location is on the map.
3. Have them identify the START position on the map. (Don't help them.)
4. Have them plot a course from the START position to the MYSTERY location on the map.
5. Have them tell you how they will get there. "I'll drive 2 blocks south on this road to Little Road and I'll turn left," etc.
6. Let them follow their directions and see where they take them. Do not let them look at the map while they're driving (that's dangerous!) but you can repeat the directions as they said them. (Write them down if you need to.)
7. If there's a problem with the directions, help them sort it out.

Talk about:

- How to read a map
  - Where to find North (South, East and West)
  - Map scale and how to estimate the distance you'll be driving
- How to follow directions
- What to do if a friend suddenly yells, "Turn here!"
- What to do if you miss your exit on the highway

If you have a GPS—great! Make sure your teen knows how to use that safely too. But being able to follow directions and read a map are important skills for drivers. Don't let the GPS substitute for the map in this lesson.

GPS Tips:

GPS systems can be big distractions. Never attach them to them windshield because they can obstruct the driver's view. If you do use one (later), let your passenger operate it. When you're alone, use the audio feature rather than the map.

After Getting a Provisional License

In this Section:

- Creating Your Teen-Parent Driving Contract
- Rules, Consequences and Monitoring
- Best Cars for Teens
- New Technologies
- The Teen-Parent Driving Contract
- Dangerous Behaviors and Situations
- Fatigue and Driving While You're Drowsy
- Maggie's Story
- Speeding
- Reid's Story
- Road Racing
- High Emotion
- Alcohol and Driving
- Meagan, Lisa and Eric's Story
- A Night to Remember
- Road Rage
- Blame Your Parents
- Daydreaming
- Tailgating
- Right-of-Way
- Motorcycles
- Railway Crossings
- Stuff That Can Get You into Trouble
- Lending the Car
- Plan, Share and Update
- Prom Night: Lacey's Story
- Parking: Safety, Etiquette and Responsibility
- Handicapped Parking
- Police Stops and Pulling Over
- GIRLS: What would you do in these situations?
- Stuff You Should Have in Your Car
- Dealing with Emergencies
- Winter Driving Tips
- Girl Power
- 5 Advanced Driving Lessons

Chapter 7
Actively Involved Parents
After Getting a Provisional License

Up until now, whenever your teen has been driving, you've been there to coach, direct and protect, but that's about to change. As soon as your teen passes their road test, they'll want to take the keys and go out there alone—or with a group of their friends. That poses a bunch of new challenges.

Before your teens drive without you at their side, you need to have your Teen-Parent Driving Contract in place. You've already been working on your family driving rules in the previous sections. Now you're going to put them together, assign the consequences for breaking the rules and sign it.

Creating Your Teen-Parent Driving Contract

This is a very important step as Sergeant Gus Ramirez of the Highway Patrol, Sante Fe County, New Mexico points out in his message to parents:

> "Educate your teens by giving them the facts to help them make good driving decisions. Then make rules they need to follow. Follow up with strict consequences for breaking the rules.
>
> Talking is great but actions speak louder than words. It won't work unless you follow through.
>
> They may hate you for saying no now but dealing with their anger is a lot easier than placing flowers on their grave."

Finalize Your Rules

Teens are not the worst drivers—but they are the least experienced. That lack of experience contributes to driver error which is involved in most crashes. It's important to eliminate as many distractions and potential problems as possible so young drivers can concentrate on driving.

You've been building your family rules. Now use them to complete or modify the contract on page 255.

When it's completed, sign it with your teen. Post it in a place where it can be seen (like near the refrigerator.)

Periodically talk about it with your teen—to keep it fresh in their minds and to find out if they're having any difficulties.

The Safe Passage Clause

You'll see that the contract includes the "Safe Passage Clause." It is very important.

Mistakes can happen. Things can get out of control. The "Safe Passage Clause" tells your teen that their safety is the most important thing. If they are ever in a situation where they need a safe ride home, you agree to pick them up or arrange another ride so they can get home safely.

If you get that call, it's important to stay calm and postpone discussions about what happened until the next day. That night, your adrenaline will be pumping. You'll be worried and maybe even angry. You could get carried away, scolding or overly emotional about what's happened. You could say things you regret. As a result, your teen might decide not to call the next time they get into trouble and that could be disastrous.

Instead, wait until the next morning to discuss what happened. It's okay to say you're disappointed. It's okay to talk about how some behaviors are inappropriate or dangerous—and why. Use the situation as a teaching moment.

But also make sure your teen understands you appreciate that they called you. Let them know that you recognize they used good judgment by asking for your help instead of risking their lives. Encourage them to continue to use good judgment and call you again, if they ever need a safe ride home.

Rules, Consequences and Monitoring

Your Teen-Parent Contract will make your expectations clear but it's useless unless you assign meaningful consequences, monitor your teen's adherence to them and follow through with the consequences immediately if a rule is broken.

So what kind of consequences should you set?

Make sure the consequences you set for breaking the family's driving rules are a deterrent, not just a slap on the wrist. And impose the penalties immediately, as soon as the infraction occurs. Not—"on Sunday morning, after the Saturday night school dance."

Use Your Judgment

You know your teens, so make the consequences meaningful to them. Penalties should relate to driving and reflect the seriousness of the offense. Although all offenses are serious, (or they wouldn't be included) some may have an explanation that should be considered, so use judgment. For example, your teen might honestly forget to buckle their seatbelt once. So a stern reminder to say "Seatbelt Check" (and do it) before they put the car in gear might be enough the first time. The second time, the consequence might be 2 weeks without driving privileges—because you don't want your teen to get in the habit of forgetting to buckle their seatbelt.

Speeding and reckless driving are serious offenses because they often lead to crashes. They require serious penalties. For example—the penalty for speeding 5-10 miles over the limit should hurt. More than 10 miles over the limit should hurt even more.

How Will You Know if Your Teen Breaks the Rules?

You won't always. You'll have to decide how you will gather information about your teen's driving and how you'll deal with it.

If your teen gets a ticket, you may have to hear about it through them or the grapevine. In some areas, the police won't provide information to parents about tickets, even though the parents own the vehicle.

You'll find ideas about how you can monitor your teen's driving in the coming pages. Electronic monitors will provide you with the actual speeds they have driven. Friends and other drivers can provide feedback too.

Give some thought to how you'll get information about how your teen is driving and how you'll deal with that information.

Suggested First Offense Fines for Speeding

If you find that your teen has been speeding (the electronic monitor indicates this or they got a ticket), you might consider these penalties:

- 5 to 10 miles over the speed limit—loss of driving privileges for 1 month
- 10 + miles over the speed limit—penalty is doubled to 2 months or more
- Street racing—Penalty is tripled plus an additional family 'fine' (or other penalty)

Speeding (defined as exceeding the posted speed limit or driving too fast for conditions) is a factor in nearly one-third of all fatal crashes.

In each case, the teen should also be responsible for paying:

- The fine associated with a ticket
- The additional driver insurance premium, if there is one

Caution!

No matter how much money you have—or how many 'connections'—don't even consider hiring a lawyer (or agent) to 'take care' of those tickets for your teen. Don't consider using those 'connections' to make the ticket 'go away'.

If you run interference so they don't have to face the legal consequences of their actions, you'll be heading down a very slippery slope. You'll be teaching your teen that the rules don't apply to them.

Second and Subsequent Offenses

Again—penalties need to escalate. They should double—at least.

You need to escalate your involvement too. If your teen continues speeding or driving recklessly, check with your local hospital or police department to see if they offer programs for teen drivers. Some offer excellent programs that allow teens to meet people who've been involved in crashes caused by that kind of irresponsible behavior. Seeing the devastation first-hand should have a serious effect.

Remember that you control the keys to the car. If your teen continues speeding or driving recklessly—take the keys away. And consider that your teen may have other problems. Alcohol and drug use are often linked to speeding and reckless driving.

Get them whatever help they need.

What if your teen gets a ticket and hides it from you?

Your driving contract addresses that. There must be trust and your teen must understand at the outset that hiding a ticket from you is a very serious offense. Determine what the additional penalty will be.

Monitoring Your Teen's Driving

If your teens are breaking the law and endangering the lives of themselves and others, you need to know right away because—you can't fix a problem you don't know exists.

Speeding tickets are like customer complaints.

In my other life, I'm a corporate trainer. One of my favorite topics is Customer Service. In that role, I try to help my students understand that—as unpleasant as it can be to hear customer complaints—they are gifts. They should not only listen to them and resolve them—***they should be grateful for them!*** Does that sound crazy?

The fact is—that for every customer who complains—many, many others had the same problem but didn't bother to complain. They simply found another supplier for that product or service. That's disastrous for business—and the long-term effect could include cutbacks and job losses. So when someone takes the time to complain, they're doing the company a favor! By complaining, that customer gives them an opportunity to explain a misunderstanding or rectify the problem, and fix the root cause to protect future business. (And often the 'complainer' becomes a loyal customer as a result.)

If There's a Problem—You Need to Know

Traffic tickets are equally unpleasant to get—but can be gifts in disguise. They make you aware of a problem so you can address the root cause—make your teen slow down and obey the law.

Other Parents Wish They'd Had that Opportunity

In 2008, in Muskoka, Ontario, there was a terrible car crash that killed three young people, including the 20 year-old driver. He'd been speeding along a very windy country road when he lost control and veered off into the lake.

His family was understandably devastated. His father found out, after the accident, that his son had several speeding tickets.

He wishes he'd known about them. Maybe he could have done something to curb his son's 'need for speed.' In any case, he wouldn't have bought his son a powerful sports car that fuelled his son's reckless behavior. But he didn't get that chance because he didn't know.

Of course—it's best if your teens NEVER get speeding or reckless driving tickets because they always obey the law. But if they take chances that put their lives in danger, you need to know.

Monitoring Your Teen's Driving or

"There's Never a Police Officer Around When You Want One"

Okay—you've got your rules and penalties in place, but everyone knows that police forces work with limited budgets and have a lot of territory to cover. No matter how diligent and hard-working your police department is, they can't be everywhere at every time.

And teens are smart. They quickly learn where the speed traps are and how to turn on the tears to avoid getting a ticket. Officers were teens once too, and sometimes give in and let kids off with a warning. (So if your teen does get a ticket—it's highly likely this is not the first time they've committed the offense. It's just the first time they got caught and ticketed!)

So How Can You Get "Eyes" on the Road?

Ask all your friends, relatives and neighbors to watch out for your teen. Make it clear they'll be doing you a big favor by letting you know how they're driving—good or bad—soon after they spot them on the road.

Explain to friends that you want to keep your teen safe and can't fix a problem you don't know about. If they see your teen doing something risky or illegal and try to 'give them a break' by not telling you, you'll miss the opportunity to address the problem and change a behavior that could endanger their life.

Explain that you're not asking them to spy on your kids and don't want to know who they're hanging out with or where they are at all hours. You're only interested in their driving.

Explain that you won't tell your teen who reported them—just the time and place of the incident. So your teen won't be mad at Grandma if she 'tells on them.' (They'll never know it was Grandma.) But be sure to get the time and place so you can verify it was indeed your teen. Mistakes could happen and you don't want to go accusing your teen of something they couldn't possibly have done.

Be Transparent

Tell your teen what you're doing and why. Be prepared for their annoyance and accusations of spying. They won't like being monitored, but their safety is more important. You don't need their okay to parent them.

And just knowing that other drivers are watching out for them is a deterrent. Your neighbor could be in that black car behind them or your colleague in the red sports car ahead. They'll never know.

Add an Incentive

You've asked for feedback good or bad. You're prepared to deal with the bad stuff, but what if someone calls and says, " I saw your daughter yesterday afternoon, in the mall parking lot. She was driving carefully and stopped for the pedestrians that were crossing the road."

Of course you'll tell her she was spotted driving safely. You might even tell her exactly what was said. What incentives can you put in place to reward her good driving? Consider these possibilities:

- An extra night out with the car
- A free tank of gas (or $10.00 towards a tank of gas.)
- Special driving privileges for a specific period of time

You may never get a call. But the possibility that people are watching is a strong deterrent for your teen. And if you do get the feedback you want—you just might be pleasantly surprised by what people have to say.

Other Ways to Monitor Your Teen's Driving

CallMyMom.org

Here's an interesting idea. You go online to callmymom.org and sign up. They'll send you a bumper sticker to put on the car your teen will be driving. It has a unique number (0504 in the example above).

Then—any driver, anywhere can call the number to report how the car is being driven. They leave a voicemail which is automatically forwarded to the contact number you've provided.

At this time, there's no fee for this service. They operate on donations—but that could change.

Tip from Lauren, the Driving Instructor:

Don't be afraid to monitor your new driver.

Use Technology. There are a number of devices out there to help parents monitor their teen's driving from afar. GPS units can tell you where your teen is and how fast they're going.

At the very least, the knowledge that you're "watching" will help your teen make better decisions on the road.

Electronic Monitoring

There's a fine line between monitoring and spying. I'm all for deterring dangerous behaviors but I don't want to know where my daughter is every second of every day. I understand that she needs some privacy and I don't want her thinking I don't trust her—***because I do***. (But I also know peer pressure can push teens to do things they wouldn't normally do. And above all—I want her to be safe.)

There are a lot of products available to help you monitor how your teen is driving. Some address speeding alone while others let you know about sudden stops and risky behaviors as well.

Trust Goes Both Ways

If you decide to use an electronic monitoring system, please tell your teen what you're doing. Knowing there's a device in the car alone is a deterrent. Installing it without their knowledge so you can catch them doing something they shouldn't, is deceitful.

Monitoring should be about building trust—not destroying it. Trust goes both ways.

You'll find links to several great products for monitoring drivers at TeensLearntoDrive.com, but there are two products I'd like to tell you about.

Cool Product! The Speed Demon

www.LiveFastDriveSlow.com

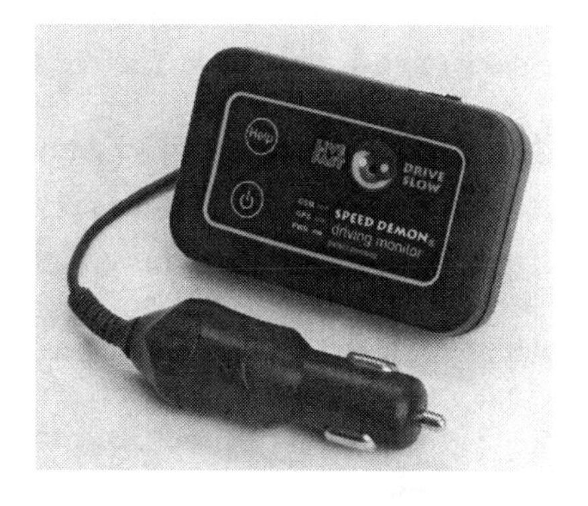

The 'Speed Demon' is a small device parents can easily install in cars to monitor how fast their teens are driving. It uses GPS technology and the T-Mobile network to advise parents when their teens exceed the speed limit. Parents set the allowed speed limits and can adjust them as their teens gain driving experience. It also helps parents monitor curfews.

Although it uses GPS technology, parents can't use it to track their kids—***unless the teens exceed the speed limit***. As long as teens drive within the speed limit, they "stay under their parents' radar too!" What an incentive not to speed!

Another reason this product is cool is because it was invented by a teen. Jon Fischer was 16 when he entered his Speed Demon-prototype in the Massachusetts State Science Fair. He'd been looking for an idea for a project he could enter, when a schoolmate died in a car crash. The victim and his friend were celebrating on the day they earned their driver's licenses. The driver was speeding and lost control of the vehicle.

Jon decided to create a device that would keep future teen drivers from a similar fate. Being a teen himself, he felt it was equally important to protect the privacy of other teens. That's why it doesn't track location unless the speed limit is breeched.

Jon is older and in college now. He's an avid aerial skier—in fact, that's what got him involved in the Science Fair in the first place. He'd wanted to take n advanced course in ski jumping acrobatics and made a deal with his dad. His dad would pay for the course (and let him go) if he entered the Science Fair. I, for one, am glad he did!

You'll find the Speed Demon at www.LiveFastDriveSlow.com. It sells for around $200.00 and there's a monthly T-Mobile fee of around $15.00.

Lemur Safe Driver Wireless Vehicle Monitors

www.LemurMonitors.com

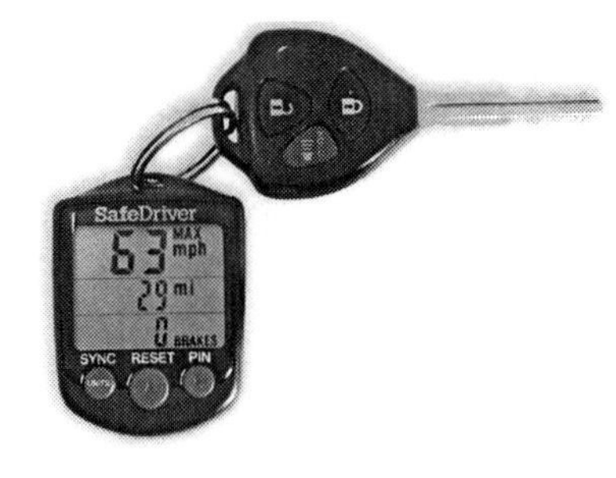

Another great product parents can use to monitor their teen drivers is the Lemur Safe Driver Monitor. One part plugs in under the dashboard. (It's so easy I did it myself!) The other part is a key fob that attaches to your keys. You can see in the picture that it looks pretty much like a remote car door opener.

The advantage of this system is that it's inexpensive and there are no monthly fees.

A possible drawback is that it only provides information about the last trip in the car, so parents using it need to be diligent about checking it every time their teen uses the car. Personally—I don't see this as a disadvantage because I think it's important to check it every time the car is used anyway. (At least at first. Later, when your teen is a little more experienced, you might agree to periodic 'surprise' checks.)

The Lemur monitor will not only give you information about how the car is being driven, it will also reinforce the fact that you are actively monitoring how they drive. (Keeping them aware that you are 'watching' is important!)

After each time your teen uses the car, check the key fob to find out:

- The maximum speed the car was driven
- How many times the car was stopped very suddenly
- How far the car travelled

You can use this information to talk to your teen about how and where they are driving.

Check the Resources Section of TeensLearntoDrive.com for more information or check out www.LemurMonitors.com

Best Cars for Teens

This is also a good time to think about what kind of car your teen should be driving. Some parents promise their teens cars for their sixteenth birthday, but is that really the way to go?

Should you buy a car for your teen?

The first year of driving solo is the most dangerous for teens, so it's important to keep especially close watch during this time. It's a lot easier to monitor and manage driving when the vehicle is a shared family car. So in most cases, it's wise not to buy your teen a car during this critical period, even if you can easily afford it.

If you must get a car for your teen, consider carefully what vehicle you should buy. (You might also think about changing the family vehicle to something with additional safety features if that's what your teen will be driving.) You'll find some tips about vehicles in this section.

Also think about what kind of stake your teen should have in the vehicle.

People Value What They Earn

It's human nature. When we work hard for something, we tend to cherish it and protect it. Freebies and gifts, though appreciated, aren't as valued. (Subconsciously, we think, "Easy come, easy go!") So think about what kind of a stake your teen should have in the car. Should they pay for -

- The down payment
- The monthly payments
- The insurance
- The gas
- Repairs—caution about this one. Teens may put off necessary repairs if they don't have the money. Perhaps it's better to pay for the repairs yourself and then arrange a reimbursement schedule with your teen.
- A combination of the above?

By contributing to the cost of the vehicle and/or the upkeep, they will probably try to keep it in better condition too.

Shared Vehicle Rules

If you'll be sharing a vehicle, it could be wise to set some ground rules. It's always easier to set the rules upfront and adjust them when necessary. It's much harder to impose rules at a later date. Think about things like:

- Cleanliness of the vehicle on the outside and tidiness inside
- When the car is returned, how much gas do you expect to find in the tank?
- If something in the car isn't working properly or it's making a funny sound, how quickly do you want to be notified? (Keep in mind that in most cases—the sooner you know, the less costly the repair.)

Best Cars for Teens

Some people think it's best to get their teens big, old clunkers that provide lots of metal around their drivers. The idea is that if you put your teen in a tank, they'll be protected from outside forces. And that will work if they're involved in fender-benders.

But big cars are hard to maneuver and older vehicles don't have the most up-to-date safety technology. However—size does matter! Small cars don't provide much protection. I shudder to think of what would happen to someone driving a 2-seater in a high-speed crash!

Mid-size seems to be the way to go. The Insurance Institute for Highway Safety recommends passenger cars weighing between 3,500 and 4,500 pounds. They'll cost a little more to run (gasoline) but will provide better protection.

5 Great Sites to Help You Choose the Best Vehicle

The following sites provide great information to help you research your vehicle and compare its safety ratings and maintenance costs.

- **www.safercar.gov**—This NHTSA website rates vehicles according to how they performed in front & side crashes and gives rollover ratings.
- **www.iihs.org** - This site is sponsored by The Insurance Institute for Highway Safety. It rates vehicles as Good, Acceptable, Marginal or Poor in front, side and rear crashes. It also allows you to evaluate comparable vehicles to find the best vehicle in a particular class.
- **www.autosafety.org/video-archive**—The Center for Auto Safety has all kinds of auto information.
- **www.theautochannel.com/media/index.html**—The Auto Channel provides information about various makes and models as well as listing the costs you can expect to pay for maintaining the vehicle.
- **www.odi.nhtsa.dot.gov/recalls/recallsearch.cfm**—This NHTSA site will show you any recalls that have been issued on that vehicle.

Vehicles to Avoid

Some vehicles are clearly poor choices for teens. They include:

- Sports cars and other high performance vehicles that have too much power and encourage reckless driving.

- Pickup trucks and SUVs that are more prone to rollover crashes.
- Small cars. They don't absorb the impact of a collision as well as mid-size or larger cars.
- Older vehicles without airbags and other safety devices

New Technologies

Safer SUVs

Variable Ride-Height Suspensions

Some vehicles offer a new suspension feature that raises or lowers the ride height of the vehicle while it is moving. The advantage to this system is that it increases stability by lowering the center of gravity, making the vehicle less likely to roll over if it becomes unbalanced.

These Variable Ride-Height Suspensions (VRHS) are called different names by different manufacturers. Some are automatic while others require the driver to engage them. If you have the second kind, make sure you know how to use it.

Which Vehicles are Most Likely to Roll Over?

SUVs are more likely to be involved in rollovers because they tend to be top heavy. Smaller, lighter SUVs are particularly prone to rollovers.

How to Check the Rollover Rating of a Vehicle Before You Buy It

NHTSA has rated vehicles based on data compiled from more than 86,000 single-vehicle crashes. The ratings are available free of charge at www.safercar.gov. Look for "Search 5-Star Safety Ratings." Then enter the year, manufacturer, model and specifics of the vehicle and it will give you the rating. '5 Star' is the top rating.

Integrated Spotter Mirrors

These mirrors have an inset smaller mirror that shows the area normally considered a blind spot.

My Key

This is a very cool technology from Ford. It allows parents to customize a special key for their teen. Then parents can set certain parameters so when teens use it:

- The vehicle's top speed is limited
- The maximum volume of the radio and audio devices is lowered so they can still hear what's happening outside the car

When that special key is used, the vehicle will also:

- Signal the driver when the speed hits 45, 55 and 65 miles per hour
- Chime every 6-seconds (for a full five minutes) if the driver doesn't buckle-up (The audio system won't work until they buckle-up either)
- Give an earlier low-fuel warning

Note: 'MyKey' has so many benefits, that parents /coaches might even consider using it themselves.

Rear View Camera Systems

Cameras at the back of the vehicle show the driver what's behind them when they're backing up.

Hands-free and Voice-activated Communications and Audio Systems

Most automobile companies offer some form of hands-free calling and audio. Although hands-free is better than hands-on, these systems are still distracting.

Check your local laws to find out what systems are allowed in your area.

Chapter 8
Need-to-Know Info
After Getting a Provisional License

The Teen-Parent Driving Contract

I can already hear you—"Why do I need a stupid contract?"

Your Teen-Parent Driving Contract will make your parents more comfortable, but it's for your protection too. It makes sure you understand what your family rules are so you don't make a mistake that will get you in big trouble.

And since your parents know you've read and agreed to the rules, it could lead to more driving time for you too!

The Safe Passage Clause

The contract also provides you with 'Safe Passage' home if you need it. If you're ever in a jam and need a safe way to get home, your parents promise to help you—no matter what the time or circumstances. They just want you to be safe.

How does it work?

Let's say you're at a party and you totally lose track of time. Your curfew was eleven o'clock and it's almost 3:00 a.m. You've been drinking and you know you shouldn't drive but you really don't want to call your parents because that will wake them up and they'll be mad because you completely missed your curfew. Then they'll go ballistic when they find out you were drinking! You might think you'd be better off driving home. You could be really careful—take the back roads, then sneak into the house and they'll be none the wiser, right?

Wrong! First of all, they're probably frantic because you aren't home. Even if you did make it home safely, they'll be waiting and now—you'll be late AND you drove while you were impaired! You would have just managed to make a bad situation a whole lot worse.

But as bad as that can be—it could be so much worse. You might not make it home at all. By driving impaired you could kill yourself or someone else.

So, alternately, you could invoke that Safe Passage Clause and call your parents to tell them you need a safe ride home. They promise not to yell at you (once they get past screaming, "Thank heaven, you're alright!")

If they forget and start getting mad at you, simply remind them that they promised you safe passage. Then they'll come and get you—no questions asked.

The next day, after everyone's gotten some sleep and things have calmed down, you can talk about what happened and sort things out together.

Will they still be mad at you for blowing off your curfew and drinking when you were the driver? Sure. You know what you did was wrong, but you also made a smart, very mature decision. You chose not to drink and drive. You took responsibility for your actions. That has to earn you some brownie points somewhere along the line.

Dangerous Behaviors and Situations

Congratulations! You passed your road test! I'm sure you're looking forward to the freedom of being able to drive without an adult looking over your shoulder. But—with freedom—comes additional responsibility.

The decisions you make while you're in the driver's seat alone, will affect all the people around you. You'll be faced with life and death choices where there are serious consequences for mistakes—no matter how innocent.

This section will provide you with a lot of information about potentially dangerous situations so you'll make wise driving decisions.

Fatigue and Driving While You're Drowsy

Everyone gets a little tired sometimes, but when you're really sleep-deprived, you're in no shape to drive.

Sleep is NOT an Option!

It's a Necessity!

Human beings NEED 3 things to stay alive:

1. Water
2. Food
3. Sleep

Getting enough sleep is just as important as the first two—but in our culture we often associate sleep with laziness. That's wrong and we need to change it.

When we don't get enough sleep, we start to fall apart. After 18 hours without sleep, we function as though we're impaired (with a blood alcohol concentration of 0.08).

> NHTSA estimates that *one million* crashes each year result from driver inattention. A lot of those crashes are due to drowsiness.
>
> •••••
>
> 45% of teens sleep less than 8 hours on school nights—while they need around 9 hours per night
>
> NSF's 2006 *Sleep in America* poll
>
> •••••
>
> "Healthy people CANNOT sleep too much. When they get enough sleep, they wake up."
>
> D.Drobnich, The National Sleep Foundation

So—if you wake up at 6:00 o'clock in the morning, by 11p.m. that night, you:

- Can't concentrate very well
- Don't react as quickly as you normally do
- Aren't processing information properly
- Have poor decision-making skills
- Are less coordinated than usual

If you're sitting on the sofa, watching TV, this isn't a big problem. You'll probably just doze off and catch up on the sleep you're missing. But if you're behind the wheel of a car—you're already a danger to yourself and others! And if you fall asleep behind the wheel—you may never wake up!

The NHTSA estimates that drowsiness is the cause of more than 100,000 major crashes each year. 76,000 people are severely injured in those crashes and 1,500 people die.

But the real numbers are probably much higher. There's no breathalyzer-type test for exhausted drivers and a lot don't survive their crashes so police can't ask them what happened. Instead, police departments look at certain factors to figure out if the driver fell asleep.

When drivers fall asleep at the wheel there are some telltale signs. Typically:

- It happens at night (highest percentage of teen crashes)
- It happens between 2:00 p.m. and 4:00 p.m. (after school)
- It involves a single vehicle that drives off the road
- It happens on a highway or high-speed roadway
- It results in serious injuries or death
- There's no indication that the driver tried to brake or avoid a collision
- The driver is alone
- The driver is often a young man (between 16 to 29)

Drowsiness is a significant problem that increases a driver's risk of a crash or near-crash by at least 4 times

NHTSA Data 2006

More Bedtime Tips

Don't eat, drink, or exercise within a few hours of your bedtime.

Don't leave your homework for the last minute.

Try to avoid the TV, computer and telephone in the hour before you go to bed.

•••••

At least once a week—

- 28% of high school students fall asleep in class
- 22% fall asleep doing homework
- 14% arrive late or miss school because they oversleep

NSF's 2006 *Sleep in America* poll

•••••

Who is most at risk for drowsy driving?

- Teens (especially boys)
- Shift workers
- Commuters
- People who drive long, straight sections of road

Teens and Sleep—(or Lack of Sleep!)

A lot of teens like to stay up late but that's not the only reason they don't get enough sleep. Sometimes they go to bed early and ***still*** can't get to sleep even though they know they have to get up early the next morning.

It's not their fault. There are several factors that keep them awake, including their body clocks (circadian rhythms)—which are beyond their control. But there are a few things they can do to make it easier to get to sleep.

Darrel Drobnich, of the National Sleep Foundation, offers these suggestions:

- Keep the room cool and make it as dark as possible
- Spend the hour before bedtime doing something quiet and relaxing
- Go to bed at the same time every night
- Avoid caffeinated beverages in the evening, including coffee tea, colas, power drinks and chocolate

Parents: If your teens don't get enough sleep during the week and sleep till noon or later on the weekend—let them. It's not just 'laziness.' They really need it. Teens are still growing and maturing and their bodies need sleep to regenerate and function properly. Sleep is not optional. It's critical!

Signs that You Aren't Getting Enough Sleep

Here are some signs that you aren't getting enough sleep:

- You have a lot of trouble getting out of bed in the morning
- You power-sleep on the weekends
- You fall asleep in class
- There are circles under your eyes
- You doze off at the movies or while waiting for friends
- Sometimes you have trouble concentrating on things
- You get headaches in the morning

Drowsy driving is common among teens.

- 51% admit to having driven drowsy in the past year
- 15% drive drowsy at least once per week.

(NSF's 2006 *Sleep in America* poll)

• • • • •

Our internal body clocks program us to be sleepy twice a day:

- 1st during the middle of our nighttime sleep period
- and again 12 hours later, between 2:00 and 4:00 in the afternoon (siesta time)

So—how tired is *too* tired to drive?

If you've been awake for 24 hours, you drive the same way you would if you had a blood-alcohol level of 0.10 percent. Your judgment is impaired so you're likely to miss a stop sign or misjudge distances. Your reactions are slowed so you can't respond fast enough to what's happening around you and your coordination is off, so you can't handle the vehicle the way you normally would either.

Lack of sleep can also cause aggressiveness toward other drivers, which can lead to road rage.

And just like when you're impaired by drugs or alcohol, you'll probably think your driving is fine, until you fall asleep and crash full force into a tree or another car! Because the fact is, that once your body is that tired, you can't stay awake, no matter how hard you try to fight it!

In the U.S.–Driver drowsiness and fatigue cause at least:

56,000 crashes each year
40,000 serious injuries
1,550 deaths
$12.5 Billion in monetary losses

• • • • •

20% of drivers admit they fell asleep at some time

NHTSA data

• • • • •

In Canada—Driver drowsiness and fatigue cause:

Up to 21% of crashes each year
2,100 serious injuries
400 deaths

• • • • •

20% of drivers admit they fell asleep during the last year

Canadian Council of Motor Transport Administrators

• • • • •

Teens know that driving when they're very tired is dangerous.

Many speed up so they can get home faster!

Teen Unsafe Driving Behavior Study- NTHSA 2004

What's a Sleep Debt?

If you've been awake for 24 hours straight, you know it, but a lack of sleep over several days can catch up with you too.

Basically—adults need 7 to 8 hours of good quality sleep each night. Teens need more—around 9 hours—because their bodies are still growing and maturing. So—if you've been staying up late and getting up early for several days in a row, that can add up to a dangerous situation too.

You need to do the math.

If you fall asleep (**not** *go to bed*) each night at 11:00 p.m. and wake up each morning for school at 6:00 a.m.—you're only getting 7 hours of sleep each night. So by the time Friday night rolls around you've accumulated a sleep debt of 10 hours.

Night	Required Sleep	Actual Sleep	Sleep Debt
Sunday	9 hours	7 hours	-2 hours
Monday	9 hours	7 hours	-2 hours
Tuesday	9 hours	7 hours	-2 hours
Wednesday	9 hours	7 hours	-2 hours
Thursday	9 hours	7 hour	-2 hours

Your Total Sleep Debt is **10 hours**

You'll need to sleep in until 11:00 a.m. on Saturday and Sunday mornings to wipe out that sleep debt. If you don't, it will continue to accumulate until you **cannot** keep yourself awake any longer (no matter how hard you try) and that's very dangerous.

But it would really be best if you could try to get 8 ½ hours of sleep each night during the week so you wouldn't have so much catching up to do on the weekends. When you stay up really late on the weekends and then sleep in till 2:00 p.m. each afternoon—you throw your sleep schedule completely out of whack! Then it's really hard getting back into a routine again on Sunday night for the following school week.

The following story shows how dangerous sleep debt can be.

The Last Day of School

The week had been brutal—three final exams in four days! Steve had been living on Red Bull and coffee so he could study for one exam after the other. His last exam ended at 7:00 pm on Friday. He'd gone to the pub and kicked back with his buddies for a couple of hours to celebrate the end of the year. He didn't drink any alcohol because he was a responsible guy and knew he had a long drive ahead of him.

Around 11:00 p.m. his buddies went back to the residence with him to help him load his car. The rule was that he had to be out of the residence within 24 hours after his last exam. Since it was Friday and his summer job started on Monday, he wanted to have the weekend to settle in back home and reconnect with friends before the nine-to-five began.

He didn't realize how much stuff he'd accumulated this year. There was the TV, computer, music system, clothes, sports equipment, books, bedding and all the photos and knick-knacks his mom had made him take. It took all three of them to jam everything in and close the trunk.

By the time he'd said goodbye and gotten on the road, it was after midnight. Steve turned up the radio and headed for the highway.

For a few hours, he was fine. Then exhaustion hit him. He started yawning and couldn't stop. His eyes were sore and he couldn't concentrate. Several times he veered to the side of the road until the sound of the rumble strips snapped him back. Steve opened his window to let some fresh air in and pinched the back of his neck to stay alert. He thought about pulling over for a nap but he was almost home. It seemed silly to stop now when he'd be in his own bed in half an hour.

Steve knew he was tired but he underestimated how dangerous his situation was. One second he was yawning and the next second he veered off the road into a tree.

• • • • •

The police knew Steve had fallen asleep at the wheel because he'd hit the tree at full speed. There were no skid marks on the road—just a smashed laptop, a soccer ball and a photo of his family.

Drowsy Driving: Talk about It

(Answers are on page 239)

Using the details from the story, complete the chart below.

Road Conditions	Visibility	Site of Crash
☐ Dry ☐ Wet or icy	☐ Not a factor ☐ Poor - foggy, heavy rain, etc.	☐ City street ☐ Intersection ☐ High speed thruway or highway
Light Conditions	**# of Vehicles in Collision**	**Teen Passengers (not including the driver)**
☐ Daylight ☐ Dark: Late night or early morning	☐ 1 ☐ 2 or more	☐ None ☐ 1 only ☐ More than 1
Driver's Experience Level	**Driver's Physical Condition**	**Driver's Mental Condition**
☐ Less than 1 year ☐ 2 to 3 years ☐ More than 3 years ☐ Unknown	☐ Alert ☐ Impaired by drugs ☐ Impaired by alcohol ☐ Extremely tired	☐ Focused on Driving ☐ Distracted ☐ Other
Was Driver Error a Factor?	**Wearing Seatbelts?**	**The Crash Happened:**
☐ Yes ☐ No ☐ Unknown	☐ Yes ☐ No ☐ Unknown	☐ Close to home ☐ Far from home

1. Based on your analysis, what factors contributed to this crash?

2. What should Steve have done when he realized he was very tired? (Hint: remember—he was very close to home)

3. What clues indicated that Steve was too tired to continue driving?

4. What can drowsy drivers do to stay awake? Circle your answer/s.
   a) Grab a cup of coffee
   b) Open the window to let in fresh air
   c) Crank up the radio and sing along
   d) Pull over at a safe place and take a nap
   e) Pull over and take a walk
   f) Drink a power drink
   g) All of the above
   h) None of the above.

TIP: Coffee will give you a "buzz" of alertness but it takes 20 minutes to kick in.

Drink a large coffee or caffeinated power drink and then take a 20-minute nap. When you wake up, the caffeine will kick in and you should be good for another hour or so of driving.

• • • • •

Did you know that messing with people's sleep cycles is a means of torture in some countries?

What are the warning signs <u>immediately</u> before someone falls asleep at the wheel?

Answer: There are none! Drivers who have survived crashes like this usually don't remember falling asleep. One second they were driving along. The next second they were sound asleep.

Drowsy Driving and Driver Fatigue

If you are exhausted, there is nothing you can do to stop yourself from falling asleep.

There are 3 types of driver exhaustion:

1. Drowsy driving is from lack of sleep and/or extreme physical exertion.
2. Fatigue can be from traveling long, straight stretches of road—often alone.
3. Fatigue can also be from driving in severe weather conditions like heavy rainstorms or blizzards.

How to Deal With the 3 Types of Driver Exhaustion

1. From <u>lack of sleep and/or physical exertion</u>—you need to get off the road in a safe place and take a nap. Set the alarm on your cell phone for 20 minutes and doze off. (See Tip inset.)
2. From <u>driving long, straight stretches of road</u> try these tips to stay alert:
   - Keep the car temperature cool.
   - Take a break at least every 2 hours so you can:
     - Take a 20-minute nap
     - Go for a brief, refreshing walk
     - Switch drivers

3. From driving in very bad weather—pull off the road in a safe place and relax until it's safe to proceed. If the weather is that bad it's too dangerous to drive and you weren't making much progress anyway.

Road Trip Tips

Before you set out on a road trip:

- Get enough sleep (8 ½ to 9 ½ hours). You need to be well rested.
- Skip the burger and fries or the big, greasy breakfast. Heavy foods make you sleepy. Eat a lighter, healthier meal instead
- Avoid alcohol (duh!)
- Take along a passenger who can talk to you and share the driving.

Check Your Medications

Some medications make you drowsy. Make sure you read the warnings on the labels of any drugs you're taking. Some—like allergy medications—have alternate non-drowsy formulas.

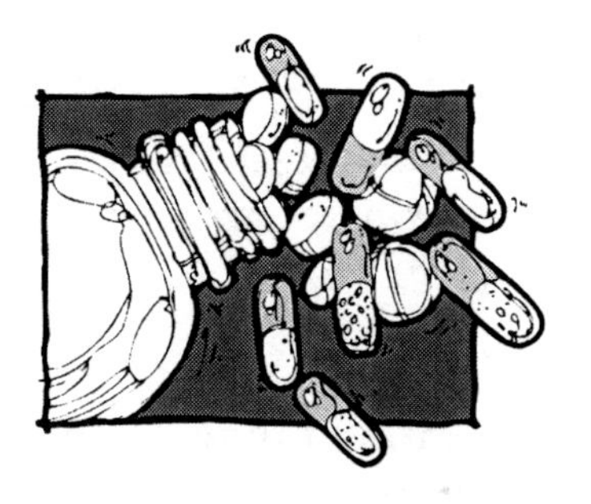

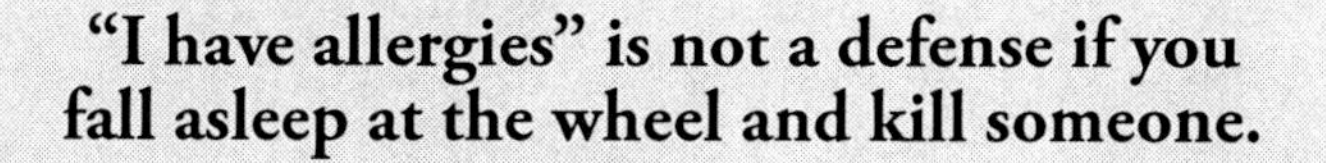

"I have allergies" is not a defense if you fall asleep at the wheel and kill someone.

Sleep is a necessity, not a luxury.

If you don't take care of yourself you could cause a crash and kill yourself or someone else.

Read on to find out what happened to Maggie McDonnell and her family.

Maggie's Story

It was an ordinary day. The July sun was shining and Maggie was happy. She had lots of friends and plans for the weekend. Exams were over. She'd just completed her second year at college and was on track to become a social worker, which was what she'd always wanted.

Maggie McDonnell was tall and graceful with long chestnut hair and big, blue eyes. She was a wonderful dancer and loved entertaining her family by pirouetting around the living room. Even at 20, she was their baby and they adored her. Life was good!

That Wednesday morning, the traffic was light on the parkway as she neared the restaurant where she worked as a hostess. It was Maggie's day off but she'd taken an extra lunch shift to help out a co-worker who couldn't make it.

Suddenly—out of nowhere—a car that was headed in the opposite direction veered across three lanes of traffic and hit her head-on. The driver didn't try to swerve or brake. He smashed into her car at the worst possible angle at full force! Maggie died within minutes! The beautiful girl whose life was just beginning—was gone.

• • • • •

But that's not the end of her story. The tragedy didn't end there. When Maggie's father identified her body, he was crushed and fell into a deep depression. He never uttered Maggie's name again. Over the course of the next seven years, he suffered a series of strokes and he died.

Her mother was overcome with grief and suddenly found it too difficult to get up in the morning. It would be two years before she would be able to start living her life again—although it would never be the same without Maggie.

And countless friends and relatives would be stunned and horrified by what happened next.

The driver who killed Maggie was not a teenager. He was an adult—in fact, he was a teacher's aide. He admitted to being awake for more than 30 hours before he got behind the wheel of his car. As he drove along, he'd been experiencing head snaps (those micro-sleeps where you doze off briefly and then snap back) and had veered out of his lane several times before he hit Maggie. He knew he was too tired to drive but he chose to drive anyway.

He didn't apologize for killing Maggie. He said, "Plain and simple I fell asleep." although there was nothing plain or simple about it. He was charged with vehicular homicide and prosecuted but after 2 long trials, he walked away with a $200 fine.

Imagine if Maggie was ***your*** sister. Imagine if her parents were ***your*** parents. Does that sound fair?

• • • • •

Of course it isn't. As a result of the injustice of this situation, the law was changed in New Jersey. In the future, if someone in that state falls asleep at the wheel because they've been awake for 24 hours or more, they will go to prison. And other states are making changes too.

Drowsy driving is something that's so easy to control. All you have to do to be safe on the road is take a nap. You could save your own life. You could save the life of a girl like Maggie and you could spare countless friends and relatives from such sadness.

You might drive while you're drowsy once and be fine.

You might do it 10 times and be fine.

But you never know which time will be the time when you fall asleep at the wheel and crash your car.

The only thing you can be sure of is that—that time—will be the last time!

A Message from Maggie's Mom

Carole McDonnell, Maggie's mom, talks to groups of teens as often as she can, to warn them about the dangers of drowsy driving. This is her message to you:

"Prom night is one of the most dangerous nights of the year but not for the reason you think!

Most teen drivers think alcohol is the biggest problem, so if they don't drink, they'll be safe. But they're wrong. There's a much bigger threat to teens on prom night and every single teen who drives is at risk. The problem is—lack of sleep.

During the weeks leading up to prom, what are you doing? In some places, you're writing exams. In other places, you're attending classes. In either case, you probably aren't getting enough sleep between school, your excitement about the prom and the things you need to do to get ready for it. So by the time Friday rolls around, you're already sleep-deprived!

Then—most schools require you to attend classes on Friday if you want to go to prom so you drag yourself around to classes all day. When the final bell rings—the race is on! The girls run from hairdresser to nail salon. The boys rush to pick up their tuxes. Then everyone has to get ready.

Excitement keeps everyone going through the evening and the dance, but by the early morning hours, everyone's energy level starts to drop and exhaustion hits. When it does—you don't want to be behind the wheel of your car because you'll fall asleep. No matter how big or smart or conscientious or athletic you are—you cannot make yourself stay awake when you're that tired!

If your passengers are all your best friends, you could kill or critically injure every one of them! And if you survive the crash, you could face serious charges and prison. Why take that chance when there are so many other fun ways you can get to the prom and stay safe?"

"***And Parents***—don't let your kids stretch prom night into a weekend of festivities unless you're sure they get sufficient sleep first. Sometimes teens plan activities like a day at the beach or an amusement park for the day after prom and that's a recipe for disaster because they're already severely sleep-deprived. Insist that they all take a good, long break—especially the driver—and get lots of sleep first. Then they can regroup safely, and have fun!"

Options for getting to and from the prom, without driving:

- Rent a limo—share the cost with a bunch of friends
- Rent a bus—this can be a lot of fun, especially for a large group (consider school buses, travel coaches and city buses)
- Get an older sibling to be your 'chauffeur' for the night
- Ask your parents to drive you (this may not be the coolest option but it will keep you safe.)
- Hire a driver
- Be creative!

Food for thought:

Why does Prom have to be on Friday night? Why not Saturday, when everyone's had a chance to rest?

Teen drivers are most at risk:

- Early morning driving to school
- Late afternoon driving home from school.
- Late at night, coming home from an event

Morning Drive Tips

One of the most dangerous times for teens is in the morning on the way to school. Don't just jump out of bed and go. Give yourself a few minutes to wake up and try these tips:

- Drink a caffeinated beverage 30 minutes before you leave home.
- Eat breakfast.
- Shower and dress after breakfast to give that caffeine time to work.

• • • • •

Should These Teens Drive Today? Answers are on page 240.

Read the stories below and decide whether or not these teens are safe to drive today:

1. Christina is 17 and working as a lifeguard at a theme park 60 miles away. She works a 9-hour shift on Friday and goes out to a concert/party afterward. It's in another city and she doesn't get home until 3:00 a.m. on Saturday morning.
   She's scheduled to work another 9-hour shift on Saturday—starting at 8:00 a.m. She sleeps in 'til 6:30 a. m. and begs her parents to let her drive to work today. Is it safe for Christina to drive to work today?

   ____

   ____

2. Will and Barb are going to the prom. They haven't made all their plans yet but there will probably be parties before and afterwards. They don't have a lot of money so Will plans to drive in his family's car. Is that a good idea?

   ____

   ____

*6 hours of sleep or less **triples** your risk of getting in a crash!*

Family Rules about drowsy driving.

Decide on your family rules for drowsy driving. Write them in the space below:

____

____

Speeding

How Fast is Too Fast?

Teens—Circle your answers below.

Based on the posted speed limits below, at what speed do you think you would be 'speeding'?

(Note: miles per hour to kilometers per hour calculations are approximate.)

1. If the posted speed limit is 30 mph (50 kph), you would be considered 'speeding' at:
   - 35mph (56 kph)
   - 40mph (65 kph)
   - 50mph (80 kph)
2. If the posted speed limit is 50 mph (80 kph), you would be considered 'speeding' at:
   - 55mph (90 kph)
   - 60mph (97 kph)
   - 65mph (105 kph)
3. If the posted speed limit is 70 mph (113 kph), you would be considered 'speeding' at:
   - 75mph (120 kph)
   - 85 mph (137 kph)

Some people think it's okay to exceed the speed limit as long as they keep up with the speed of other traffic. Many driving instructors even teach students that, but the fact is that any speed over the speed limit is dangerous and can get you a ticket.

Some teens admit they speed late at night when the roads are empty.

SPEED

- Reduces the amount of time you have to avoid the crash,
- Increases the likelihood of crashing
- Increases the severity of a crash once it occurs.

•••••

Speeding is a factor in more than 50% of fatal teen crashes.

•••••

Teens say they speed—

- To keep up with traffic
- Because it's fun

2005 Allstate Foundation study

•••••

When speed increases from 40 mph to 60 mph, the energy released in a crash more than doubles.

(IIHS, 2003)

•••••

Highways Aren't Race Tracks. The drivers around you aren't professional drivers either. They are completely unpredictable.

(No wonder most teen crashes happen between 9:00 pm and 6:00 am !)

The faster you go, the harder it is to control your car and the longer it takes to stop it. Speeders can't slow down quickly enough to avoid sudden obstacles or slowing traffic. They often run yellow lights and cause serious collisions at intersections.

And your quick teen reflexes won't help you. A sudden swerve to avoid a crash could flip your car and land you in a ditch (or worse!)

Adjusting Your Speed for the Conditions

The posted speed limit applies to ideal light conditions on good, dry roads. If it's dark or raining hard, or the roads are wet or icy, you need to adjust your driving to those conditions. And that means driving below the posted limit in many cases.

The Changing Profile of Teen Speeders

In 2005, an Allstate Foundation study reported that male speeders outnumbered females by 4 to 1, but that's changing.

In fact, some insurance companies are raising the rates for teen girls because they've become faster, more aggressive drivers.

A 2010 Allstate study reported:

- 48% of girls admit to driving 10 mph over the posted limit.
- 16% of girls describe their own driving as aggressive

BEWARE: Most speeders also run yellow lights.

2005 Allstate Foundation study

Reid's Story

I wish this page could be in color so you could see Reid's piercing aqua-blue eyes and thick black lashes. He had movie star good looks and a smile that could light up a room!

At 17, school was a struggle for Reid but he had talents and personality to spare. With a rich tenor voice and a gift for whistling, he might have been headed for the American Idol stage—if he could just have gotten past his stage fright!

He made friends with other teens easily but he was the Pied Piper when it came to little kids! Reid loved them and they loved him back. He helped out at his church's Sunday school where volunteers were called 'shepherds.' That suited Reid because he always had a 'flock.' When little ones would howl as their parents tried to leave them for the first time, Reid would come over and squat down beside them. He'd talk to them gently on their level and then lead them away by the hand. By the time their parents returned, they'd be having such a good time that they wouldn't want to leave.

Early one December evening, Reid fell asleep on the sofa while watching a movie with his mom and sister, Martha. Around 8:00 p.m. he woke up alone. Martha had gone upstairs to read and his mom had gone to a meeting at the church. (His Dad, Tim was away on business.) Since the night was still young, he decided to visit his friend, Mike, who lived in the next town. He sent a text (Reid had lightning-fast texting fingers) to his parents letting them know where he was going, because that was the family rule. (They needed to know where he was going and when he'd be home.)

Reid jumped in his car and drove down the road. He didn't get too far before he met a couple of girls he knew from the neighborhood. It was a cold, wet evening and they didn't have anything to do so Reid's plans changed. The girls got in the car and the three of them decided to go for a ride together. They headed for the highway, in the opposite direction of Mike's house.

With no particular destination in mind, they drove for a while and talked. Reid must have missed his exit. He probably felt a little panicked as the clock passed 10 p.m. and he realized he was lost. He knew the girls had a strict 10:30 curfew.

Maybe he sped up to get them home on time, because the police department's crash reconstruction specialist estimated he was driving about 10 mph over the highway's 65 mph speed limit. Ten miles over the limit doesn't sound like a lot but it was dark and Reid didn't know the area where he was driving.

He drove into a curve too fast and tried to brake when he realized how sharp the turn was. He skidded and overcorrected. The car went into a series of spins. It slammed into the guardrail at the worst possible angle on the driver's door. Reid was badly hurt and lost consciousness.

Smoke started rising from the car. Luckily, an off-duty fireman was the first person on the scene. He pulled Reid and the girl in the front seat out the front passenger door before the car burst into flames. The girl in the backseat was able to get out on her own.

Reid Hollister died at around 3:00 the next morning. The girls had injuries but recovered. They have little memory of what happened that night. It looked like they were all wearing seatbelts but no one knows for sure. The seatbelts melted from the heat of the fire.

• • • • •

Now there's a hole in Reid's family that can never be filled. His father, Tim Hollister has written a book about how he deals with his grief over losing his beloved son. (Check our website for details.) He's tried to channel some of his sorrow into becoming a teen safe driving advocate so other families will not have to suffer the loss that his family has.

Tim was part of a group that helped rewrite Connecticut's Graduated Driver Licensing laws so they better protect learning drivers. He's also started a blog called "from Reid's Dad" (www.fromreidsdad.org) that advocates teen driving safety. It's well written, has a unique perspective and comes from one of the most knowledgeable voices in teen-driver safety advocacy. Check it out.

Reid's Story: Crash Analysis

Using the details from the story, complete the chart on the next page.

(Answers on page 241)

Road Conditions	Visibility	Site of Crash
☐ Dry ☐ Wet or Icy	☐ Not a factor ☐ Poor - foggy, heavy rain, etc.	☐ City street ☐ Intersection ☐ High speed thruway or highway
Light Conditions	**# of Vehicles in Collision**	**Teen Passengers** (not including the driver)
☐ Daylight ☐ Dark: Late night or early morning	☐ 1 ☐ 2 or more	☐ None ☐ 1 only ☐ More than 1
Driver's Experience Level	**Driver's Physical Condition**	**Driving was:**
☐ Less than 1 year ☐ 2 to 3 years ☐ More than 3 years ☐ Unknown	☐ Alert ☐ Impaired by drugs ☐ Impaired by alcohol ☐ Extremely tired	☐ Purposeful ☐ Recreational
Was Driver Error a Factor?	**Wearing Seatbelts?**	**The Crash Happened:**
☐ Yes ☐ No ☐ Unknown	☐ Yes ☐ No ☐ Unknown	☐ Close to home ☐ Far from home

1. Based on your analysis (above) what do you think caused this crash?

____

____

2. How could the driver have avoided this crash?

____

____

Family Rules about Speeding

Decide on your family rules about speeding. Write them in the space below:

____

____

____

Road Racing

WATCH IT ON VIDEO—Go to TeensLearntoDrive.com to watch videos about Road Racing.

Family Rules about speeding and road racing.

Decide on your family rules about speeding and road racing. Write them in the space below:

____

____

High Emotion

Picture this:

You just had a HUGE fight with your boyfriend or girlfriend. The worst ever! You leave the house and shut the door. *Do you close it gently and quietly?* No! You slam it!

You head down the driveway. *Are you walking slowly?* No! You're stomping or running down the driveway because you're angry. Then you jump in your car and roar away, laying rubber just to make your point!

As you're driving, you keep running through everything they said. Your foot automatically presses harder on the accelerator and your mind drifts off the road.

Are you safe? No way! Even the best drivers make critical errors when they're angry or upset. You can't help it. Your body reacts to how you're feeling and your mind focuses on what's troubling you at the moment. (And that's not the road!)

So—if you can help it—don't drive when you're angry, very worried or upset. Let someone else drive or take a walk to calm down before you get behind the wheel.

If you can't help driving (you have to get an injured friend to the hospital) then make a real effort to focus on your driving. Concentrate on staying within the speed limit and keep your eyes and mind on the road. (Getting to the hospital fast is important but if you speed or take foolish chances—you may not get there at all!)

• • • • •

If your friend is really upset, offer to drive them or ask someone else to drive. And don't be a bozo. If you have to give someone bad news—don't do it by text or on the phone. Show respect for the other person and consider their safety. Deliver bad news in person and make an effort to stay calm so emotions don't escalate. Don't let them get behind the wheel when they are very upset.

Alcohol and Driving

This chapter ***is not*** about whether or not you should drink alcohol and it's ***not*** about how old you should be when you make that decision. Those are separate discussions you need to have with your parents.

This chapter ***is*** about keeping you safe if you do drink (whatever your age) or if you're ever in a position where you're depending on a ride from someone else who's been drinking.

It's also about being a good friend by making sure the people you care about don't make the biggest mistake of their lives by driving when they're impaired.

• • • • •

Following is a true story that shows how a bad decision one night can have a devastating effect on everyone involved.

A Day at the Beach

Part 1: Meagan's Story

Meagan walked into the room with her hands at her sides. The silky red bridesmaid's gown draped elegantly around her. "You look gorgeous!" her mom said.

Renee stood for a moment and admired her daughter. She looked so beautiful and grown up. Where had the time gone? Before she knew it, Meagan would be finished college and perhaps, she'd be a bride herself, instead of a bridesmaid in her brother's wedding. Renee was proud just looking at her, but she was also confused. Meagan had called her in a panic saying the store had sent the wrong-sized dress.

"But I really don't see the problem," she continued. "It fits you perfectly!"

Meagan grinned and lifted her arms. Swoosh! The dress dropped to the floor and Meagan was left standing in her underwear! "Now do you see the problem?" she responded.

They both burst into laughter as Meagan stooped to retrieve her gown. Then Renee made a few phone calls. The dress would be altered in plenty of time for the wedding, which was just weeks away. Meagan knew her mom could fix anything.

That's why Meagan called her mom again the next day and asked her to come pick her up at Carmen's apartment. She had another problem that needed Mom's touch. They decided they'd go to lunch in a nearby restaurant and include Renee's mom in the party.

Now—Meagan's twin sister, Carmen, had just moved into a new apartment and it was a disaster! She'd dumped her stuff and then gone away for the weekend with a friend—knowing she'd have a horrible mess to deal with when she returned. Meagan was staying in that disaster zone temporarily too.

Lisa and Meagan

But when Renee came to pick her up, Meagan dragged her mom through the boxes in the living room into Carmen's bedroom. It was an oasis! Meagan had unpacked everything and arranged it all. The room was perfectly organized and Renee knew Carmen would be thrilled when she got home. She was so proud of Meagan for doing such a kind thing to help her sister.

They drove to the restaurant and talked about Meagan's problems in the car. She'd been worried about a couple of high bills she'd run up but had no means of paying. One was for her cell phone. The other was for a new credit card she'd applied for without talking to her parents. They worked those problems out too—so another disaster was averted and three generations enjoyed each other's company over lunch.

Later Meagan returned to the apartment and called her friend, Lisa. Lisa was babysitting but agreed to pick Meagan up when she finished. Lifelong friends, they liked just hanging out together and talking. They went to the beach and it was after midnight before they got back in Lisa's car and headed home.

Part 2: Eric's Story

Eric Smallridge was the boy next-door. An Eagle Scout turned college senior; he was handsome and friendly and had never been in any serious trouble before the day that changed his life.

The Day at the Beach

Eric and one of his friends drove to the beach. After parking Eric's Jeep Cherokee, they pulled the cooler out of the back and carried it down to the beautiful white sand beach. Nothing tasted better than an icy cold beer on a hot, sunny day—and they had come prepared!

Ten other friends joined them at their usual rendezvous spot. They brought more beer for all to share. It was a fun time of sun, surf, Frisbee, beer and lots of laughs. By late afternoon they were sweaty, sun burned and covered in sand, so they decided to call it a day. On the way home they stopped for a quick snack before showering, changing clothes and heading back to the beach to eat dinner, see a live band and enjoy a little beach nightlife.

Everything went as planned and that evening they traded jokes and stories as they moved from restaurant to restaurant. They ate and drank more beer. No one was binge drinking and there were no shooters or drinking games. It was just a long, fun day of enjoying friendship and beer.

After midnight, things started winding down and Eric headed back to his Jeep to go home, but when he turned the key—nothing! The battery had been giving him trouble lately and it had finally died. He asked his friends if any of them had jumper cables. They did not. But one of his friends, Michael, recognized that Eric probably should not be driving. He tried to talk Eric out of getting behind the wheel, but Eric convinced him that he would be careful and everything was going to be fine. Two of Eric's other friends borrowed jumper cables from someone in the parking lot. Michael used his truck to start Eric's Jeep and then everyone went their separate ways.

Just a few minutes later, Eric was driving home down the center lane of the highway. A car traveling in the right lane suddenly caught his eye as it pulled up next to him and began pushing over into his lane. The right lane was ending and, rather than slowing to merge, the driver of that car sped ahead to merge into the center lane in front of Eric. With no place else to go, Eric instinctively swerved to the left—unaware that a car had just pulled into that lane!

• • • • •

One second Lisa and Meagan were chatting happily as they headed home from the beach and the next second their back bumper was struck by Eric's Jeep. Their car spun into the median where it crashed into a tree. They were killed on impact

A Strange Twist of Fate

News of the crash spread quickly across the campus. When Michael heard what had happened he was horrified. In no way was he responsible for the crash, but he was still overcome with guilt.

It turns out—he knew Lisa and Meagan well and had referred to them as his "sisters." He was grief-stricken when he realized he had jump-started the car of the driver that ran them off the road and killed them.

• • • • •

There could be no 'happy' ending for this story—Meagan and Lisa were gone forever, three families were totally devastated, Michael was racked with guilt, and Eric was sentenced to spend the next 22 years of his life behind prison bars—but there was healing.

Some believe it was a miracle. Others think it's crazy. The process was long and too complicated to describe here but Lisa and Meagan's families forgave Eric for what he did. That forgiveness opened a new path for them all.

All three families (Meagan's, Lisa's and Eric's) committed to sharing their story about the consequences of drinking and driving. They don't want any other families to have to experience the loss and sadness they feel.

Renee Napier, Meagan's mom, now visits high schools and colleges across the United States to talk about what happened and to urge teens to plan ahead when they go partying so they won't drink and drive. Sometimes Eric's parents and older brother, a law enforcement officer, join her. Eric will join her too one day—which will be sooner than was originally thought.

You see, Meagan and Lisa's families petitioned the court to reduce Eric's sentence and they were successful. His sentence was reduced to eleven years.

In the meantime, Eric has a very personal message for you about what can happen if you choose to drink and drive.

From Eric Smallridge, aka Inmate P22679

Eric in Prison

Dear Teen Drivers:

I thought the worst that could happen is I'd get pulled over and get a DUI.

I knew people who got DUIs in high school. It really didn't seem like that big a deal. They paid their fine, lost their license for six months and caught rides with friends until they got their hardship license. An accident where someone gets killed, well, that was just not going to happen.

But it did happen ...

and I had been drinking. And now, I have been incarcerated for a little over two years with plenty of time to think about the consequences of drinking and driving. Every day, I wish that I had realized the seriousness of a DUI and heeded the advice "not to drink and drive."

I had a great life ...

—full of opportunity and promise, with a wonderful family, lots of friends, a beautiful girlfriend, and I had just received my bachelor's degree in Management Information Systems. Anything and everything a young man could have wanted in his life, I had. Then, in a split second, it was all gone. It may be too late for me, but I really hope that telling you about the miserable realities of my life in prison will help you make better choices than I did.

Prison is like "Groundhog Day"

You may have seen the television show "Oz." The show was about an extremely violent, maximum-security prison. I think it's a bit exaggerated. Prison is more like the movie Groundhog Day, which is about a guy (Bill Murray) who keeps repeating the same day over and over again.

Prison is very repetitive. My daily routine hasn't changed at all since I arrived: Wake up at 4:45 a.m., breakfast at 5:00 a.m., count time 6:30 a.m., report to work at 7:00 a.m., work until 10:00 a.m., return to the dorm for 10:30 a.m. count, lunch at 11:00 a.m., back to work until returning to the dorm for 3:30 p.m. count, dinner at 4:00 p.m., back to the dorm, 5:30 p.m. count, 9:00 p.m. count, and finally, lights out at 10:00 p.m. Sleep is a blessed relief because at least then my mind can be in another place and time.

> If you asked Eric what he did on Feb. 7th or Oct.12th last year, he could tell you exactly!
>
> Why—does he have a photographic memory?
>
> No. Because, in prison, he does exactly the same things at exactly the same time—everyday. There's no fun—just boredom.

A guy had his finger bitten off ...

Now, don't get me wrong, prison can be a very violent place. After all, many people here are incarcerated for horrible, violent crimes. There are murderers, rapists, child predators, drug pushers, aggravated batterers and more. Since I've been here, people have been stabbed, others severely beaten, and on one occasion, a guy had his finger bitten off. The institution where I am is supposed to be one of the least violent. I'll leave it to you to imagine what goes on at other institutions.

But that's not the hard part ...

While violence is ever-present, it isn't what makes prison life so hard to endure. One of the hardest things is thinking about all that I had taken for granted in my life, and how horribly I have messed up not only my life, but also the lives of so many others.

If I were to talk about all the things I took for granted as a free man, I'd be writing for a very long time. But the list of really important things begins with my freedom itself. When I was a free man, I never even thought about what freedom meant to me. Now, I think about it all the time. I have no freedom of choice. I am told what to wear, what to eat, when to eat and how fast to eat.

The menu is repeated week after week, and you eat what they give you or you don't eat. I cannot choose to use the bathroom by myself or take a shower by myself.

I live in a dorm with 69 other "roommates" that I didn't choose, and most of whom I don't even want to associate with. Our bunk beds are barely 24" apart, and there is no way to isolate myself from them or their constant noise. If I have a headache or am not feeling well, the best I can do is pull my bed covers over my head.

There is no privacy in prison

The guards must be able to see me at all times, no matter where I go. All inmate movement is controlled. There are actually red lines painted on the sidewalks, and we must walk inside the red lines at all times.

Another thing I took for granted while free was the ability to pick up a phone and call my family and friends whenever I felt like it.

2 telephones for 70 men!

Phone access is very limited in prison. It literally takes months to get a phone number approved so I can call it, and I am only allowed to have 10 approved numbers on my calling list. There are only two telephones to use for all 70 men crammed in each dorm, and they are only turned on a few hours each evening. When I do get to make a phone call, the calls are limited to 15 minutes, and I have to call collect knowing that the person I am calling will be charged anywhere from $8 to $20 (depending on their service provider). No one can ever call me, not even in times of family emergencies, such as when my grandmother passed away very unexpectedly this summer.

> If you think you ***need*** to talk on your cell or text while you drive—think about how you'll stay in touch in prison, after the crash.

Visiting with family and friends had always been a huge part of my life that I had taken for granted. It is especially difficult during the holidays and other special occasions like marriages and reunions. I never realized how very precious all those moments were and how much they meant to me, or how much it meant to my family and friends that I be there with them. Now that isn't an option for any of us.

In prison, no one can just "come for a visit."

The only way I can visit with anyone is if they go through a long and frustrating application process. Only 15 people can be on my approved visitation list at one time, and only five of them can come to see me on a given day. Those that are approved to visit have to drive about 100 miles each way and if five people are already there, they get turned away. Visitation conditions are far from ideal, and privacy is nonexistent. We are allowed one hug as they enter and one when they leave.

My friends and family have to be thoroughly frisked

On a busy weekend, there may be upwards of 180 people visiting, and everyone sits across from each other at these long common tables where sometimes everyone is trying to talk over each other just to be heard. The worst part is that I never imagined that my friends and family would have to be thoroughly frisked, and I would have to be strip searched before and after every visit.

1 small TV with 3 channels for 70 men

If you've seen movies where inmates have televisions or computers, forget it. There is one small television that gets three or four local channels for 70 inmates. It is placed in a small area with the only two tables we have for writing or playing cards.

> Forget about your favorite TV shows or video games!

Life in a dorm is loud and crowded.

Hopefully, you now know that prison is a miserable place that you never want to experience for yourself. So far, I have told you about the frustration and the boredom, the violence that erupts occasionally, the constant noise of so many inconsiderate inmates and the unnerving startle when the guards suddenly shout at someone for good reason or just because they can. I've told you about some of the things I used to take for granted when I had my freedom, but I still haven't told you about the very worst part of being in prison.

The worst part of being in prison is ...

- just being here. Every fence topped in circles of razor wire, every closed door, every wrinkled blue uniform, every barred window is a constant reminder of the wasted years ahead of me and the many innocent people's lives that have been adversely affected because of the accident I so ignorantly thought could never happen.

The two people I think about most ...

are the two that died in the crash I didn't think could ever happen. Meagan Napier and Lisa Dickson were only twenty years old. They had their whole lives ahead of them. I think about them all the time—and it hurts. Every day I ask God why I wasn't the one to die instead of them. If only I could trade places with them, so they could realize the great lives they should have had. But I can't, and they can't, and I will live with that every single day for the rest of my life.

I think about Meagan and Lisa's families and friends a lot, too. I agonize over what I could possibly do to ease their grief and return their loved ones to them. But I cannot do that either, and it is more painful than any amount of physical torture that could be inflicted upon me.

Writing this has not been easy for me.

It is really hard to talk about my existence as Inmate P22679—the feelings of worthlessness, the fear that I will no longer be capable of contributing to society when I am finally released from prison, the feeling that I have failed myself and my family and the sorrow I feel for the loss of two beautiful human beings—Meagan and Lisa.

I'm writing this for them …

their families and my own family. It never seemed possible that my life could turn out this way. And I bet, you don't think yours could either.

If you have a drink, driving simply is not an option.

Don't risk it, not even once, because it only takes a split second to go from a great future to Inmate P22679. Please don't hesitate to designate a driver, call a friend or a cab. Otherwise, you may be riding in a police car or, God forbid, a hearse.

If you drink, don't drive,
because I am living proof that it CAN happen to you."

Eric Smallridge

Alcohol and Driving: Talk about It

(Answers are on page 242)

"A Day at the Beach" Crash Analysis

Using the details from the story, complete the chart below.

Road Conditions	Visibility	Site of Crash
☐ Dry ☐ Wet or icy	☐ Not a factor ☐ Poor - foggy, heavy rain, etc.	☐ City street ☐ Intersection ☐ High speed thruway or highway
Light Conditions	**# of Vehicles in Collision**	**Teen Passengers (not including the driver)**
☐ Daylight ☐ Dark: Late night or early morning	☐ 1 ☐ 2 or more	☐ None ☐ 1 only ☐ More than 1
Driver's Experience Level	**Driver's Physical Condition**	**Driver's Mental Condition**
☐ Less than 1 year ☐ 2 to 3 years ☐ More than 3 years ☐ Unknown	☐ Alert ☐ Impaired by drugs ☐ Impaired by alcohol ☐ Extremely tired	☐ Focused on Driving ☐ Distracted ☐ Other
Was Driver Error a Factor?	**Wearing Seatbelts?**	**The Crash Happened:**
☐ Yes ☐ No ☐ Unknown	☐ Yes ☐ No ☐ Unknown	☐ Close to home ☐ Far from home

1. Based on your analysis, what factors contributed to this crash?

____

____

2. What should Eric have done instead of driving home?

____

____

Now—you might be thinking to yourself that you'd never get carried away and have too much to drink like Eric did, but it can happen so easily. Just look what happened to Justin in the story below.

A Night to Remember

When Justin accepted the keys from his Dad, he knew the rule: 'no drinking and driving.' So he'd limit himself to one beer tonight.

(Okay—so he hadn't talked to his Dad about the one beer thing but one beer really didn't count. He'd still be way under the legal alcohol limit so even if he got stopped by the police, they'd have to let him go. Besides—there's no danger in one *beer*. Heck—it was mostly water anyway. Not like real alcohol.)

First he picked up his girlfriend, Jennifer, then his best friend, Brad. Everyone was pumped. Brad had just started dating Chelsea. Chelsea's dad was a big shot in the movie industry so they had this incredible house with an amazing pool and home theatre and everything. Chelsea had invited them all for a swim and barbeque. Her parents were way cool and had made arrangements to go out for the evening so the four of them were on their own—except for the guy her parents ***had hired*** to grill the steaks and serve them dinner!

Justin had never seen anything like this in his life and he was major impressed. The pool area was all tropical plants and waterfalls. There was a huge swimming area outside and you could swim through this cave thing into the house. It was so cool.

Justin says beer isn't like real alcohol.

Is that true?

Which of these drinks has the most alcohol:

A. 5 oz. Glass of white wine (12% alcohol)
B. 5 oz. Glass of red wine (12% alcohol)
C. Cocktail mixed with 1 ½ oz. of liquor (40% alcohol)
D. 12 oz. bottle of beer (5% alcohol)

Answer: They all have the same amount of alcohol. Alcohol is alcohol so beer produces the same effects as any other alcoholic beverage.

However, many bartenders (especially at parties) don't measure the amount of alcohol they put into drinks. One slushy drink or cocktail could hold several shots

(1 ½ oz. portions) of alcohol. Wine is often served in glasses that hold much more than 5 ounces.

That doesn't make beer any better. It's just easier to measure how much alcohol you're consuming.

The Barbeque Guy was hustling around the grill. It was like watching one of those TV cooking shows. He was choppin' and peelin' and flippin' all kinds of fruit and veggies. Even watching him was fun!

Next to him was a bar with all kinds of liquor and fruit and little umbrellas and stuff. Chelsea picked up the tray that was already loaded with four pineapples. She passed them out. Justin didn't think it would be right to ask for a beer instead so he just took one. It was filled with some fruity, icy rum drink. It tasted more like a slushie than alcohol and it was good. They all sipped and swam until dinner was ready. By then the pineapples and the refill pitcher were empty.

The table was really fancy, like an expensive restaurant. There were linen napkins and flowers and crystal glasses. Some barbeque! Justin was more used to the backyard burger kind of thing. He felt very adult and really lucky to be invited. He and Brad held out the chairs for the girls when they sat at the table. Just like in the movies.

BBQ Guy poured each of them a glass of white wine. Brad got to test it and everything. Then BBQ guy served the salad. Justin didn't like the 'hunk of lettuce and tomato' kind of salad, but this was incredible. There were nuts and barbequed veggies and things in it. He felt obliged to drink the wine while he was eating. He finished everything.

Next came the steaks—the best he'd ever had—and a glass of red wine. He knew the wine was really good because the label was fancy. He didn't really like red wine but he drank it because everyone else did and it just seemed like the right thing to do. They talked and laughed and had the most incredible time. Justin had to remind himself that this whole night was real.

> Each year, drinking by college students, ages 18-24, contributes to an estimated:
>
> - 1,700 student deaths
> - almost 600,000 injuries
> - almost 700,000 assaults
> - 90,000+ sexual assaults
> - 474,000 engaging in unprotected sex.
>
> In 2001, 2.8 million college students drove a car while under the influence of alcohol.
>
> (Hingson et al, 2005)
>
> • • • • •
>
> In 2003, there were 6,409 traffic fatalities among 15-20 year-olds.
>
> More than 1/3 were alcohol-related.
>
> Source: NHTSA FARS Query, 2004
>
> • • • • •
>
> 2010—In a recent High School survey more than 50% of students admitted to getting into a car when they knew the driver was under the influence of drugs or alcohol.

After dinner, they sat around the pool again. They swam a bit while BBQ Guy cleaned up. Finally, BBQ Guy asked who wanted coffee. Justin knew he'd better have some because he was feeling a little buzzed and needed to sober up a bit. Everyone raised their hands except Brad who hated coffee.

Five minutes later, BBQ Guy was back with three tall glasses wrapped in napkins and topped with whipped cream. He said they were Irish coffees. Justin tasted his. It was delicious but he could taste booze in it. He'd rather have had plain coffee because he knew he needed to clear his head before the drive home. But the girls were drinking theirs and saying how good they were and he just couldn't say no. He did manage to say "I'd better have a couple of plain old coffees after this because I have to drive home."

Brad piped in with, "Go ahead. I'll drive if you want. I haven't had as much to drink as you and I don't mind driving."

Justin thought about it. It was the perfect solution. He didn't know exactly how much Brad had to drink but he was a good guy and a good driver. Besides, if they got stopped on the way home, ***he*** wouldn't get hit with the DUI—not if ***he*** wasn't the one driving!

"Thanks Brad, that'd be great." Then Justin turned to BBQ Guy and smiled, "In that case, you can keep these babies comin'." Everyone laughed as BBQ Guy headed back to the bar to whip up another round of Irish coffees.

The "Night to Remember" Quiz

Answers are on page 242.

1. Why did Justin drink the pineapple drink and the wine when he planned to have a single beer?
   a) Because he was afraid to say "no"
   b) Because everyone else was drinking them
   c) Because they looked so cool
   d) Because they made him feel very sophisticated and mature
   e) All of the above
2. What is the main reason Justin's parents don't want him to drink alcohol when he's driving their car?
3. If Justin finishes his fifth drink at midnight, when will he be alcohol-free and safe to drive?
4. If Justin wants to sober up quickly what can he do?
   a) Drink lots of hot, black coffee
   b) Take a cold shower or jump in the pool
   c) Take a 20-minute nap
   d) None of the above
   e) Any of the above.

Safe Ride Tips:

There are always options when you plan ahead.

- Take turns being the designated driver.
- Pool your money for cab fare.
- Hire a friend or sibling to pick you up.
- Walk.
- Take public transportation.
- Stay over with a friend.
- For large groups on special occasions—hire a limousine or a bus.

"A Night to Remember": Talk about It

(Answers on page 243.)

Discuss the following questions with your parent/coach.

1. Justin was the driver this evening. He'd promised his dad he wouldn't drink and drive. What do you think of his idea that one beer didn't count?
2. Do you think it is smart to let Brad drive?
3. Jennifer was depending on Justin for a ride home. What should she do?
4. Chelsea's parents let her have this party and serve alcohol to her friends even though they weren't home. Was that a good idea?

Make a Plan Before You Go

You have to admit—this was one incredible night. There were so many 'firsts'. First time at this fantastic place. First slushy pineapple drink. First time being served by someone like the BBQ Guy, etc. It's easy to understand how Justin got carried away.

But every evening out is a 'first' of some kind or an anniversary of something else. First date. First time at a new club. Birthday. Two-month anniversary. Your team won. Your team lost. There's always a reason to celebrate or drown your sorrows.

That's why you need to plan ahead. Before you leave the house, make sure you know how you're going to get home—safely.

Every time you accept the keys to the car,
YOU ARE the Designated Driver.
If you don't want that responsibility—don't drive.
Walk, take a cab or catch a ride with someone else who will stay sober.

Have a Back-up Plan

If you drive, it's your responsibility to stay sober and get all your passengers home safely. But sometimes mistakes happen. If you planned not to drink but end up drinking, you need to have a back-up plan so you can still get home safely.

Use the **Safe Passage Clause** in your Teen-Parent Contract. Don't be afraid to call your parents for a ride home. They'll appreciate the fact that you used good judgment and didn't drive impaired. Regardless of the time or circumstances, they promised not to yell at you. They'd rather pick you up at 2:00 a.m. across town, than identify your body at the morgue in the morning.

When you're older and away at college, it might not be possible to call your mom or dad for a ride, but you still need a back-up plan. Maybe make a pact with a group of friends to support each other this way. Maybe keep some emergency money in your wallet, so you can take a cab if you need it, but always have a plan and don't be afraid to use it.

If you knew you could save a life, would you?

Drunks don't know they're drunk. They think they're 'buzzed' or 'happy'. They feel empowered and think they can do anything. So asking a drunk if they're okay to drive isn't helpful. No matter how much they've had to drink, they'll always answer 'yes' so someone else needs to make that judgment for them. If you're their friend, that someone could be you.

Remember the story 'A Day at the Beach"? Michael knew Eric was impaired and shouldn't drive. He didn't cause the crash, but he could have prevented it.

If you were Michael, what could you have done to keep Eric from driving?

What would you do to prevent your friend from driving drunk?

Be a Hero

If you do the right thing and keep a friend from driving drunk, you could save their life or spare them from a 20-year prison sentence. They might thank you the next day—but probably not.

If, on the other hand, you don't stop them from driving drunk and they die or kill someone else—you'll suffer from the guilt of knowing you didn't stop them. If they survive, they might even blame you for letting them drive.

It's a thankless job but somebody NEEDS to do it.

Facts about Seatbelts and Alcohol

The more alcohol teens drink, the less likely they are to buckle up. That applies to drivers *and* passengers.

80% of teens (15 to 20) who die in car crashes where alcohol was involved, were not wearing seat belts.

• • • • •

Parents: Don't take chances

If a teen driver comes to pick up your teen, address the driver by name. Remind them that they're the Designated Driver tonight and that you're trusting them to drive safely with your son or daughter in the car.

"Hi Ian. I see you're the Designated Driver tonight. Kelly is almost ready to go. I'm trusting you to stay sober and drive safely with her in the car and bring her home by eleven p.m. tonight."

Will Kelly be mortified? Probably, but that's a small price to pay for making sure Ian understands his responsibility and brings her home safely.

Tips for taking the car keys away from a drunken friend:

- Talk to them about surrendering their keys while they're still partying, instead of when they go to leave. That way, if they won't listen, you have the option of quietly taking their keys. Let them think they lost them and you can 'find' them in the morning.
- Take the friend aside. Don't confront them or embarrass them in front of other people.
- Tell the person you care about them and don't want them to get hurt. Try to keep it light-hearted rather than scolding or judgmental.
- Tell them you've arranged for them to get a ride home with someone else or invite them to stay over.
- If you don't know the person well, try to get their friends to help you keep that person from driving.
- If they won't listen, and insist on driving, you need to do something else. You don't want to damage anyone's property but you might consider something simple like letting the air out of their tires.
- In an emergency, consider these options;
  - Call someone else to come and get them like their parents, their sibling, their friend or your parents.
  - If all else fails, call the police. You can do it anonymously. Explain the situation and ask for help. Your friend never needs to know you called and you could be saving their life.

If you're hosting a party:

- Collect the car keys as people enter. If they aren't sober when it's time to leave, don't give the keys back.
- Be prepared to do whatever is necessary to make sure your guests get home safely.
- Keep in mind that, in some places, you could have a legal responsibility if someone drinks too much at your home and then crashes their car.

A Final Note of Caution

About Alcohol and Insurance—

If you crash your car when you're impaired, you could find your insurance will not cover the expenses.

They might pay out initially and then sue you to recover what they paid.

You could also find that your insurance rates go through the roof afterwards—if you can find a company willing to insure you at all!

If you are out partying on Friday night and get home safely with your designated driver, that's great! Good job!

But before you jump in the car to go to work the next morning, make sure you're fit to drive. If you're feeling at all buzzed or hung over—you need to catch a lift with someone else who is stone cold sober.

As I'm writing this, a young woman in Minnesota has been charged with Vehicular Homicide. She was driving to work at 8:45 in the morning after partying the night before. She'd had a few hours of sleep and thought she was okay to drive.

She was going a little too fast when her car hit some black ice and she lost control. Her friend in the back seat was killed in the crash.

The accident may have happened anyway. If she'd been completely sober, that would probably be the end of the story. But she wasn't. She still had a lot of alcohol in her system from the night before. Enough, that she was still legally impaired. Now—if she's convicted, she could spend the next 20 years in prison.

She's 19 years old and, regardless of the outcome of her trial, her life will never be the same again. Her good friend is gone forever.

Remember—it's not about the DUI. It's about survival. Don't ever risk your life or the lives of your family and friends by driving impaired. Make a better choice.

And keep in mind—that if an impaired driver is involved in a crash, their insurance might initially cover the costs. However, the insurance company will probably sue them later to recover what they paid out. Insurance protects sober drivers—not impaired ones.

Family Rules about Alcohol and Driving

Decide on your family rules for drinking and driving. Write them in the space below:

____

____

Road Rage

It's hard to stay calm when someone cuts you off or flips you the bird—especially when your friends are yelling, "Did you see that? You're not going to take that, are you?"

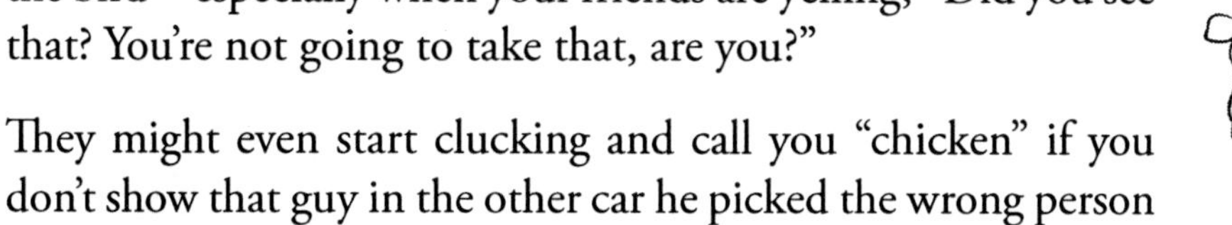

They might even start clucking and call you "chicken" if you don't show that guy in the other car he picked the wrong person to mess with!

It's hard to resist pulling up beside his car and giving him the evil eye. You might even want to yell some choice four-letter words out the window—or cut him off to even the score!

But the problem is—you don't know anything about that guy. He could be a biker on his way to do a 'hit' and one more body wouldn't trouble him a bit. Or a granny with a shaky trigger-finger who's so terrified of being a victim—she carries a revolver in her purse! Or a Dad who just lost his kids in a custody battle and has nothing to lose! And anything you do will provoke them!

And even if the altercation never gets violent—who do you think the police are going to believe started it? The nice guy in the leather jacket, the Granny, the Dad—or you, the teen driver with adrenaline gushing out your ears? This really is a fight you can't win.

But you don't want to lose face with your friends either, so what can you do?

Blame your parents!

Just tell your friends what will happen to you if your parents get a whiff that you were involved in a road rage incident.

Blame Your Parents

Behold the Lesson of Humunga Kowabunga

When my nephew, Bryan, was about eight, he went to a Disney World water park with a large family group. He was awed by the giant waterslide Humunga Kowabunga and daringly declared that he was going to ride it!

His younger cousins marveled at his bravery and followed him around all day. Periodically they would ask if it was time for him to ride.

Now, after his declaration—Bryan had watched other kids come ripping down that slide at breakneck speeds and he was having second thoughts. But his cousins didn't know that. So every time they asked, he gave an excuse. It was too early. Or he was hungry. Or he'd just eaten. Until it came to the very end of the day.

His cousins were waiting. Humunga Kowabunga was waiting. Bryan said he was ready but decided he'd better make a pit stop in the restroom first.

A few minutes later he emerged with a scowl on his face. "Ah darn!" he cried. "I just stubbed my toe and now it's bleeding. I waited all day to go on Humunga Kowabunga and now I can't even go!"

His cousins crowded around him to see the toe and strained to see the microscopic spot of blood. They said sympathetic things to make him feel better. Bryan was still their hero.

Your Parents Are Like that Stubbed Toe

That toe wound (which may have been self-inflicted) saved Bryan's neck and his pride. It provided the excuse he needed to back out of riding the waterslide without having to admit he was afraid.

Of course you're a lot older but the principle is still the same. When it comes to road rage, you may not be afraid of that other driver but you should be afraid of what will happen if your parents find out you were involved in a road rage incident. You could lose your driving privileges for a long, long time!

Tell your friends exactly what will happen if your parents find out. (And understand that parents often ***do*** find out because other drivers are quick to report road rage incidents.)

Your friends might be willing to take that chance—but they aren't the ones who will have to live with the punishment!

Important: Don't be afraid to blame your parents whenever someone wants you to do something you know you shouldn't do. Whether it's getting in the car with someone who's been drinking or speeding on the highway—tell your friends you can't do it because it will cost you your license.

Tips for avoiding becoming part of a road rage incident:

- Don't give them the evil eye (even though you really, really want to!)
- Don't even give them the satisfaction of knowing they made you mad. Look straight ahead and pretend you didn't even notice what a stupid thing they did. Tell your friends to look straight ahead too—like the other driver doesn't even exist.
- Don't make eye contact.
- If they're flashing their lights and beeping behind you, pull over and let them go by.
- Never chase them or cut them off.
- If you did cut someone off accidentally—mouth "Sorry" and let it go.

WATCH IT ON VIDEO—Go to TeensLearntoDrive.com to watch a videos about the real dangers of road rage (and how stupid the people who get involved look.)

Daydreaming

A vivid imagination is a wonderful thing to have but driving requires concentration. Getting carried away by your thoughts is very dangerous when you're sitting in the driver's seat. I know this from experience.

I'm a good driver—(even better now—after researching this book!) but I had a scary experience several years ago. I was driving along on a busy city street when I must have gotten caught up in my thoughts. I was jolted back to earth when I realized I'd just sailed through a red light!

Nobody honked or yelled to alert me, but my subconscious mind saw that red light. After I cleared the intersection (thank heaven there were no cars coming!) it finally got the message through to me.

I pulled over to the side of the road as soon as I could. My hands were shaking and I was really unnerved. I could have been killed or hurt someone else very badly.

I was very lucky that day and it taught me a lesson. Now when I'm driving and I feel my mind start to wander, I bring it right back.

Tailgating

> A lot of teens admit they tailgate when the car ahead isn't driving fast enough.
>
> NHTSA Publication: DOT HS 810 670 Sept 2006

Tailgating is driving too close to the car ahead of you.

Have you ever tailgated someone?

If you tailgate and the car ahead stops suddenly—whose car do you think will get wrecked? YOURS! And if you rear-end someone, it's automatically your fault in the eyes of the law. That means you pay for the damage to both cars—even if they stopped deliberately to mess you up.

Now if you're thinking "that's what insurance is for"—understand that even if your insurance covers the damage, you'll have to pay the deductible, which is probably around $500. But that's not all! If you thought your insurance was expensive ***before***, wait until you get the new price which is based on a crash where you were clearly at fault! It could double or more!

Tailgating is stupid and dangerous. The person ahead of you might even get annoyed and slow down or develop road rage.

What should you do if someone tailgates you?

It's scary when someone tailgates you because you know they'll hit you if the traffic stops suddenly. You might be tempted to slow down to punish the tailgater, but don't. Just pull over and let the speed demon go.

And then try not to laugh when you pull up next to them five miles down the road.

Right of Way

It's important to know who has the right of way and to obey the rules. If you ever have to go to court to defend yourself, having the right of way will win your case.

But having the right of way is no consolation if you wind up in a wheelchair because the other driver didn't obey the rules. So you also need to drive defensively.

My daughter Emily is always saying things like "We can go. He ***has*** to stop because he has the stop sign." And she's right. He *has* to stop—but the fact is—he may not. He might be distracted or stupid or drunk or not see it—and even though he has the stop sign—he may not stop.

So watch the other drivers on the road and learn to predict what you think they will do. Is that driver slowing down enough to stop when he reaches the stop sign? Is that person who's signaling a right turn slowing down enough to turn?

Don't take unnecessary chances because you believe you have the right of way.

Who has the Right-of-Way?

Read through these situations and determine who has the right of way. (Answers are on page 244)

1. You pull up to an intersection at the same time as another car. There are stop signs in all directions. Who has the right of way?

   ____

2. You are turning left. You've waited for a break in the traffic and then a boy dashes out to cross the road just as the light turns yellow.

   ____

3. You are pulling out of your driveway onto the road. Another car is coming toward you on the road, but it's going slowly.

   ____

Motorcycles

Motorcycles are a lot harder to see than cars and trucks. Some riders speed and weave in and out of lanes, which makes it even tougher.

And motorcyclists are vulnerable because they don't have the protection of a big metal vehicle around them. Sometimes they even wear shorts or short-sleeved T-shirts and there's nothing between their bare skin and the road!

> More than 1/3 of motorcycle crashes happen at intersections.
>
> •••••
>
> Make sure you know your hand signals because that's how most motorcyclists signal what they intend to do.

So drivers need to be really vigilant to watch out for motorcyclists.

Here are some tips:

- Don't try to share the lane with a motorcycle. They're smaller than cars but they still need the whole lane.
- Allow plenty of room around the motorcycle. Don't crowd or tailgate.
- Be aware that motorcycles sometimes turn unexpectedly. Their turn signals are hard to see and they often use hand signals.
- Be very careful turning left in front of motorcycles. They're approaching faster than you think.
- The turn signals on motorcycles don't shut off automatically like cars' signals do and sometimes the driver forgets. So they may not turn when you expect them to.
- Double-check your mirrors before changing lanes if there's a motorcycle in the area.

Railway Crossings

When it comes to a showdown between a car and a train—the train will win every time.

Every year thousands of cars and trucks are crushed at railroad crossings. Most often the occupants don't get out in time. Why would anyone want to take that chance?

Some railroad crossings have big red lights and gates that lower to keep cars off the tracks.

Some have nothing more than a sign at the side of the road.

Railway Crossing Safety Tips

When you approach a railway crossing, slow down and stop. Look right, then left, then right again.

If there are no trains in sight, proceed across the tracks as long as there is plenty of room on the other side of the road. You must be able to clear the tracks on the other side.

> Never stop on the tracks. If you get stuck on the track—get everyone out of the car and to a safe distance immediately. Then call the police.

If a train is coming, leave plenty of room for the train to pass (at least 20 feet or 5 meters from the gate or sign)

After the train has passed—look right, then left then right again, before you cross the tracks. There have been many cases where cars tried to cross the tracks after one train passed but didn't realize there was second train behind it or one coming from the other direction.

> **If there are signals—wait until the lights stop flashing and the gate goes up before crossing**

A personal note of warning—sometimes there are no signs!

Several years ago, I was exploring country roads with my Mom. My daughter was in an infant seat in the back. Lured by a garage sale sign, I turned into a private driveway and headed toward the farmhouse, which was some distance away. The van windows were up, the radio was on and we were talking.

Suddenly—I stopped the car. Before I could say a word, a train sped by us—within a few feet of where we were!

There were no signs. The tracks were completely invisible from where I stopped. To this day—I don't know what made me stop. Maybe my guardian angel. Or my subconscious mind noticed there was a straight row of bushes on either side of the road, and a slight incline ahead. But there is no doubt that we would all have been killed if I hadn't stopped.

I didn't expect to find railroad tracks running across a private driveway.

So when traveling country roads and private lanes—take extra care if trains run through the area.

Stuff That Can Get You into Trouble

Driving safely is part of the responsibility of every driver. Once you have the keys to the car, there are lots of other things that can get you into trouble too.

Lending the Car

Neither a borrower nor a lender be

For loan oft loses both itself and friend.

—William Shakespeare

Discuss with your parent how to handle situations like the one below. Then answer the questions. (Answers are on page 244.)

One afternoon, you're hanging out with some friends when one of them says, "Gimme your keys. I just want to grab a pizza."

You try to say no but everyone's watching and your friend says, "What's the matter? Don't you trust me? It's 2 blocks away. I'll be back in 30 seconds."

1. Would other drivers be covered by your insurance? How much is the deductible?

____

____

2. Who would have to pay for damages to the car if they had an accident (even if it wasn't their fault)? Who would pay the deductible?

   ___

   ___

3. If someone was injured in the crash (including the driver or passengers) who would be responsible for paying for their bills?

   ___

   ___

Lending the Car: Could this happen to you?

A friend spots your keys on the table and can't find you to ask permission to borrow your car so he just grabs them. He takes the car because he figures you wouldn't mind.

What should you have done to avoid this situation?

___

___

If you think this could never happen to you, tune in to "Judge Judy" (or one of the other TV judges) for a week. You'll see plenty of teens and young adults who thought it could never happen to them either!

Family Rules about Lending the Car

Decide on your family rules for loaning the car. Write them in the space below:

___

___

Plan, Share and Update

Do you think your parents are too nosey? Do you wonder why they always want to know where you're going and who you'll be with? Do you think they don't trust you?

It isn't that your parents don't trust you and they don't plan on spying on you either. But they love you more than anything else and they were teens once too. They know that sometimes things can go wrong and you might need help. And if you need help, they want to be able to get it to you (and your friends) as quickly as possible because they want you all to get home safely.

Your parents want you to have fun. Really. And they respect the fact that you're getting older and becoming more independent. And—believe it or not—they don't just sit at home waiting for you to call. (*Parents do have their own lives you know.*)

You never know when you might need their help, like Lacey did in the following story.

Prom Night

Two weeks before the prom, while on a senior year retreat, Lacey Gallagher was voted "Friend to Everyone," because she was. Quiet by nature, she always had a quick smile and a kind word for classmates at Little Flower High School.

Lacey was a great student. She loved high school and had big plans for college too. She'd applied for a double major in Psychology and Special Ed because she loved working with children with special needs.

She was back at the gym too, working out to get in top shape so she could play college soccer. (Lacey had been so devastated by the recent deaths of both her grandmothers, that she'd quit playing soccer for a while.) She loved the game and had scholarship options.

Tonight was prom night and Lacey had planned every detail. Her white satin dream gown had been specially designed for her and was hanging in the closet. She'd scheduled a manicure and a hair appointment. She'd even arranged to take her tiara to the hairdresser so her long blond hair could be styled around it. But by mid-afternoon, things started to fall apart.

The prom was on a Friday night so a bunch of her friends had planned an after party in the Pocono Mountains. Several classmates had cabins they could stay at and they'd organized fun events to last the weekend including a big barbeque on Saturday night.

Lacey had never gone to an after party before but this time she wanted to go. She loved her friends and knew they'd all be graduating soon and going their separate ways. This could be their last chance to hang out together before the next phase of their lives began.

But sorting out the last minute details of exactly where she'd be staying and how she would get there was difficult. And to make matters worse, her cell phone wasn't working, so she had to keep emailing everyone. Her boyfriend, Pat, wanted to go with some of his friends. Lacey wanted to go with hers. There'd been a lot of drama that afternoon, and by the time the limousine arrived to take them to the prom, the final details still hadn't been ironed out. Lacey would be going to the Poconos but exactly where she'd be staying and how she'd get there was still unclear.

Leaving everything to the last minute was not like Lacey. She was a planner and usually so well organized. But time had just run out. Lacey knew her mom, Denise, was really uncomfortable about letting her go away for the weekend without knowing the details of where she'd be and how she'd get there. What if there was some kind of emergency? Lacey told her mom not to worry and promised to call her as soon as things were sorted out.

Her younger sisters watched in awe as Lacey swept down the stairs like Cinderella going to the ball. The crystal tiara shimmered in her hair and her strapless ball gown floated behind her. She glowed in every photo they took before she floated out the door and was whisked away in the waiting limousine.

• • • • •

It was an incredible night! They all danced and laughed until after midnight. Then they piled back into the limo for the short drive to a friend's house where they changed into sweats and jeans. They wanted to be comfortable for the longer drive into the Pocono Mountains for the weekend festivities. At some point, the final plans were decided but, in all the excitement, Lacey forgot to call her mom.

• • • • •

That night Denise Gallagher fell asleep on the sofa, clutching the phone. She'd been waiting for that call from Lacey when she dozed off. Instead, Denise was jolted awake at 3:00 a.m. by a call from the mom of Lacey's friend, Katie. There'd been a car accident!

Denise and her husband, Frank, were terrified. Although they hadn't known which car Lacey would be travelling in—they had known she was travelling with Katie so they knew Lacey was involved in the crash. The problem was—they didn't know what to do or where to go to help. The one night that they didn't know where Lacey was, turned out to be the night that she needed them most—and they didn't know where they should start looking!

Frank jumped in his car and headed toward the turnpike; while Denise called everyone she knew to try to get him directions on where to go.

The turnpike was smothered in dense fog. It was very hard to see. Eventually the traffic stopped moving. A crash had happened on the turnpike and traffic was backed up for miles. People were getting out of their cars and talking.

Frank realized this was the scene of the crash he was looking for. He found a highway patrol officer who advised him that several students had been taken to a nearby hospital. There was a lot of confusion and misinformation. Eventually, Frank and Denise learned there had been a fatality in the crash. Tragically, it was Lacey. She had not been wearing a seatbelt and had been thrown from the vehicle.

• • • • • • • • • • •

Two and a half years later, Frank and Denise are still devastated by their loss. It doesn't seem real that Lacey is never coming home. Her Mom talks about that night in a hushed voice so she won't break down in tears. She has an important message for the parents of teens:

A Message from Lacey's Mom

"Trust your instincts. If you're uncomfortable with something—don't just let it go.

The night Lacey died was hectic. I watched her as she rushed around getting ready and asked her a lot of questions about her plans for the evening and the weekend.

> Street guide books, GPS systems and websites like mapquest.com or Google Maps can help sort out complicated or incomplete directions. Every car should also have a street guide or map in it and drivers should know how to use it.

Although Lacey had planned every detail of the prom, she'd decided to go to the after-party in the mountains at the last minute.

Last minute changes and weekends away made me very uncomfortable. As she got ready to leave, I realized she still didn't know exactly where the party was or how she was going to get there.

I knew it would be late and dark and that the limousine we'd arranged could not take the kids to that party. That worried me and I talked to Lacey about it. I didn't like the idea of last minute plans but I trusted Lacey. She was one of the most responsible kids I knew and a true planner. She had always used good judgment and had just turned 18. I knew she'd be going to college next year so I figured I needed to let her grow up. I let her go to the prom that night, without a firm plan, on the promise she would call me when she got to the dance and let me know exactly what was happening.

I hugged her when she left and told her how beautiful she looked. I reminded her to call—but that was the last time I spoke to her.

The boy who crashed the car that night was only 17. He had a restricted (provisional) license and should not have been driving a carload of teens on the highway at 3 o'clock in the morning. He didn't have the experience to be driving at high speed in dense fog and after a very long day, it's likely he fell asleep at the wheel.

He also wasn't wearing his seatbelt and none of his passengers were wearing theirs either, including my Lacey.

My message is this: Prom night is very dangerous—even when drugs and alcohol are not involved.

Parents—Make sure you know the restrictions on your teen's license and enforce them. Don't let your teen drive (or ride!) in unsafe conditions.

And make sure you know where your teens are going and who they'll be with. Don't just say 'okay' when they tell you what they want to do.

And Teens—Trust your parents. They want you to have fun and be happy but they want to keep you safe most of all."

"Prom Night" Crash Analysis

Using the details from Lacey's Story, complete the chart below.

(Answers are on page 245.)

Road Conditions	Visibility	Site of Crash
☐ Dry ☐ Wet or Icy	☐ Not a factor ☐ Poor - foggy, heavy rain, etc.	☐ City street ☐ Intersection ☐ High speed thruway or highway
Light Conditions	**# of Vehicles in Collision**	**Teen Passengers (not including the driver)**
☐ Daylight ☐ Dark: Late night or early morning	☐ 1 ☐ 2 or more	☐ None ☐ 1 only ☐ More than 1
Driver's Experience Level	**Driver's Physical Condition**	**Driving was:**
☐ Less than 1 year ☐ 2 to 3 years ☐ More than 3 years ☐ Unknown	☐ Alert ☐ Impaired by drugs ☐ Impaired by alcohol ☐ Extremely tired	☐ Purposeful ☐ Recreational
Was Driver Error a Factor?	**Wearing Seatbelts?**	**The Crash Happened:**
☐ Yes ☐ No ☐ Unknown	☐ Yes ☐ No ☐ Unknown	☐ Close to home ☐ Far from home

1. Based on your analysis (above) what do you think caused this crash?

____

____

2. How could the driver have avoided this crash?

____

____

Parking: Safety, Etiquette and Responsibility

Parking Lot Safety

Parking lots are ideal locations for crimes like purse-snatchings, auto theft, and car break-ins, as well as abductions.

Keep the following tips in mind for parking lot safety:

1. Park in a well-lit area where there are lots of cars and people.
2. If you work late, ask a Security Guard or friend to walk with you to your car. You might feel a little silly, but better safe than sorry.
3. Don't park next to large trucks or vans. They block your view and make it difficult for other people to see you as you're getting in and out of your vehicle.
4. Make a note of where you parked.—especially in large lots. Write down the lot and space number on a piece of paper or in your cell phone, or take a picture with your phonecam. If you forget where you parked and get really lost—don't wander

aimlessly. Notify Security. They have vehicles that can drive you around and help you find your car.

5. Don't leave packages or valuables in plain sight. Put them in the trunk or take them with you.
6. Trust your instincts. Don't get out of the car if you don't feel safe. If you see someone who looks suspicious nearby, move to another spot or wait until they leave. When you do get out; get out quickly, lock the door and set the alarm if you have one.
7. If you're lucky enough to have a remote, know how it works and use it properly. Will one click open just the driver's door—while two clicks open all the doors? Know where the panic button is and don't be afraid to use it.
8. When returning to your car, scan the area around it and have your keys ready. If you feel unsafe or see anyone that looks or acts suspiciously—return to the store and notify Security.

Parking Where You Shouldn't

Parking tickets add up. If you try to hide them, you'll lose your parents' trust and they'll probably find out anyway. In some places, you can't get your annual license plate sticker until all tickets against the vehicle are paid.

(Picture your Dad getting in line to renew his plate. The line is long and he's probably a little grumpy. He finally gets to the counter—only to find he has to pay your 3 tickets first! Dinner might not be so pleasant that night!)

In some 'no parking' zones you car can be towed. If it is, you'll have to pay the tow fee and all outstanding tickets—plus a hefty impound fee which gets bigger every day the car remains in the impound lot!

Parking Tips

Don't listen to your friends when they say, "No one ever gets a ticket here" because if you do get a ticket, they won't pay it for you.

Before you pull into a spot, make sure you'll have enough room to get out. I watched a young guy proudly squeeze into a tight spot once—only to realize he couldn't open the car doors to get out of the car!

When you parallel park, make sure you've left enough room for the cars in front of and behind you to get out too.

WATCH IT ON VIDEO—Go to TeensLearntoDrive.com to watch videos related to parking.

Handicapped Parking

"Meet me at the car at noon" Josh shouted over his shoulder to Luis, as he raced down the hall to his first class. He slipped into the classroom just before the teacher closed the door.

Now that his Dad was working from home, Josh drove to school almost every day. It had taken weeks of begging and bartering before he and his dad came to an arrangement concerning the car. As long as his dad didn't need it, he could take it. In return, he filled the gas tank once a week, and drove his grandmother to her doctor's appointments—which weren't very often. (Sometimes his grandmother even slipped him a few bucks toward the gas. Sweet!)

Being totally mobile was very cool—and it didn't hurt the popularity index either. Plus—his dad's SUV had all the upgrades. Not like his mom's old van. Sure—he'd drive the van in a pinch but he was grateful for the SUV. He knew a lot of heads turned when he drove down the street. And he liked the power.

Most mornings he picked up his best friend Luis. At noon they'd go out to lunch with a bunch of kids—usually to the food court in the mall or to the local burger hangout.

By the time lunch rolled around, there was a group of kids hanging around the car. After a short discussion, they decided to go to the mall. Today's group included Arlene, who Josh liked.

Josh slid in behind the wheel and started the ignition. Five minutes later, he turned into the mall parking lot. It was pretty full. They drove up and down the aisles but couldn't find a spot that wasn't a hike to the entrance.

Suddenly, Josh got a great idea. He turned into a spot right in front of the door that had the wheelchair symbol painted on it.

"You can't park here," Arlene said. "It's handicapped."

"No problemo" Josh announced as he reached under the seat and pulled out the "Handicapped Parking" sign he used when he took his grandmother to her appointments. He slid it onto the dashboard and opened his door to a chorus of 'cool's from the back seat.

Everyone piled out the doors. Josh double-clicked the remote door lock and they all headed into the mall to grab some lunch.

Talk about It: Handicapped Parking

What do you think of Josh's 'innovative' approach to getting a parking spot?

Answer the following questions: (answers are on page 245).

1. If a law enforcement officer caught Josh misusing the Handicapped Parking sign, what could happen? Could the officer:
   a) Take away his Handicapped Parking sign?
   b) Give him a fine? If so—how much?
   c) Impound the car?
   d) All of the above.
2. How would that affect:
   - His grandmother?
   - His relationship with his father?
   - His ability to borrow the car?

> ***Bottom Line—***
>
> ***Be Socially Responsible:***
>
> Thank your lucky stars that you have two strong legs and don't need to use handicapped parking spots.
>
> Leave them for the people who need them because that's the right thing to do.

WATCH IT ON VIDEO—Go to TeensLearntoDrive.com to watch videos about handicapped parking.

Family Rules about parking in Handicapped and other restricted areas

Decide on your family rules for parking. Write them in the space below:

____

____

Police Stops and Pulling Over

Some day, you may get pulled over by a police officer or a state trooper. It could be a random safety check or because you broke a traffic law.

Trooper K.M. Blumenstock of the Highway Patrol offers these tips for staying safe if you get pulled over:

1. Immediately put on your hazard lights (4-way flashers) to show that you are preparing to pull over to the side of the road.
2. Turn off your RADIO and remove your Blue Tooth device.
3. Remove the key from the ignition and place it on the dashboard.
4. Do not remove your seatbelt or get out of the car. Keep your hands on the steering wheel.
5. Greet the officer with "Good Morning", "Good Afternoon" or "Good Evening".
6. Give the officer the documents he asks for (probably your license and the registration papers for the vehicle.)
7. The officer will tell you why you were pulled over. Answer their questions politely and truthfully. Explain why you did what you did.

Understand that police officers and state troopers are people too. They are moms and dads, aunts and uncles and grandparents too. Be polite and respectful when you talk with them, because that's the right thing to do. (You are much more likely to get a reduced ticket or a warning if you're polite, respectful and follow these rules.)

Then make sure you learn from the experience and never make the same mistake again. When you get home, tell your parents what happened and why. They will probably find out anyway and will be less angry if you are upfront and honest with them. If you broke one of the rules of your driving contract, accept your punishment like an adult. The punishment may hurt but your honesty will go a long way toward proving to your parents that you are trustworthy and responsible.

In case of emergency, Trooper Blumenthal also suggests that you equip your car with a blanket and a few flares. They should be stored safely in the trunk and make sure you know how to light and use the flares.

Stuff You Should Have in Your Car

Every car should have an emergency cell phone. Keep it charged and programmed with the following:

- Your Name and Home #
- Parent's Names and Home #s
- Parent's Office #s
- Parent's Cell #s
- Insurance Agent's #
- Insurance Policy #
- Doctor's Name and #
- Roadside Assistance Information
- Local Emergency #
- Local Police Non-Emergency #

TIP: Create a contact in your cell phone list named "ICE" That's short for "In Case of Emergency." Put the names and telephone numbers of the people who should be contacted if you need help there. Police and paramedics are being trained to check for the ICE contact in your cell phone.

Also—print out a list of the emergency numbers and keep it in the glove box.

You should also keep the following things in your car—just in case.

In the car:

- Your car's Owner's Manual (glove box)
- Cell phone (secured in car)
- This book (in glove box or nearby)
- A pen (secured in glove box)
- Windshield hammer—you can buy this inexpensive item at an auto shop. Use it to break the windshield for an emergency escape. Secure it somewhere that you can reach it if you need it but it won't become a projectile if you stop suddenly.

In your trunk:

- Tire Gauge
- Lug nut wrench
- Spare tire & jack
- 3-in-1 (or similar) oil in a Ziploc bag
- Collapsible gas can
- Jumper cables—at least 2.5 meters (8 feet) but longer is better.
- A few bottles of water
- First Aid Kit
- Duct tape (for temporary hose repairs)

IMPORTANT TIP—Don't throw out your old cell phone!

Keep it fully charged and leave it in your car.

In an emergency—you can use this phone to connect to 911—even though it's not on a cell plan. Really!

Regulations in the US and Canada require all cell phones to connect to 911—even if they are not connected to a current cell provider.

You can't use it to make random calls and the 911 operator will not call your boss to tell him you'll be late, but if you need police or an ambulance—this phone will do the trick.

- Flares
- Flash Light (battery-less is best) otherwise have extra batteries too
- Windshield washer fluid
- Windshield ice scraper with snowbrush

When you're leaving on a long trip or driving in bad weather, you should also have:

- Blanket
- Food or snacks (nutritious rather than sugary)
- Warm clothing (hat, heavy jacket, scarf, gloves, etc.)
- Necessary medications
- Collapsible shovel
- Wedge of wood you could use to keep your vehicle from moving if you had to change a tire
- A couple of flares

Stuff You Should NOT Have in Your Car

Anything that's loose in your car can become a missile if you have to stop suddenly. So make sure you secure loose articles before you start the car.

Don't put knick-knacks on your dashboard (like plastic statues) or hang trinkets from your mirror. Fuzzy dice block your view and that CD that looks so pretty in the light can become a razor blade in a crash.

Be careful with vanity license plates that identify the owner as female too. "HOTGIRL" might invite attention from people you really don't want to meet.

Never have an open bottle of alcohol in your car. If you need to transport any kind of alcohol that's been opened, make sure it's securely closed and stored in the trunk.

Great Gifts for Teen Drivers

CAUTION: These gifts probably won't be greeted with squeals of delight like the techie gifts in the big box store's TV ad. They're more like the flannel jammies your Granny used to send. (You didn't appreciate those until the furnace stalled on a really cold night.)

Teen drivers can use:

- Auto Club Membership
- An Emergency Gas Card
- Jumper Cables
- Emergency Cell Phone with Car Charger
- First Aid Kit for the Car
- Keyless Car Entry System with Remote
- New Tires
- New Windshield Wipers
- Good Quality Sunglasses

But don't get:

- Girlie decorations for your daughter's car.

It's safer if creeps don't know the driver is a young woman.

Dealing with Emergencies

Roadside Assistance Plans

Roadside assistance plans come in many packages. Auto Clubs like AAA and CAA provide excellent roadside service, but there are other groups that provide roadside assistance too:

- Some cell phone plans offer them. (Check with your service provider.)
- OnStar and other in-car systems
- Sometimes new cars (purchased or leased) have plans through the manufacturer or the dealer
- Tires—Dunlop Tires provide free roadside assistance packages for most tire-related emergencies—when you purchase selected products. (Check their website at www.dunloptires.com)
- Insurance—Allstate Motor Club (www.allstatemotorclub.com) provides full service memberships throughout the US. (Membership is not available in Canada.)

Roadside Assistance Plans provide peace of mind because in an emergency, help is just one phone call away. No matter where you are. No matter what time of day.

Flat Tires

One day you're driving along, minding your own business, when all of a sudden:

> The steering wheel gets "heavy" and the car pulls sharply to one side—or -
> Your ride suddenly gets very bumpy—or-
> Someone sees you and yells: "Hey kid! You've got a flat tire!"

Chances are—you have a flat tire! So what do you do?

You need to slow down gradually and pull over in a safe spot as quickly as you can. Don't continue to drive on it. You could damage the wheel and other parts of the car and your repair bill will soar into the thousands! But worse, you risk losing control of the car and getting into a serious accident. You really need to get safely off the road ASAP.

When you're stopped in a safe place, get out of the car and walk around it. You may see which tire is flat immediately. If you can't tell which tire is flat, use your handy-dandy tire pressure gauge to check your tires.

If you're lucky and have a Roadside Assistance plan, you can call their emergency number and wait in the comfort of your car until a pro comes to change the tire for you. But you should still know what to do—just in case you get stranded somewhere that help is not available.

Changing a tire is dirty, nail-breaking work and, with luck, you may never need to do it. But just knowing that you *could* do it, if you needed to, is empowering! Knowing what to do and being able to take charge in an emergency could also make you someone else's hero.

What causes a flat tire?

- Punctures from sharp objects like nails or glass
- A faulty tire valve
- Vandalism
- Car accidents
- Worn out tires can get damaged very easily

What to Do if You Get a Flat Tire

There are many steps to changing a tire and every car is a little different. Your Owner's Manual is the best source of information for how to change a tire on your car so make sure you keep it handy in the glove box.

It can also be dangerous if you're on a busy road or you don't follow the instructions correctly. Be sure to review that section in your Owner's Manual so you know where the jack and other equipment are located. Watch the videos on our website too. Then talk with your parent/coach about how they want you to handle a flat tire. Do they want you to:

- Call them
- Call your Roadside Assistance Provider or
- Change it yourself?

Tips for Changing a Tire

- Before you do anything, make sure:
- The car is in a safe place and on flat ground (You need enough space around the car that you'll be able to work without being in danger of getting hit by another car.)
- The car is in "PARK" and you've set the parking brake

- If you drive a standard car (manual transmission) make sure you put the car in gear. DO NOT leave it in "neutral".

You must also:

- Get everyone out of the car and move them away from the car to a safe location
- Turn the engine off
- Turn on your emergency flashers and lift the hood to warn other cars that your car is out of service
- Wedge a piece of wood (or other solid object) behind one or two other tires to make sure the car won't slip or move while it's on the jack

Get your tools ready. You'll need:

- Your Owner's Manual
- The car's jack
- A lug nut wrench
- The spare tire
- Something to put the lug nuts in as you remove them (like a box)
- 3-in-1 oil in case you need it to loosen lug nuts
- A cloth or paper towel to wipe your hands on

WARNINGS:

- **Cars can slip off jacks.**

NEVER get under a car that's held up by a jack.

• • • • •

- **If you have a small-size spare—**

If your car has a "donut" (small-size) spare, you need to exchange it with a full-size replacement as soon as possible. Don't keep driving on it.

Check your Owner's Manual for the maximum distance you can drive on it. (It's approximately 50 miles or 80 kilometers.) You should also reduce your speed.

WATCH IT ON VIDEO—Go to TeensLearntoDrive.com to watch a video on how to change your tire.

Tire Trivia Word Search Puzzle

Answer the questions below. Then find those words in the word search puzzle on the next page. (Answers are on page 246.)

1. If you hit a curb you could mess up the ____________ of your tires.
2. Most tires have tread ______.
3. Check your tire pressure when your tires are _______.
4. A tire _________ will measure your tire pressure.
5. Every month you should do a visual _______ to make sure there are no nicks or bulges in your tires.
6. You'll need this to hold your car up. ________
7. You'll need this to remove the lug nuts. __________
8. Check the Owner's _______ for more information about your tires.
9. If you don't have tread barrs, you can use a U.S. _______ to check the tread.
10. You'll usually find the correct __________ for the tires on your vehicle written in the driver's side door jamb.
11. If you don't want to change your own tire, make sure you have a __________ assistance plan.
12. ______________ your tires to ensure they wear evenly.
13. Tires are made of this. __________

14. Make sure this is in good condition in case you get a flat. _______________
15. Loosen the lug nuts in this pattern. ______________
16. You can add air to your tires at a service _____________.
17. ____________-inflated tires cause a lot of crashes.
18. Never get ___________ a car that's supported by a jack.
19. When you replace the tire, make sure this is facing out. ______________
20. ___________ in the steering wheel can mean an unbalanced tire.

```
                A P H
          J C F M W R E W K
        I Q L C I P J W J U Q A W
     V C N N P L W S X D X Q K F Q R O
    X U Z G C A T Q I T Z P I E S R D W O
   U U V U M T L T X R C K C Z S O I Z P V F
   Q V F O R R N H Z P P F Q L F D T N E S T
  C C G E J W D M G G H L O S U Y M H W F F B K
  L A S Z V T N F E S U U G C N V V W C C S M B
 L D V D Z T L R Q T Y O T J U I B E S S Q P U K D
 I W V O A L U A R U I       Q B D J B L M G Z F X
 R A F B E L G D V N           J N D Y P A Z O H U
S T P A L T E W U S             L B O C I H H H O X
P H G S O H N R P D             J E R H O G K T P S
U X E R U S S E R P             N M O B V A Q G C I
 V F C F M C N M M D           P W R M J E J D T J
 V J W E T C C D N Z R       C J L D V T P X P E G
 M C E I S I H B L G M C T Y S S Y D A H M O Q N V
  K O E V I B R A T I O N O I T A T S M Z X X G
  N N B G D P U J R F L J J P A O B D O N V J K
   M T K W G E D I S D A O R R X E A K G F U
   F H F E L T N U V C C U K E F I B H C W W
    G E J D R F N K C B H N R D I G J D Z
     L P S K D D Y B A T B A K N B B M
        S A E E E E C J B P M N U
          Q R C H L D B S O
                Y J L
```

Out of Gas

Don't drive until you almost run out of gas. It's bad for the car and can leave you stranded. If you always fill your tank before it drops below one quarter, you won't have to worry about running out of gas.

But if you do run out of gas ...

1. Turn on your emergency flashers to let other motorists know you're in trouble.
2. Move your vehicle safely onto the shoulder of the road, if possible.

If you have a roadside assistance plan, use your cell phone to call that service provider. (The number is already programmed into your cell phone, right?) Then wait for the motor club's emergency vehicle to bring a filled gas container to you. Stay in your car or move to the side of the road while you wait. Choose whichever is safer based on the conditions of the road and visibility.

If you don't have an auto club membership, but you have a cell phone—ask a friend or family member to go to a gas station and bring you a container of gas. If that won't work, call a local gas station or tow truck service. Discuss the fee before you commit to the service. It may be quite high.

If you **don't have a cell phone** and there's no help around, you'll have to get some gas. Walk in the direction of the closest gas station. Take your cell phone, your collapsible gas can, your wallet, your emergency credit card, your flashlight (if you need it) and a bottle of that water you keep in the trunk. Dress appropriately.

When you get to the gas station, if you don't have a gas can, you'll need to buy one. Sometimes they'll loan you one if you leave a deposit. Buy enough gas to start your car but not so much that you can't carry the can back to where you left the car.

You'll also need a funnel or something to use as a funnel (like a rolled up newspaper). Many gas stations provide disposable paper funnels that will work just fine.

At this point you might consider calling a taxi to take you back to your car.

When you get back to your car remove the yellow plastic tube from under the cap in your gas can. Put the yellow plastic tube into the gas tank the way you would if you were filling your car. Stick the funnel into the other end of the plastic tube. Carefully and very slowly—pour the gas into the funnel.

When you're finished, pack everything you used up carefully. Put the gas cap back on your tank. Drive to the nearest gas station.

Don't forget to return the gas can if you borrowed it—and get back your deposit.

Your Battery: What to Do When You're Feeling Powerless!

One morning, you're running late. (Things always happen when you're running late!) You jump into the car and turn the key. There's a click and then ...nothing! What do you do?

The problem could be the battery and that's good news because, if so, there's a quick fix. But first you need to make sure the battery is the problem.

How to Diagnose a Battery Problem

Try the lights, windshield wipers, heater or radio. If they don't work either work—the problem is probably the battery and a jump-start will get you moving again.

If the engine turns over ("Rrrrrrr—Rrrrrrrr") but doesn't "catch," the problem is more likely the starter and jumping the battery isn't going to help you.

IMPORTANT: Jumping a car battery isn't difficult and you can do it but you must follow the instructions carefully.

Cautions:

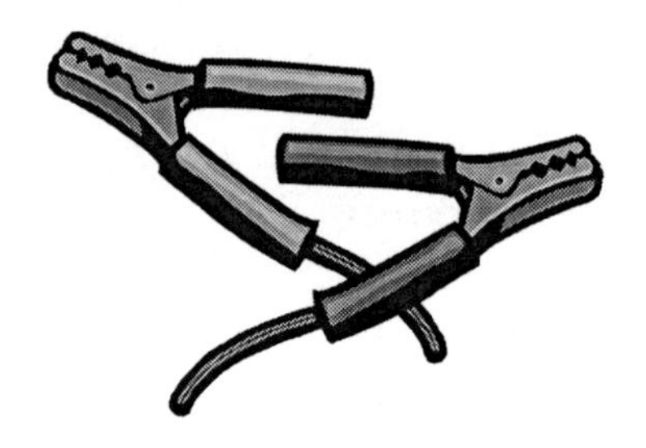

- Don't touch any metal parts on the battery or the jumper cables while you're doing this or you could get a shock.
- Use a rag to clean the battery contacts if you need to. Don't touch any white powdery substance because it could be battery acid and that could burn you.

How to Jump-Start a Battery with Jumper Cables

Read through all the instructions before you get started.

1. Make sure your car's engine is turned off. (Remove the key if you want to be sure.)
2. Also make sure your radio is in the off position so you can hear what's happening outside, when the car starts up.
3. Check that your car is in "PARK."
4. Drive the booster car into a position so its battery will be near your car's battery. The cars will be face-to-face or side-by-side depending on where each battery is located under the hood.
5. **CAUTION:** Make sure the cars aren't blocking traffic.
6. Turn off the engine of the booster car. Make sure it's in "PARK" too.
7. Unroll your jumper cables so they are straight and untangled. You'll see that each end has 2 metal claws. One claw (at each end) is red and the other claw (at each end) is black. The red one is always positive. (Remember: Red is "hot". That means RED will carry the current from one car to the other. Fire is hot. A really hot fire is "REDHOT".)
8. The black claw is always negative.
9. Locate the positive terminal on the DEAD battery. It is marked with a + (plus) sign. Use a Kleenex or a rag to clean around the base of the terminal to make sure you have the correct one. (The positive terminal is also slightly larger than the negative one.)
10. Note: The terminals are metal. You may have to lift a plastic cover to access the metal terminals underneath.
11. Locate the positive terminal on the BOOSTER car.
12. Now you're ready to begin attaching the cables. Follow the order outlined in the box below.

CAUTION: Do not touch the claws together.

How to ATTACH jumper cables:

1. **At the DEAD Battery:** Attach Red claw to Positive terminal.
2. **At the BOOSTER Battery:** Attach Red claw to Positive terminal.
3. **At the BOOSTER Battery:** Attach Black claw to Negative terminal.
4. **At the DEAD Battery:** Attach Black claw to a Ground.

13. Once all the claws are in place, start the BOOSTER car.
14. Try to start the car with the DEAD battery.
    TIP: If it doesn't start—check the connections at each battery to make sure they're secure. Jiggling each claw a little should do it . (But don't remove them)
15. When the car starts, remove the cables in the reverse order of how you installed them.

• • • • •Important• • • • •

Keep the engine running for at least 20 minutes to recharge the battery.

LATER: Figure out why your battery ran down. Did you leave the headlights on? Did you leave an appliance plugged in when you turned off the car? Understanding why the problem occurred today will help you decide how to prevent it from failing again in the future. If the problem is really that your battery is old and won't hold a charge—it's time to get a new battery.

Jumper Cables

When it comes to jumper cables—the longer, the better. Sometimes it's tough to get both cars close together and long cables can reach where shorter ones won't. Cables should be ***at least*** 8 feet long (2.5m). 12 feet or 16 feet are better (but more expensive.)

POP QUIZ: Your BATTERY (Answers are on page 247.)

1. When you try to start the car, you hear a click but no engine-starting noise. What do you do next?
   a) Panic and call someone for help.
   b) Try the lights or windshield wipers to see if they work.
   c) Get out your jumper cables.
   d) Hold the key in the "on" position until the car starts.
2. If the windshield wipers work, but the car won't start, what could the problem be?
   a) An electrical failure
   b) The engine is dead
   c) The battery is weak or dead
   d) How should you know? You're not a mechanic!

3. How can you identify the positive battery terminal?
   a) It's smaller
   b) It's the one that's grounded
   c) It has a plus sign and is larger than the negative one
4. True or False: The red cable-claws connect to the positive battery terminals.
5. As soon as the engine starts you must:
   a) Leave the car running for 20 minutes
   b) Disconnect the cables as quickly as possible
   c) Disconnect the cables in the correct order
   d) All of the above.

6. To recharge the battery you must:
   a) Plug it in to an electrical outlet
   b) You can't recharge it. You have to replace it
   c) Let the engine run for at least 20 minutes
   d) Leave the battery connected to the booster car until the battery reads "full"

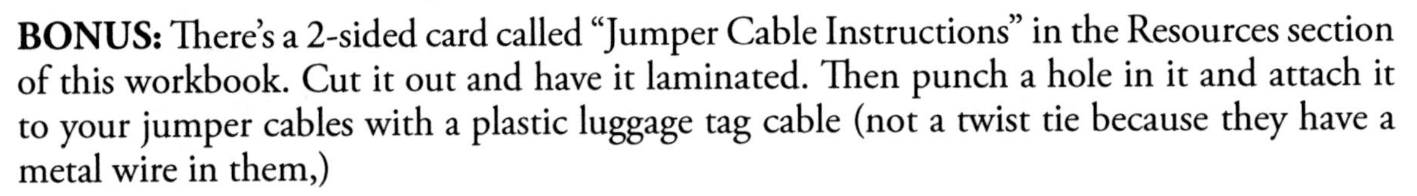

BONUS: There's a 2-sided card called "Jumper Cable Instructions" in the Resources section of this workbook. Cut it out and have it laminated. Then punch a hole in it and attach it to your jumper cables with a plastic luggage tag cable (not a twist tie because they have a metal wire in them,)

Then you're sure to have the instructions handy when you need them.

Winter Driving Tips

Thanks to the Bridgestone Winter Driving School in Colorado for their help with this section. You'll find more information about them in the Resources Section at the back of this book.

5 Things You Should Do Every Fall to Prepare Your Car for Winter Driving Conditions

Below is a list of things you should do every fall to prepare your car for winter. A good mechanic can do the things you can't do yourself.

1. Tires—Use winter tires in winter conditions
   Yes—there's a difference! All-season tires are a compromise that will not perform as well as a winter tires. Traction can vary as much as 50%!
2. The Suspension—Have it checked.
   Shocks and struts are critical to handling and every bit of vehicle performance helps on ice and snow. Road adhesion is directly influenced by shock absorber or strut performance. Worn shocks or struts can cause excessive weight transfer, which reduces the ability of the tires to grip the road.
3. Your Battery—Have it tested before winter arrives.

A dead battery is an annoyance during the summer but can become life-threatening during a winter blizzard. Even new batteries can lose as much as 40 % of their cold cranking ability in cold weather, and worn batteries lose even more.

4. The Exhaust System—Check for leaks. Carbon monoxide is a silent killer. Don't let a simple exhaust leak ruin a trip or your life.
5. Winter Wiper Blades—Replace worn wiper blades with new winter blades.

Every Time You Drive Your Car in Winter ...

1. Warm up your car briefly and clear off all snow and ice. Visibility is crucial.
   - Clear the front, rear, and side windows.
   - Brush the snow off the hood so it doesn't blow onto the windshield when you're driving.
   - Brush the snow off the roof so it doesn't obscure the rear window and the windshield of the car behind you.
   - Clear the headlights and taillights so you can see and be seen.

Wear Quality Sunglasses—They help highlight changes in the terrain and road surface even in low-visibility conditions.

2. Remove snow and ice from the wheel wells with your ice scraper. (It affects how your vehicle handles.)
   TIP: To help prevent snow build up on a slushy day spray the wheel wells with silicon.
3. Turn On Your Headlights. Whenever daytime visibility is poor, turn on your headlights. Remember this rule of thumb: Wipers ON—Lights ON

When it's Cold Outside, Use Extra Caution:

- On Bridges and Overpasses because they're icier than normal roads. They're colder because they don't have warm ground under them.
- In shady areas near large trees, buildings, mountains and billboards because they're icier than areas in full sun.
- At intersections where lots of drivers brake in the same area causing the ice to become smooth and polished.
- On hills where numerous drivers spin tires in the same area.
- Near "Phantom Shoulders" on roads. Snow plows clear the roadway using side-mounted "wings" that push the snow to the side at the same level as the road. There might be a soft shoulder underneath or even a ditch.

Stuck in Snow?

Use your floor mats for traction!

Simply turn the mats upside down and place them under the drive wheels as a traction aid.

• • • • •

To stop on ice ...

Brake harder early and then become lighter on the pedal as the car slows. This allows for precise adjustment in the event that a surprisingly slippery spot is encountered.

Be Prepared

You never know what can happen when you're on the road in wintertime. You could get stuck in snow or be delayed for a long time due to weather or traffic slowdowns. So be prepared for whatever happens. Make sure you have:

- Adequate winter clothes including winter boots, gloves, hats
- Supplies like food, water, cell phone charger,
- Emergency equipment including a blanket or sleeping bag, shovel, flashlight (with extra batteries), tow strap, and jumper cables.

Girl Power

This One's for the Girls

There's a fine line between cautious and paranoid. No girl wants to look like a baby who's afraid of her own shadow. However, the freedom that driving brings also brings vulnerability. Women are more susceptible to certain crimes than men.

Always trust that "little voice" in your head that warns you when a situation doesn't feel right or someone creeps you out. Take whatever action is needed to get to safety.

6 Simple Rules for Girls

1. If you're alone and use a remote keyless system to open your door, click once to open the driver's door when you get to your car. Don't double-click to unlock all the doors
2. Lock the doors as soon as you're inside the car.
3. Don't buy the Tinkerbell seat cushions or accessorize your car with other girlie stuff. It's safer if outsiders don't know the car belongs to a woman. (Even though it would look really, really cool!) No girlie license plate either!
4. Don't leave your purse or other valuables in plain sight. If you put them in the trunk, do it before you get to your destination. (see #5)
5. When you're shopping: don't take your parcels out to the car, put them in the trunk and then go back to do more shopping. If you need to off-load some parcels, put them in the trunk and then drive to another parking spot far enough away that someone watching, can't see you. (Yes- there are thieves that stake out parking lots—just waiting for shoppers like you to bring them brand new goods they can return for cash or sell on Ebay!)
6. When you're stopped at a light, keep the car in gear and your foot on the brake. (Your doors are already locked, right?) Make sure you leave plenty of space between you and the car ahead (at least 1 car length.) If someone threatens you, honk your horn to draw attention and then drive away as soon as the light changes and it's safe to go.

GIRLS: What would you do in these situations?

(Answers are on page 248.)

1. One evening you're driving along alone and notice a car following you. The driver points to your tire and beckons you to pull over.

   ____

   ____

2. What if you think the car behind you (in question #1) could be a police car?

   ____

   ____

3. You've had dinner at a local restaurant with friends. As you head toward your car in the parking lot, you notice a man who looks out of place. He's talking on a cell phone near your car and you'll have to go past him. What do you do?

   ____

   ____

4. At night you go to the local convenience store to pick up some milk. The parking lot is big, and dark. Where do you park?

   ____

   ____

5. You and your girlfriends are driving around and a car full of guys starts following you. They're honking and yelling and want you to pull over. The driver looks pretty cute. What do you do?

   ____

   ____

6. You're stopped at a light. A car bumps you from behind. The driver beckons you to pull over. It's late at night and there are no other cars around. What do you do?

   ____

   ____

7. There's a disabled vehicle at the side of the road? The driver holds up a gas can and asks you for a ride to the nearest gas station. What do you do?

   ____

   ____

Driver's Review Crossword Puzzle

(Answers are on page 249)

Across

1. When you go partying, always have a designated ________.
3. The driver is responsible for making sure every passenger wears one of these.
5. Eating, drinking, texting and changing CDs are dangerous ___________.
6. Your seatbelt will not protect you if you ____ your seat.
9. Always signal before you change ______.
11. You should change the oil in your car approximately every ______ months.
13. Share your _____with your parents before you leave.
15. Driver- ______ is the major cause of crashes involving new drivers.
16. ________ crossings may be marked by a sign, flashing lights or a gate.

Down

2. Pedestrians always have the right of way at these.
4. Driving too close to the car ahead of you is called ___________.
7. _____-hand turns are most difficult because you have to cross a lane of traffic
8. Most teens don't get enough of this.
10. Your ______ is the most important thing to your parents.
12. This person is ultimately respponsible for your safety.
14. Never ______ your family vehicle without your parents' permission.

Chapter 9

Structured Practice

After Getting a Provisional License

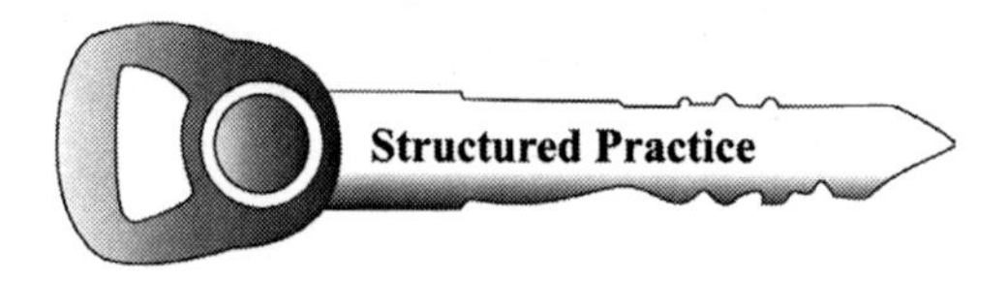

Earning your provisional driver's license is a big step. Now you are able to drive alone, under certain conditions. Make sure you both (driver and coach) understand those conditions and ensure that the driver's contract you created together aligns with those conditions.

Print your Parent-Teen contract and sign it. Keep it in a place where it is a visible reminder of your driving rules and the consequences for breaking them.

Continue to talk about how things are going. ***Teens***—tell your parents about any difficult situations you run into. Remember—they are there to help For example—if you have difficulty backing out of the driveway at your friend's house onto a busy road, talk about it. Maybe more practice would help or you could learn to back into the driveway instead. Or maybe you can brainstorm alternate places to park so you could avoid that situation altogether.

If your friends are pressuring you to do things you know you're not supposed to—talk about that too. Together you can deal with anything.

Parents—Remember to keep the communication door open. If your teen comes to you with a problem, you want to seize the opportunity to help them solve it. Stay calm and be supportive.

Continue to monitor your teen's driving and enforce the consequences when a contracted rule is broken.

Lesson Checklist

Check off the lessons below as you complete them.

- ☐ LESSON 21: Multi-Lane Highways
- ☐ LESSON 22: Driving with Friends
- ☐ LESSON 23: Highway Driving After Dark
- ☐ LESSON 24: Night Driving in Rain or Snow
- ☐ LESSON 25: In Case of Accident!

LESSON 21: Multi-lane Highways

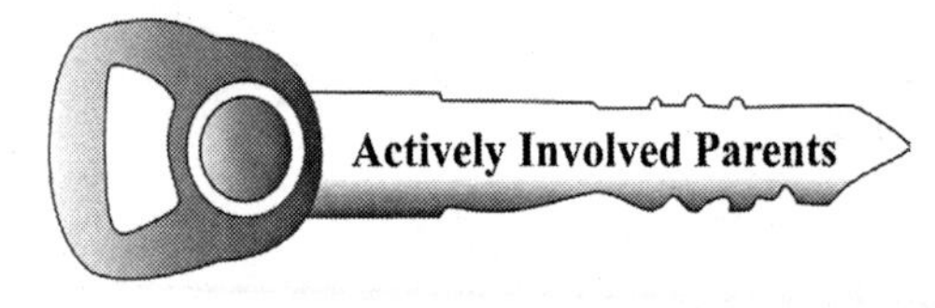

Parents/Coaches: Multi-lane highways pose a whole new set of difficulties. Merging is tricky. Each lane has a different purpose and people are constantly moving between them. Some drivers ignore all the rules. They don't look or signal before they change lanes. They speed and tailgate and it's up to your driver to be vigilant to avoid being hit by them.

The videos this week have great tips for merging and "cornering" at higher speeds.

This week work through the following topics. Check them off as you complete them.

- ☐ Dealing with Emergencies Part 2 (page 202).
  - ☐ Dead Battery
- ☐ Girl Power (page 206)
- ☐ Lending the Car (page 186)

Go to TeensLearntoDrive.com. Select the link to the "Free Video Library" from your "Favorites" (per instructions on page 3) Under Driving Lesson 21" select:

- ☐ "Structured Practice" to watch videos related to your in-car session.
- ☐ "Need-to-Know Info" to watch videos that relate to the "Need-to-Know Info" sections listed above.

Check them off when you complete them.

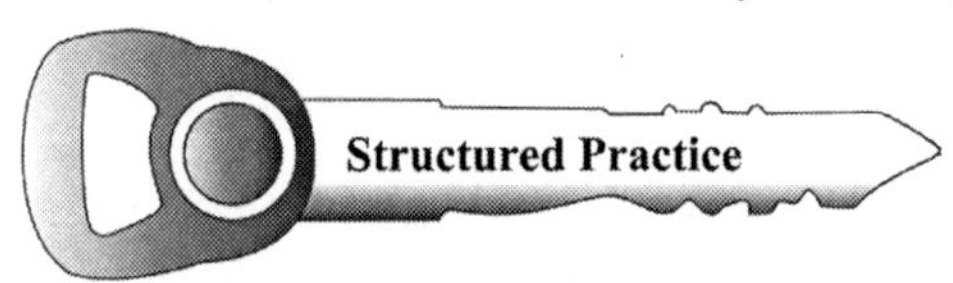

Location: A multi-lane highway or freeway.

Conditions: Clear, dry, daylight

Note about this lesson:

Save the highway-driving lesson until your teen has mastered basic road skills and 360-degree road awareness. Graduated licensing programs may specify when teens can begin learning to drive on high-speed freeways and multi-lane expressways so check the restrictions in your area.

Talk about:

- The difference between steering a car at low speed versus high-speed when very slight movements will change the direction of the vehicle
- How to use toll roads
- The kinds of signs on the highway
- How to figure out where you are on a highway
- What to do if you miss your exit
- Where to get gas or food when you're travelling on the highway
- How to get help if you need it

Remember to keep an eye on the exits and landmarks you pass.

If you ever need assistance, you'll need to be able to tell your 'rescuers' where to find you:

"I'm on Highway 16 heading east about 2 miles past exit 42."

LESSON 22: Driving with Friends

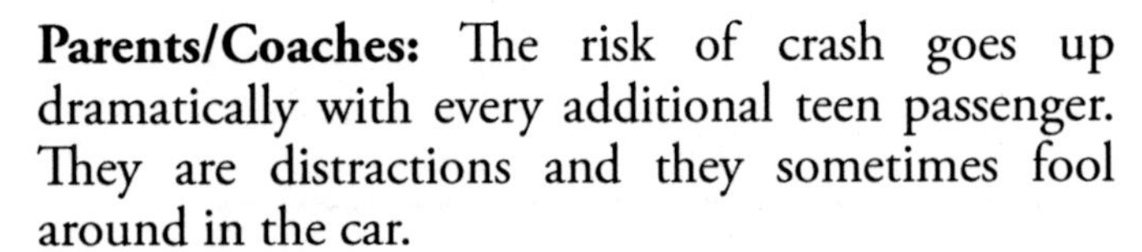

Parents/Coaches: The risk of crash goes up dramatically with every additional teen passenger. They are distractions and they sometimes fool around in the car.

This week's lesson is to make sure your teen understands that it's up to them to maintain focus on the road and control of their passengers. Make sure they know what action to take if their passengers:

- Become too rowdy
- Shout directions at the last second—like "Turn here!"
- Try to cover their eyes or deliberately bump them when their driving

It's also important that they understand the importance of their role as the designated driver. They are responsible for the lives of their passengers.

This week review the following topic. Check it off as when you complete it.

☐ Passengers (page 67)

Go to TeensLearntoDrive.com. Select the link to the "Free Video Library" from your "Favorites" (per instructions on page 3). Under Driving Lesson 22" select:

☐ "Structured Practice" to watch videos related to your in-car session.
☐ "Need-to-Know Info" to watch videos that relate to the "Need-to-Know Info" sections listed above.

Check them off when you complete them.

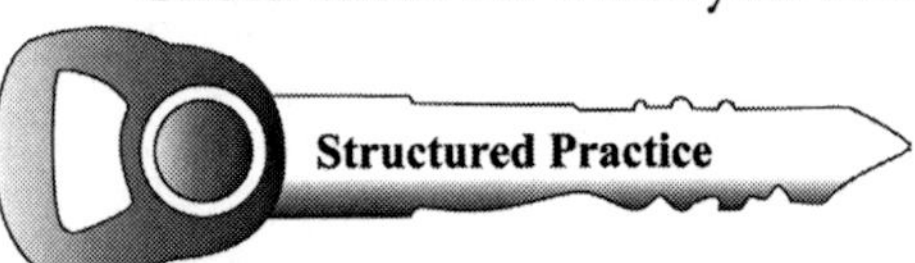

Location: Varied roads.

Conditions: Daylight or after dark—whenever and wherever you need practice.

LESSON 23: Highway Driving After Dark

Parents/Coaches: Darkness, blinding glare from approaching headlights and high speeds are a dangerous combination.

Make sure your driver knows how to identify their exit at night. They should also know how to identify the exits before and after the ones they'll use most frequently.

This week review any chapters you may have skipped or refresh your memory about some of the chapters you did early on. There's a lot to know and now that you're more experienced, you'll be able to absorb things you didn't before.

Go to TeensLearntoDrive.com. Select the link to the "Free Video Library" from your "Favorites" (per instructions on page 3). Under Driving Lesson 23" select:

- ☐ "Structured Practice" to watch videos related to your in-car session.
- ☐ "Need-to-Know Info" to watch videos that relate to the "Need-to-Know Info" sections listed above.

Check them off when you complete them.

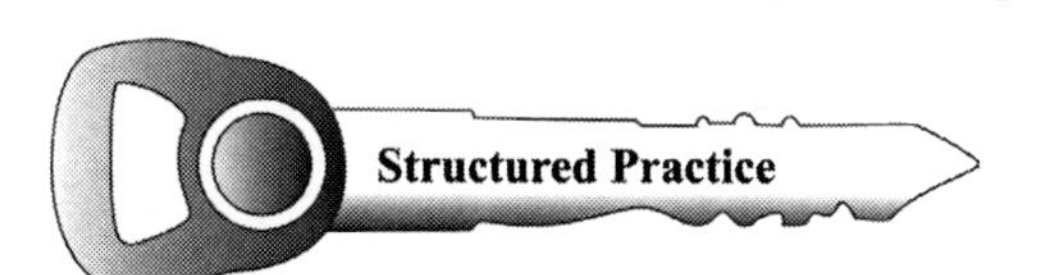

Location: A multi-lane highway or freeway.

Conditions: After dark

You've driven on the highway and you've driven at night. Now it's time to put them together. This takes lots of practice. At high speeds you 'out-run' your headlights so you can't see as far ahead of you. Plus, everything looks different at night.

Talk about:

- ☐ How to identify your exit
- ☐ What to do if you miss your exit
- ☐ What to do if you become too drowsy to drive
- ☐ Headlights and adjusting your speed at night
- ☐ When to turn on your bright lights and when to turn them off

LESSON 24: Night Driving in Rain, Snow and Fog

Parents/Coaches: Driving at night is difficult. Driving at night in the rain is even tougher. Make sure that the first time your teen drives after dark, in the rain—you're there to maintain 360 degree awareness and coach them through this tricky lesson.

Go to TeensLearntoDrive.com. Select the link to the "Free Video Library" from your "Favorites" (per instructions on page 3). Under Driving Lesson 24" select:

- ☐ "Structured Practice" to watch videos related to your in-car session.
- ☐ "Need-to-Know Info" to watch videos that relate to the "Need-to-Know Info" sections listed above.

Check them off when you complete them.

It's difficult to see at night. It's even harder to see when it's raining , snowing or foggy at night.

It's also very difficult for other vehicles to see you. Remember to slow down in these conditions and pull over in a safe place if you can't see well enough to continue.

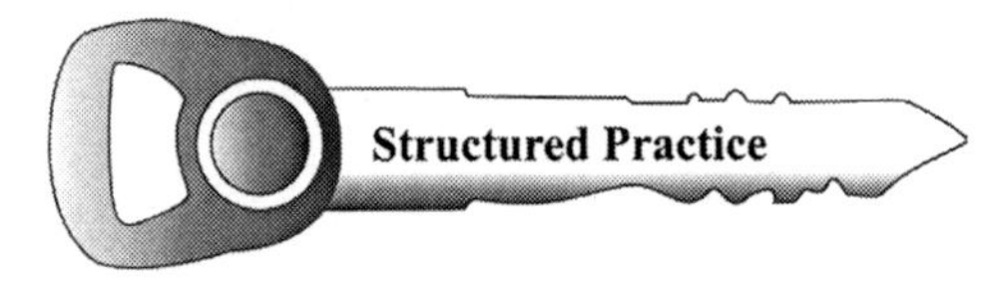

You've driven at night in clear weather and you've driven at low speeds in rain, snow and fog. Now it's time to put them together.

Tips for Night Driving in Snow and Fog:

- Leave headlights on low beam when driving in snow and fog.
  This will minimize reflection and glare, improve visibility, and reduce eye fatigue.
- When oncoming cars approach: focus on the right side of the roadway to help maintain good vision.

LESSON 25: In Case of Accident!

Parents/Coaches: Most teens will have a crash at some point. Thankfully, most will be fender benders but it's important that they don't panic. They need a clear action plan they can follow.

This workbook provides a step-by-step plan for what to do including:

- What information to exchange with the other driver
- When to notify the police
- What information to collect for your insurance company and to "make your case"
- What to say
- What NOT to say

This week work through the following topics. Check them off when you complete them.

- ☐ In Case of Accident (page 223)
- ☐ Review the Accident Report (page 276)

Go to TeensLearntoDrive.com. Select the link to the "Free Video Library" from your "Favorites" (per instructions on page 3). Under Driving Lesson 25" select:

- ☐ "Structured Practice" to watch videos related to your in-car session.
- ☐ "Need-to-Know Info" to watch videos that relate to the "Need-to-Know Info" sections listed above.

Check them off when you complete them.

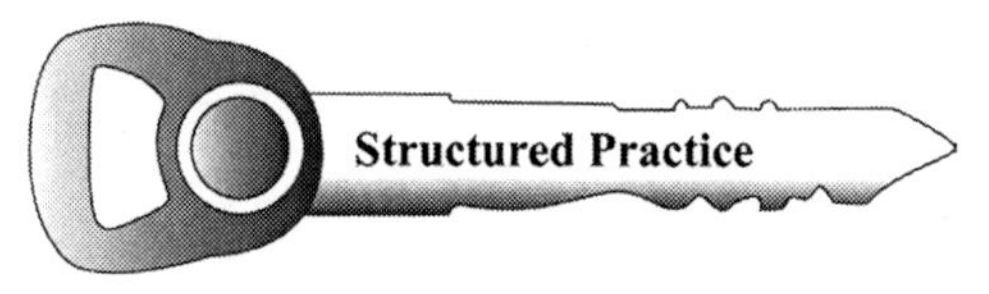

Rehearse how you would handle emergency situations like:

- Running out of gas
- Getting in a fender bender
- A serious collision

After Getting a Full Driver's License

In this Section:

- They're Not Out of the Woods Yet!
- Your Family Driving Contract
- A New Program that Could Save Your Teen's Life
- Insurance Basics
- Insurance FAQs
- What to Do if You're Involved in an Accident
- A Final Word of Caution

Chapter 10
Actively Involved Parents After Getting a Full License

They're Not Out of the Woods Yet!

You'll notice that the chapters are getting much shorter. You've done your job as instructor and coach but your job as parent isn't finished yet.

By now, *hopefully*, your teen has been driving for a few years. If they are still living under your roof, it's important to continue monitoring their driving and enforcing consequences when necessary.

However, it's likely there are some changes ahead. They may be going off to college or getting jobs and moving into their own apartments. In either case, it will be very difficult continuing to support them in the ways you have up until now. But you don't want to abandon them either. These are still dangerous years.

Like it or not, there's a lot more exposure to drugs and alcohol once kids move out of the house. Keep talking to them about making wise choices. Even if your teen doesn't have a car and won't be driving while away, it's important to remember that a lot of teens and young adults die each year as passengers too.

Encourage them to build support networks that include designated drivers or public transportation on nights out. Remind them of Eric Smallridge's story and the fact that it only takes one bad decision on one night to change their lives forever.

When they come home, talk with them about how things are going. If they have a vehicle, help them check the fluids and the tires and make sure it's running properly.

If they have a car …

Make sure they plan their road trips home safely. Encourage them to get sufficient sleep before they begin the drive home and drive during daylight rather than after dark. If the drive to and from school (or their new home) is a long one, suggest they find someone to help them share the drive. (Some parents like to share the drive to college with their teens. It's a great chance to talk. Then they fly home.)

Moving away from home provides independence and opportunities that make teens feel very adult, but keep in mind that the teen brain doesn't mature fully until around age 25.

Your Family Driving Contract

With a Full Driver's License, teens can drive at any time, anywhere with anyone. All legal restrictions have been removed but you can still impose your own restrictions by creating a new set of Family Driving Rules in a contract. It won't be as easy to enforce but it will help to remind your teen that you care about their safety and expect them to drive responsibly.

If they do break a rule, it's still important to enforce the consequences.

Breaking News about a New Program that Could Save Your University Student's Life

There's a new program that's being trialed at a university in British Colombia, Canada. I hope it will be offered all over North America to the parents of university students. You can help ensure it's available for your teen.

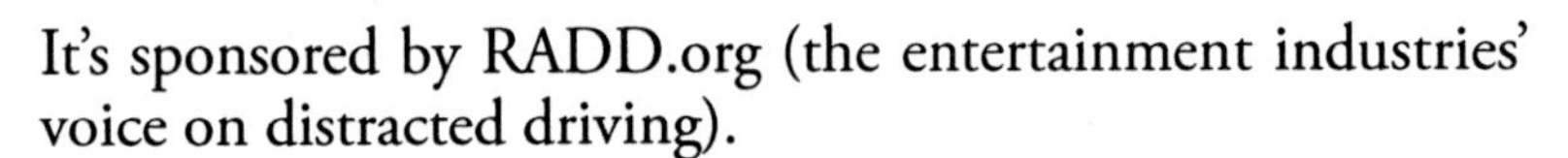

It's sponsored by RADD.org (the entertainment industries' voice on distracted driving).

Here's how it works:

1. Parents prepay for taxi trips and "load" them onto a credit-type card.
2. They give the card to their student.
3. If that student needs a safe ride home, they call any local taxi and use one of the prepaid trips to get home safely. The taxi company will automatically assign a ***high priority*** to their call. (Your student needs no money—just the card.)

Think of the possibilities—if a friend abandons them or they've been drinking or a date turns bad, or in any other situation where they're stranded or in jeopardy and you aren't there to help—you can rest assured that they'll always have a safe ride home.

How to Sign Up

I love this program and will do everything I can to make sure it's available for Emily. If you want to make sure this program will be available at your student's university or college—contact RADD through their website at RADD.org

You'll also find additional details and updates in the Resources Section of TeensLearntoDrive.com.

Chapter 11

Need-to-Know Info

After Getting a Full License

Insurance Basics

Up until now, you've probably been covered under your parents' plan, but it's time to learn a little about insurance because one day soon, it will be your responsibility.

You can't legally drive anywhere without insurance. Some companies offer 'insurance' that will provide you with a certificate that allows you to drive legally but provides almost no coverage. If you're strapped for cash, these policies can look tempting but you need to understand that you or your family could be bankrupted if you caused a crash where people were injured or property was damaged. And you'd be leaving your victims in an even worse position.

The rules for how much insurance is required, differ from state to state and province to province. Some places allow people to drive with as little as $10,000 of coverage. That would not go far to provide medical care or hospitalization.

There are lots of options for insurance coverage but you want to make sure you're adequately covered for:

- Damage to your vehicle
- Damage to other vehicles
- Damage to property caused by your vehicle
- Injuries to yourself, your passengers, passengers of other vehicles, and pedestrians
- Theft of your car
- Theft of the contents of your car (This is often covered by home insurance.)

Insurance costs a lot of money, especially for teen drivers. You may be tempted to save some money by underinsuring or cheating on how you insure your vehicle. That would be a huge mistake. If, heaven forbid, you're involved in an accident, the damages could total millions of dollars! And if you've fudged your application, you could find you aren't covered after all! You could also find that your future insurance cost is much higher, after the insurance company catches you in a lie.

Your insurance agent will advise you about what kinds of insurance you need and how much your deductible should be.

Tips to Save Money on Insurance Premiums

Car insurance for teens is very expensive because they have the greatest risk of getting into an accident. You need to be adequately insured but you don't want to pay any more than you have to either, so make sure you shop around to find the best rate. Ask a lot of questions.

Here are some tips for lowering your insurance premiums:

- Take an approved driving course. Most insurance companies offer a discount for new drivers who have taken a driving course they have approved. (Check that the course is approved and investigate the discount before you take the course.)
- Ask your insurance company about additional discounts. Some companies provide discounts for students with a good grades or who drive occasionally.
- Drive a mid-sized or large car—not a compact or a sports car. They're safer in a collision and less likely to be used for racing so they cost less to insure.
- Choose a car with safety features like front & rollover airbags, anti-lock brakes and OnStar.
- Choose a car with anti-theft features like an alarm system or GPS tracking system.

More Money-Saving Tips

Drive responsibly so you don't get speeding tickets or tickets for dangerous driving. (Those tickets provide demerit points, which will cause your insurance premiums to skyrocket overnight!)

Don't leave packages or valuables lying around in the car where someone walking by will see them. One break-in will also send your premiums through the roof.

Insurance FAQs

1. What is a deductible?
   Your deductible is the amount of money you're going to pay from your own pocket every time you make a claim on your insurance. One way to lower your insurance premiums is to raise your deductible. (If you agree to pay more out of your own pocket if you have a crash, the cost of your insurance goes down.)
   The key is to find a balance. If your deductible is too low, your insurance rate could be sky high. However, if you set the deductible too high, and have an accident—it might not be worthwhile processing a claim.
2. Will your iPod, cell phone or GPS be covered if they're stolen from your car?
   Probably not. If they aren't permanently attached to the car, they probably aren't covered. They may be covered by your parents' homeowner's policy, but that's where the deductible comes into play. It may not be worth processing the claim.
   So don't leave them in the car—especially where they are visible to anyone walking by.
3. If you modify your car with special rims or other upgrades—will that be covered by insurance?
   Check with your agent. You may have to add those upgrades to the policy and pay extra to have them covered.

TIP: Keep all the receipts for the extras you add and take photos—just in case.

Insurance Fact: Teen boys have traditionally paid significantly more for insurance than girls, however, that's changing. Many insurance companies are raising the premiums for girls because statistics show they are becoming more aggressive drivers.

What to Do if You're Involved in an Accident

Following are some common questions and answers about what to do if you're involved in an accident.

When should you report an accident?

Call 911 immediately if there are any injuries.

The first priority is to make sure everyone is safe and out of further danger. Then call 911 immediately to get help for those who need it.

- **If the damage looks minor and there are no injuries, should you still call the police?**

Yes. Although most places say 'call the police if the damage to your vehicle is over a certain amount of money, how can you estimate how much a repair will cost? Repairs that look minor can be very expensive.

Another problem concerns injuries. You may feel okay immediately after the crash or attribute any physical discomfort to the stress and shock of the crash. A day or two later you might realize you actually sustained an injury.

The problem is—if you didn't call the police, there's no accident report and without that—you're probably out of luck as far as getting your insurance to cover your medical bills.

A good Rule of Thumb is to call police if:

- Anyone is hurt
- You suspect the other driver is drunk or on drugs
- The other driver acts suspiciously or threatens to hurt you
- An airbag deploys (Someone could be hurt more than they think)
- The damage to a vehicle or property is more than a few scratches
- You or your passengers feel any discomfort

A police officer may come to the scene or, in some areas, if the damage is minor, you may be asked to go to an Accident Reporting Center.

Should You Move Your Car to the Shoulder of the Road?

Yes if—you can do so safely as long as:

- no one is injured
- the damage is minor
- there's no smoke or sign of fire near the vehicle
- there's no gasoline dripping from the car
- there's no dispute about who caused the accident

No if –any of the above criteria have not been met. If you can't move the car, make sure you and your passengers are in the safest possible location while you wait for help to arrive.

How can you signal other motorists that the car was involved in a crash?

Raise the hood and turn on your emergency flashers. If you have red emergency cones place them on the ground, 10 to 12 feet behind the car. This will signal the cars behind you that the lane is blocked and they will need to go around your vehicle.

What happens if your car isn't drivable?

You'll have to call a tow truck (or the police will.) You have to decide where to have it towed. Make sure you remove any valuables from the car first including:

- Your cell phone, iPod, GPS
- The car's registration and any personal documents
- The car seat if a child is sometimes a passenger in the car
- Your wallet, purse or money
- The garage door opener and keys
- Any other personal items of value

Exchanging Driver Information

If you're involved in an accident with another vehicle, NEVER leave the scene before you exchange driver information. If there are injuries and the police have been called, stay until you've had a chance to speak with the officer.

You are obliged by law to exchange contact and insurance information with the other driver. That means they have to give you their information too.

Make sure you give them:

- Your name and address
- Your Driver's License number
- The name of your insurance company and the policy number

Make sure that you get all that information from the other driver as well. Also note the license plate number on their vehicle.

In most cases, you can hand them your license and Proof of Insurance and they'll give you theirs. You each make your notes and hand the documents back.

More Tips for What to Do and NOT Do—after a Crash

1. If you have a cell phone that takes photos or a camera, use it to take pictures of the scene, the other driver and the witnesses. Be discreet. Don't get in anyone's face. Your objective is to gather evidence, not to provoke the other driver.
2. Don't reveal your insurance limits or other financial data.
3. Don't admit fault.
4. Fill in the "Accident Report" in the resources section of this workbook.
5. If the police come to the scene, request a copy of their report. They'll tell you how you can get one.
6. As soon as possible, go to a quiet place and write down what happened with as much detail as possible. Ask any witnesses who were in your car to do the same and provide you with a copy.
7. Contact your insurance company as soon as possible to report the accident. Hopefully you have programmed this number into your cell phone. Otherwise you'll find it on your Proof of Insurance (which should be in the glove box.)
8. Keep all of the documents you create and your photos together in a safe place. You may need them if the insurance company denies your claim or your case ends up in court.

A Final Word of Caution

Soon you'll be out on your own and out from under your parents' watchful eyes. Please remember the lessons you've learned here and the stories you've heard about all the lives that were lost or changed forever because someone made a bad decision ONE TIME.

One time. That's all it takes. Just ask Chris Marcone.

A Message from Chris Marcone

Dear Teen:

My name is Chris Marcone and I am an inmate in the Florida Department of Corrections. In March of 2008, I was sentenced to thirteen years in prison for an automobile accident that I caused. My decision to drink and drive caused the death of an innocent thirteen year-old girl. I was charged and convicted of DUI manslaughter along with three related charges. Although, in the end, it's a life sentence for my victim's family and friends along with my family and me. One selfish, irresponsible decision that I made all on my own, caused a lot of innocent people a lifetime of pain and suffering.

Since I was around thirteen years old I've been hanging out and partying with friends, never really getting into any kind of serious trouble or having any kind of problems. I wasn't hurting anyone and I wasn't doing anything different than what everyone else I knew was doing. I even drove after having a few drinks thinking I was all right to drive. I figured I'd just take it easy—be extra careful and everything would be all right. For a long time that worked.

But on April 12th, 2007 everything wasn't all right anymore. After a night of drinking and hanging out with friends, I got behind the wheel of my car when I was drunk. I didn't even get a block away when I crashed. I ran a stop sign because I blacked out. The worst part was I T-boned an oncoming car and seriously injured three people and led to the death of the young girl.

Because of my reckless actions—a life was cut entirely too short and a family lost a loved one forever. At least in prison, I have letters, phone calls, weekend visits and a release date to look forward to. All that's left for them are memories and a grave to visit. They were innocent people who were driving responsibly but were just in the wrong place at the wrong time.

Every day for the rest of my life I have to live with the guilt of all that I've taken away from the victim's family and friends and the emotional pain I've caused them. And also the pain I've caused my family. There's not a day goes by that I don't think about the accident and all the damage it has caused. I have to carry all this with me for the rest of my life.

I have to spend thirteen years in prison, separated from my family and friends. That's the majority of my young adult life behind bars. I am able to write, make calls and get visits from my family but those privileges can be taken away at any time. They are allowed only at certain times.

Most of all, those friends that I used to party with have disappeared. Even some family members have lost contact with me. A lot of pain and heartache have been caused because of one stupid, selfish mistake that could have been prevented, but can never be fixed or taken back.

If you're gonna be drinking while you're partying or any other time, you need to have some kind of plan before you start drinking. Arrange for safe transportation by a designated driver. If you are unable to drink and party responsibly, then you don't need to be doing it. It's not worth the risk. By driving drunk you're putting innocent lives at risk along with your own. By partying responsibly and driving sober, you're saving lives.

Stay safe.

Chris

Chris Marcone with his cousins

Chapter 12

Structured Practice After Getting a Full License

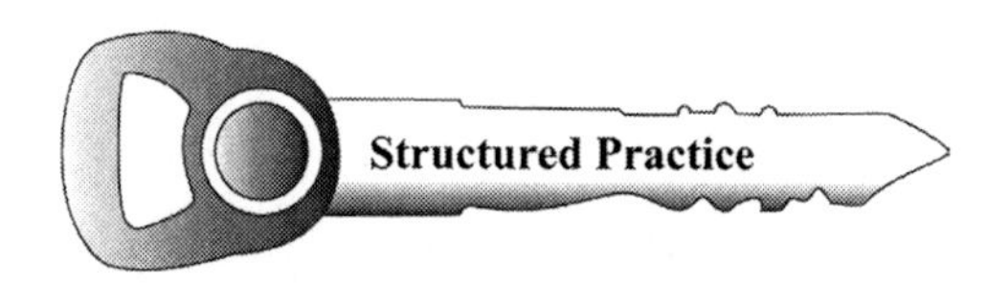

Hopefully, by the time you receive your full license, you've been driving for around two years and you're almost 18. There are no additional skills for you to practice, just a plea to remember what you've learned.

You may be tempted to relax your standards a little since you've done such a great job so far, but don't let your guard down. Your full license comes with increasingly complex situations and potential distractions. Now you can drive on the highway, after dark with friends in the car. That takes more concentration and attention—not less.

Don't start long drives until you're well rested—and don't let your friends talk you into taking foolish risks.

And please, continue to use your Safe Passage Clause when you need it. If you move away to college or to start a job, continue to drive responsibly and make an alternate plan to get home safely when you need to.

Stay safe.

Appendix

Answers

Resources

Contracts

Checklists and Helpful Tools

Answers

From page 17

The "Are You Ready to Learn to Drive" Quiz

"Always"—Each time you answered "Always" you earned 2 points so multiply the total at the bottom of the "Always" column by 2.

"Usually"—Each time you answered "Usually" you earned 1 point.

Sorry—"Rarely" and "Never" aren't worth any points.

Your score:

"Always" Total is ___________ X 2 = _____________

Add your **"Usually"** Total + _____________

Equals **<u>Your Score</u>** _____________

If you scored:

30-44 Congratulations! You've developed some pretty good habits and have the right attitude to become a good, responsible driver. Let the lessons begin!

15-29 You're on the right track but you still have some areas to work on. Start learning to drive and work on some of your personal habits at the same time.

Less than 15 Your habits and attitude would make you a dangerous and irresponsible driver. You have a lot of work to do to change your habits and attitude before you'll be ready to learn to drive.

Why are personal habits important for driving?

Some habits can be very dangerous. For example—if you're always late, you're always rushing. Rushing leads to speeding and taking unnecessary chances.

Learning drivers need to be able to follow instructions, focus their attention on the road and make good decisions. So habits that support those skills are very positive for drivers.

Before your parents turn over the keys to the car, they need to know you understand the responsibility those keys represent. Not all teens are mature enough to handle driving even when the law says they're old enough to start learning.

While driving instructors can teach driving skills, they can't teach you to have a good driving attitude.

From Page 18

The "Test Your Driving Knowledge" Quiz

1. b) 9 o'clock and 3 o'clock

2. FALSE Teens should have their cell phones with them. In an emergency, a cell phone can be a lifeline to get help from police, fire or ambulance services.

However, no one should use them (for talking or texting) while they are driving.

3. FALSE Young teens are more likely to be involved in single car crashes caused by falling asleep at the wheel.

4. FALSE 5 or 10 miles per hour over the speed limit is speeding—even if all the other cars are going the same speed. Did you know that you could even be speeding when you're driving at the posted speed limit? If the weather conditions are very bad, you should be driving at a speed LOWER than the posted limit!

5. FALSE The airbag/seatbelt combination is the best protection for pregnant women when they use them correctly.

They must sit correctly with their feet on the floor.

The seatbelt should be fastened across the hips/pelvis—never across the belly.

The shoulder belt should be across the chest—not across the neck.

In late pregnancy, it might be harder to tilt the belly away from the steering wheel so women can adjust the steering wheel toward the breastbone—not the head or the belly.

They should also keep the seat back as far as possible, ensuring they can still control the vehicle.

6. d) All of the above.

7. FALSE Cruise control should not be used when it's raining or on wet roads.

8. FALSE Airbags and seatbelts MUST be used together.

9. TRUE In a crash, a body will slide right out from under the seatbelt if the seat is reclined.

10. d) All of the above.

11. TRUE

12. FALSE Anyone can learn to operate a vehicle and drive it smoothly. The most important skills concern scanning the road for problems, awareness of the other vehicles around you and making sure you have an exit if you need it—to avoid a crash.

13. FALSE Statistics show that teens who take Driver Training courses have ***more*** crashes than those who don't.

Why? Pros believe it's because teens get a false sense of confidence when they complete Driver's Training courses.

While Driver's Training courses are a great start for teen drivers, they can't possibly teach everything and good habits need to be practiced. The eight hours behind the wheel that most courses provide, is not nearly enough.

14. d) You are ***16 times*** more likely to be killed if you are not wearing your seatbelt!

15. FALSE You should use the oil recommended by the manufacturer of your vehicle. Your Owner's Manual will tell you which one to use.

16. TRUE That's why you should never get back in your car to do something and then go back to pumping your gas.

17. e) **None of the above.** When you're very tired, nothing can keep you awake.

18. FALSE A tire gauge checks tire pressure.

19. FALSE In a crash, the person without the seatbelt will become a torpedo that travels around inside the car—crashing into other people and objects. They could die and they could kill other people too.

Your safety is your responsibility so never ride in a car (as the driver or a passenger) with anyone who is not wearing a seatbelt.

20. FALSE Flashing your headlights is rude and aggressive. It won't make the driver pull over and could make him slow down further to "show you who's boss."

21. FALSE The handicapped sign or plate is for the use of the handicapped person it was assigned to. If you are able-bodied and that person isn't with you, you can get a ticket or suffer other consequences for using it illegally.

22. FALSE

23. FALSE The operator only knows where you are if you call from a landline. If you use a cell phone, you must tell the operator where you are so they can send help.

Bonus Answer—Your body is traveling at the same speed as the car—60 miles per hour!

From Page 20

The "True or FOAF" Quiz

1. FOAF I asked my friend, Don, the Collision Investigation Expert, if anyone has ever been decapitated by a seatbelt. The short answer is "Yes—but almost never." Then he quickly added, "But you're asking the wrong question. The real question is—would they have survived otherwise—and the answer is definitely not!"

He investigated one accident where a car went into a tree at 115 miles per hour (180 km/hr). The bodies were torn apart in the crash but they stayed in the car. At that speed, there is no way they could have survived. Seatbelts save lives. Period.

2. FOAF When an airbag activates, a white powdery substance is released. Some people think it's smoke, but it's not. Airbags are made of a rough material that can scrape skin and look like a burn, but it's really an abrasion.

3. FOAF Seatbelts save lives because they keep people in the car. Passengers who don't wear seatbelts, get ejected through the windshield. If they survive the force of going through the windshield, they get killed when they hit something like a tree or land on the road and get run over by another vehicle.

4. FOAF Every passenger needs a seat belt. The seat in front will not restrain rear passengers who can be tossed around the interior like pinballs and injure or kill other passengers.

5. SOMEWHAT TRUE. There are a few states where '#77' will reach the State Police but in most places this won't work.

6. FOAF. According to snopes.com, this story is not true and has been circulating since 1993. Unfortunately a few police officers have been taken in by this one and forwarded to friends. That left the impression that this WAS a police warning. But it's not.

7. FOAF A lot of people believe this but there is no evidence to support it.

8. TRUE A spark from static electricity can ignite gas fumes that hover over your gas tank when you're filling up. The Petroleum Equipment Institute recommends the following precautions to avoid causing static fires while refueling:

- Always turn off the engine.
- Never smoke near gas pumps.
- Don't re-enter your vehicle while refueling.

9. FOAF. According to Snopes.com slimjims cannot trigger airbags to explode so there is no danger here.

10. FOAF According to Snopes.com this is not true.

11. FOAF Pennies don't work. Nor do peanut butter, breath mints or anything else. (And think of where those pennies have been! Yuck!)

12. FOAF. In fact that CD can be very dangerous. In an accident it cuts like a razor. (TIP: tin foil in the hubcaps doesn't work either.) Snopes.com

13. FOAF According to Snopes.com, death by fire or drowning accounts for less than 1/10th of 1% of crash-related deaths. And even in those cases, seatbelts save lives. Victims who don't wear them get knocked about and can become unconscious. They're the ones who don't survive!

14. TRUE It's dangerous to use cruise control when the roads are wet. Vehicles can hydroplane out of control.

15. TRUE True but highly unlikely. According to Snopes.com this was possible with the technology that was available in the eighties. With modern technology it's like being able to crack a computer password. Technically possible but virtually impossible—especially given the short time they'd have to do the job.

16. TRUE.

From page 38

Chapter 3 Review Crossword

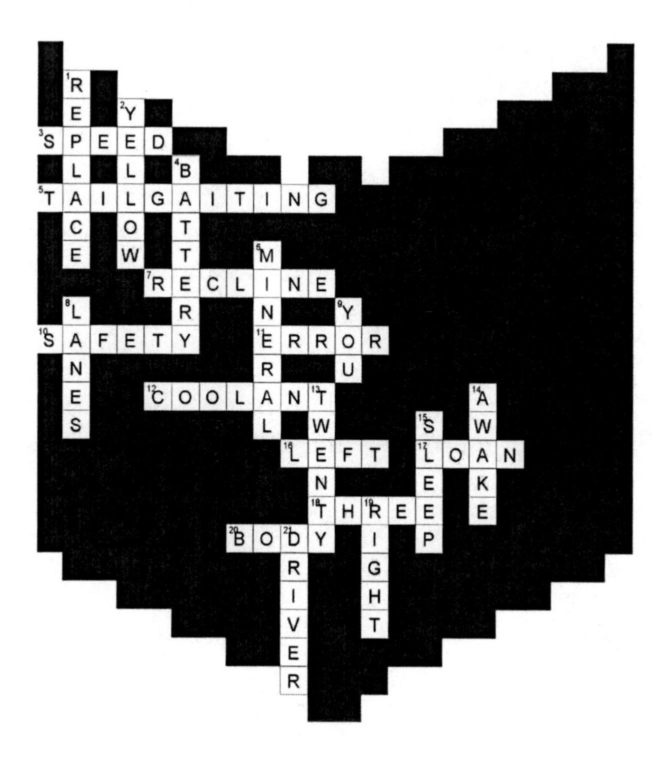

From page 55

"Katie's Story"—Crash Analysis

Road Conditions	Visibility	Site of Crash
■ Dry ☐ Wet or Icy	■ Not a factor ☐ Poor - foggy, heavy rain, etc.	☐ City street ☐ Intersection ■ High speed thruway or highway
Light Conditions	**# of Vehicles in Collision**	**Teen Passengers** (not including the driver)
☐ Daylight ■ Dark: Late night or early morning	■ 1 ☐ 2 or more	☐ None ■ 1 only ☐ More than 1
Driver's Experience Level	**Driver's Physical Condition**	**Driving was:**
☐ Less than 1 year ■ 2 to 3 years ☐ More than 3 years ☐ Unknown	☐ Alert ☐ Impaired by drugs ☐ Impaired by alcohol ■ Extremely tired	■ Purposeful ☐ Recreational
Was Driver Error a Factor?	**Wearing Seatbelts?**	**The Crash Happened:**
■ Yes ☐ No ☐ Unknown	☐ Yes ■ No ☐ Unknown	■ Close to home ☐ Far from home

1. The driver was extremely tired and probably fell asleep at the wheel. The facts that it was dark and they were traveling at high speed on a highway were contributing factors. It is very likely that Katie would have survived the crash if she had been wearing her seatbelt.

2. Katie and A.J. should have driven with his parents as they'd planned. Since A.J. was driving, he should have pulled over and taken a nap when he realized he was too tired to drive.

   In either case, Katie should have kept her seat upright and her seatbelt buckled.

From page 58

SEATBELTS: What Would You Do?

None of the things those teens suggest are safe so you have 3 options:

1. You can drive them to the theater in shifts.
2. Some can walk while you drive the others.
3. You can park where you are and all walk together.

From page 72

"Almost Home"—Think About It

3. Leeza made 2 mistakes:
   a) Leeza forgot to do up her seat belt this time—even though she usually did.
   b) Even though Leeza had the right-of-way, she should have continued scanning the intersection for oncoming cars. If she'd been watching, she would have seen that Andrew's car was going too fast to stop and she might have been able to get out of the way.

From page 73

"Almost Home"/"Lauren's Story" Crash Analysis

Road Conditions	Visibility	Site of Crash
■ Dry □ Wet or icy	■ Not a factor □ Poor - foggy, heavy rain, etc.	□ City street ■ Intersection □ High speed thruway or highway
Light Conditions	**# of Vehicles in Collision**	**Teen Passengers** (not including the driver)
□ Daylight ■ Dark: Late night or early morning	□ 1 ■ 2 or more	□ None □ 1 only ■ More than 1
Driver's Experience Level	**Driver's Physical Condition**	**Driver's Mental Condition**
□ Less than 1 year ■ 2 to 3 years □ more than 3 years □ Unknown	□ Alert ■ Impaired by drugs □ Impaired by alcohol □ Extremely tired	□ Focused on Driving ■ Distracted □ Other
Was Driver Error a Factor?	**Wearing Seatbelts?**	**The Crash Happened:**
■ Yes □ No □ Unknown	□ Yes ■ No □ Unknown	■ Close to home □ Far from home

1. The driver ran the red light because he was distracted with his cell phone. That caused the crash. Contributing factors were: it was dark and it happened in an intersection.

   The victim may also have been distracted by her passengers. If she'd been watching the car approach, she might have realized it was going too fast to stop and she may have been able to take some evasive action.
2. The driver should have pulled off the road before he used his cell phone.

From page 74

Word Search Puzzle: Distractions

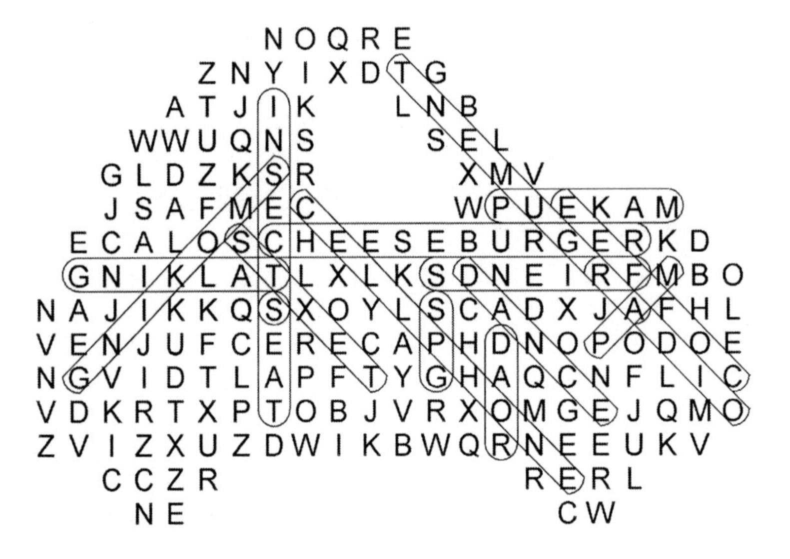

argument	radio
cellphone	road
cheeseburger	seat
coffee	smoking
dance	talking
friends	texts
GPS	
insects	
makeup	
map	

1. This kind of heated conversation can be very distracting. ARGUMENT
2. Talking on this takes your mind off the road. CELLPHONE
3. You'll enjoy this more in a restaurant. CHEESEBURGER (Hint: I like mine with cheddar, tomato and lettuce!)
4. You don't want to spill this in your lap! COFFEE
5. Some kids like to DANCE to the music but not when you're driving. (You could confuse the accelerator with the brake!)
6. When you're the driver, you're responsible for their safety. FRIENDS
7. This can help you find your way. GPS
8. Swatting these when you're driving can be more dangerous than getting stung! INSECTS
9. Girls—put this on before you leave home—not in the car. MAKEUP

10. If you don't have a GPS, use this. MAP
11. Changing this to your station can be a distraction. RADIO
12. Distractions are dangerous because they take your eyes (and your mind) off the ROAD.
13. Adjust this before you start the car or you could slide too far forward. SEAT
14. Doing this makes your car smelly and leaves yellow scum inside your windshield. SMOKING
15. TALKING with friends on your cell, takes your mind off the road.
16. Reading these messages, takes your eyes off the road. TEXTS

From page 75

Distractions Crossword Puzzle

From Page 157

Drowsy Driving: Talk about It

Crash Analysis

Road Conditions	Visibility	Site of Crash
■ Dry □ Wet or icy	■ Not a factor □ Poor - foggy, heavy rain, etc.	□ City street □ Intersection ■ High speed thruway or highway
Light Conditions	**# of Vehicles in Collision**	**Teen Passengers** (not including the driver)
■ Daylight □ Dark: Late night or early morning	■ 1 □ 2 or more	■ None □ 1 only □ More than 1
Driver's Experience Level	**Driver's Physical Condition**	**Driver's Mental Condition**
□ Less than 1 year □ 2 to 3 years □ more than 3 years ■ Unknown	□ Alert □ Impaired by drugs □ Impaired by alcohol ■ Extremely tired	□ Focused on Driving □ Distracted ■ Other
Was Driver Error a Factor?	**Wearing Seatbelts?**	**The Crash Happened:**
■ Yes □ No □ Unknown	□ Yes □ No ■ Unknown	■ Close to home □ Far from home

1. Steve was impaired by lack of sleep and fell asleep at the wheel. The facts that he was driving at night and on a highway were contributing factors.
2. Steve could have pulled over to take a nap or because he was so close to home, he could have called his parents and asked them to come and get him.
3. Steve couldn't stop yawning, his eyes were sore and he couldn't concentrate. He also veered off the road onto the rumble strips.
4. H—None of the above

If you are extremely tired, none of these things will keep you awake. A cup of coffee will provide a short burst of alertness but takes about 20 to 30 minutes to work.

From page 162

Should These Teens Drive Today?

1. No. The ride to work is dangerous because Christina must be drowsy after getting so little sleep.

   The ride home will be even more dangerous. If Christina is like most teens on summer vacation, she's been sleeping at least 2 hours less than she should all week. Friday night she only slept 3 hours so she already has a sleep debt of about 14 hours.

   Today she'll spend 9 hours in the hot sun. Her job is usually not physically active but it's tiring because lifeguards need to be very alert throughout the day. Even if she comes straight home, she'll have that 60-mile drive home. That will probably take around an hour on the highway and she'll probably be driving alone. All those factors combined make this an extremely dangerous situation. Christina should not be making this drive until after she gets a good night's sleep.)

2. No. Prom night is not a safe night for ANY teen to drive.

From page 165

Reid's Story—Crash Analysis

Road Conditions	Visibility	Site of Crash
□ Dry ■ Wet or Icy	■ Not a factor □ Poor - foggy, heavy rain, etc.	□ City street □ Intersection ■ High speed thruway or highway
Light Conditions	**# of Vehicles in Collision**	**Teen Passengers** (not including the driver)
□ Daylight ■ Dark: Late night or early morning	■ 1 □ 2 or more	□ None □ 1 only ■ More than 1
Driver's Experience Level	**Driver's Physical Condition**	**Driving was:**
□ Less than 1 year ■ 2 to 3 years □ More than 3 years □ Unknown	■ Alert □ Impaired by drugs □ Impaired by alcohol □ Extremely tired	□ Purposeful ■ Recreational
Was Driver Error a Factor?	**Wearing Seatbelts?**	**The Crash Happened:**
■ Yes □ No □ Unknown	□ Yes □ No ■ Unknown	■ Close to home □ Far from home

1. Several things combined to cause this crash. The inexperienced driver was speeding on a highway at night. He was driving in an area that was unfamiliar to him and may have been distracted by his passengers. It had been raining so the roads may have been a little slippery too.
2. He should have slowed down due to the road conditions and because he was entering a curve.

From page 174

Alcohol and Driving: Talk About It

"A Day at the Beach" Crash Analysis

Road Conditions	Visibility	Site of Crash
■ Dry □ Wet or icy	■ Not a factor □ Poor - foggy, heavy rain, etc.	□ City street □ Intersection ■ High speed thruway or highway
Light Conditions	**# of Vehicles in Collision**	**Teen Passengers** (not including the driver)
□ Daylight ■ Dark: Late night or early morning	□ 1 ■ 2 or more	■ None □ 1 only □ More than 1
Driver's Experience Level	**Driver's Physical Condition**	**Driver's Mental Condition**
□ Less than 1 year □ 2 to 3 years ■ more than 3 years □ Unknown	□ Alert □ Impaired by drugs ■ Impaired by alcohol □ Extremely tired	□ Focused on Driving ■ Distracted □ Other
Was Driver Error a Factor?	**Wearing Seatbelts?**	**The Crash Happened:**
■ Yes □ No □ Unknown	□ Yes □ No ■ Unknown	■ Close to home □ Far from home

1. Eric was impaired and should not have been driving. It was also dark and the cars were traveling at high speeds. Eric was distracted by the car to the right of him and was not aware of the other cars around him.

2. Eric knew he was going to be drinking so he should not have driven to the beach in the first place. He and his friends could have come together with a designated driver instead of driving separately.

   Since Eric *did* drive to the beach, he should have found a safe ride home. He could have gotten a ride with a sober friend or taken a cab home. Another sober friend could have driven his car home or he could have returned the next day to get it.

From page 177

The "A Night to Remember" Quiz

1. **e)** All those things contributed to Justin changing his plan and drinking what was offered. Plus—once he'd had a few glasses of the slushy rum drink, it became easier to 'go with the flow' and keep drinking.

   Alcohol decreases inhibitions and makes it easier to say 'what the heck' to doing things we wouldn't normally do.

2. The answer is not 'because he could wreck their car'—although he could. A car can always be replaced.

   Nor is it, 'because if he gets charged with DUI, their insurance rates would go way up'—although that's true too. (If Justin crashes the car, the insurance rates could double or triple—even if no one gets hurt!)

   The answer is—Justin's parents don't want him to drink and drive because they know driving impaired is very dangerous. They love Justin and want him and his passengers to be safe.

3. It takes between 1 to 1 ½ hours for each standard drink (see story insert) to be processed out of the body. Exactly how fast that works depends on a lot of factors including your size and metabolism.

   If Justin finished his fifth **beer** at midnight and he's a big, healthy guy with a fast, efficient metabolism, the earliest he'll be alcohol free would be 5:00 a.m. Otherwise, it could take until 7:30 am.

   However—Justin wasn't drinking beer. He was drinking cocktails and wine. A 'standard' cocktail includes 1 ¼ oz. of alcohol but each pineapple drink probably had the equivalent of several servings of alcohol in it. A serving of wine is 4 ounces, but most people pour a lot more than that into a glass too.

   On this occasion, Justin has consumed many more than five drinks. He needs a good night's sleep and may not be alcohol-free until after noon.

4. **d)** None of the above. There's no way to sober up quickly. Justin has to sleep off the alcohol and a 20-minute nap is not nearly enough (see answer # 3.)

   Lots of people think they can sober up by drinking lots of strong, black coffee but that doesn't really work. After a few cups, the person may sound better and may appear sober but there's still too much alcohol in their system to drive.

   Likewise, a cold shower might make someone look more alert but it won't help their perception or motor skills so they still can't drive.

   Justin should definitely not jump in the pool. Alcohol and swimming are a dangerous combination.

From page 177

"A Night to Remember": Talk About It

1. Justin promised his dad he wouldn't drink and he broke his promise. His dad would be angry about that. However, the worst thing that could happen is that Justin would be so afraid of disappointing his dad that he wouldn't call home for a safe ride and would try to drive when he's impaired instead.

   His first mistake (breaking his promise) could be worked out and his dad would eventually get over it. His second mistake (driving impaired) could be deadly and no one in his family would ever get over that!

2. Letting Brad drive is not a good option. Brad has been drinking too and even though he's not as impaired as Justin, he's still impaired. Justin thinks his biggest problem would be getting a DUI. That's what Eric Smallridge thought too.

   The DUI is a serious wakeup call but the real tragedy would be if Brad crashed the car and killed them all or killed a carload of innocent people.

3. Jennifer should do everything she can to keep Justin and Brad from driving. Maybe BBQ Guy could drive them home (assuming he is sober). Maybe they could stay overnight or Justin could call his parents, but none of them—Justin, Brad, Jennifer or Chelsea is capable of driving safely tonight.

   Under no circumstances, should Jennifer get in Justin's car if Justin or Brad insists on driving.

4. **d)** That was a bad idea because they would still be responsible if anything bad happened as a result of that decision.

   The story doesn't say how old these teens are. However—if they are underage—Chelsea's parents acted very irresponsibly—even criminally—by allowing these teens to drink alcohol in their home. Maybe they think Chelsea and her friends will think they're cool because they let her serve alcohol. Maybe they think, "Teens are going to drink anyway so at least Chelsea's safe at home." But they could be arrested just for having this party in their home—even though they weren't there at the time.

   And—even if these teens are legally able to drink, the parents and the BBQ Guy could be charged if the teens drove impaired.

   And—worst of all—if there was a car crash, they would be responsible for injuries and even deaths. How cool do you think Chelsea and her friends would think they were then?

From page 184

Who Has the Right of Way?

1. The car on the right has the right of way.
2. The boy has the right of way.
3. The car on the road has the right of way, even though it's moving slowly.

From page 186

Lending the Car

1. You'd need to check your policy for this, but many policies only cover licensed drivers over age 25, with specific exceptions. Your deductible is probably between $100 and $500 but again—check your policy. This is the amount you will have to pay even if insurance covers the crash, which is doubtful.
2. You (your parents if you're under age) would have to pay the deductible for sure and if they weren't covered by your insurance (see #1) you'd probably have to pay for everything else too.
3. You (your parents if you're under age) would probably have to pay for all of it and that could bankrupt them.

From page 186

Lending the Car—Could this happen to you?

Don't leave your keys lying around. Keep them with you, in your pocket or purse where someone can't take them without your knowledge.

From page 190

"Prom Night" Crash Analysis

Road Conditions	Visibility	Site of Crash
■ Dry □ Wet or Icy	□ Not a factor ■ Poor - foggy, heavy rain, etc.	□ City street □ Intersection ■ High speed thruway or highway
Light Conditions	**# of Vehicles in Collision**	**Teen Passengers** (not including the driver)
□ Daylight ■ Dark: Late night or early morning	■ 1 □ 2 or more	□ None □ 1 only ■ More than 1
Driver's Experience Level	**Driver's Physical Condition**	**Driving was:**
■ Less than 1 year □ 2 to 3 years □ More than 3 years □ Unknown	□ Alert □ Impaired by drugs □ Impaired by alcohol ■ Extremely tired	■ Purposeful □ Recreational
Was Driver Error a Factor?	**Wearing Seatbelts?**	**The Crash Happened:**
■ Yes □ No □ Unknown	□ Yes ■ No □ Unknown	■ Close to home □ Far from home

1. No teen should drive on prom night. To make it worse—this driver was an inexperienced and exhausted one with a restricted (provisional) license who drove at night, in foggy conditions, at high speed with a carload of teens who weren't wearing seatbelts. It could not have been worse!
2. These teens should have gone home to sleep before going to the after party, or hired someone to drive them.

From page 193

Handicapped Parking

1. d) All of the above.

Fines can be $500.00 or more. If a car is impounded, the driver has to pay the towing fee, the impound fee PLUS the ticket. So unauthorized parking in a handicapped spot can be VERY expensive, and a lot more inconvenient than walking a few extra feet from a regular parking spot. (Using a handicapped spot when the person who requires it is not in the vehicle is unauthorized use.)

The handicapped parking permit would be confiscated.

And you could also be incredibly embarrassed. News stations have done lots of undercover stories where they used hidden cameras to catch people who park illegally in handicapped spots. There are also several websites like handicappedfraud.org that post information about abusers.

How do you think your Mom or Dad would feel if a business colleague mentioned they saw their car on TV last night?

2. His grandmother would have to fight to get her permit back and it could be denied.

His father would be angry and disappointed and could take away Josh's driving privileges.

From page 199

Tire Trivia Word Search Puzzle

1. If you hit a curb you could mess up the **alignment** of your tires.
2. Most tires have tread **bars**.
3. Check your tire pressure when your tires are **cold**.
4. A tire **gauge** will measure your tire pressure.
5. Every month you should do a visual **inspection** to make sure there are no nicks or bulges in your tires.
6. You'll need this to hold your car up. **jack**
7. You'll need this to remove the lug nuts. **lugwrench**
8. Check the Owner's **Manual** for more information about your tires.
9. If you don't have tread bars, you can use a U.S. **penny** to check the tread.
10. You'll usually find the correct **pressure** for the tires on your vehicle written in the driver's side door jamb.
11. If you don't want to change your own tire, make sure you have a **roadside** assistance plan.
12. **Rotate** your tires to ensure they wear evenly.
13. Tires are made of this. **rubber**
14. Make sure this is in good condition in case you get a flat. **spare**
15. Loosen the lug nuts in this pattern. **star**
16. You can add air to your tires at a service **station**.
17. **Under**-inflated tires cause a lot of crashes.
18. Never get **under** a car that's supported by a jack.
19. When you replace the tire, make sure this is facing out. **valve**
20. **Vibration** in the steering wheel can mean an unbalanced tire.

alignment
bars
cold
gauge
inspection
jack
lugwrench
manual
penny
pressure
roadside
rotate
rubber
spare
star
station
under
under
valve
vibration

From page 203

POP QUIZ: Your BATTERY

1. b) Try the lights or radio to see if they work.

If the wipers and radio still work, the problem is not the battery.

2. a) An electrical failure

3. c) It has a plus sign and is larger than the negative one

4. True

5. c) Disconnect the cables in the correct order.

6. c) Let the engine run for at least 20 minutes

From page 207

Girls: What would you do in these situations?

1. Turn on your emergency flashers to show that you see them. Slow down to a safe speed and find a place with a lot of people around where you can pull over safely to check your tire. Never pull over in a dark or secluded place.

2. Turn on your emergency flashers to show that you see the officer and understand he wants you to pull over. Slow down to a safe speed.

   Then look at the police vehicle carefully. Police cars have a lot of expensive equipment and a certain look. If you are uncertain about whether or not it's a real police car, and the area is dark and secluded, call "911" and explain the situation to the operator. They'll tell you what to do.

3. Go back to the restaurant and ask your friends to walk you to your car. And give yourself a pat on the back for listening to that "little voice" that told you the man didn't feel "right."

   Maybe he was just a guy on a cell phone. If so—no harm. No foul.

   But if he was dangerous, you might have just saved your own life.

4. Park under a light near the door of the store. Do not park next to a large vehicle that obstructs your view. Keep your keys in your hand and your finger on the panic button of your remote as you enter the store and when you return to your vehicle.

   Push the panic button (triggering your car horn to blast) if anyone suspicious gets too close.

   It's easy to look embarrassed like you made a mistake by hitting the button if it becomes clear that the guy was harmless.

5. If the car is weaving, speeding or you feel threatened in any way:

   Do not pull over. Do not get out of the car.

   Ask a passenger to call 911 and advise the operator of your situation. Follow the instructions of the 911 operator.

   It really is not a good idea to pull over, however, if you don't sense a threat and you're getting a lot of pressure from your friends to pull over:

   - Choose a spot that's well lit, where there are a lot of other people around.
   - NEVER pull over in a dark or deserted area
   - NEVER let any of your passengers get into their car.
   - NEVER follow them to another location.
   - NEVER drink or eat anything they offer you.
   - NEVER drive home (with them following) because then they'll know where you live.

   And keep in mind that just because a guy is cute, it doesn't mean he's nice or harmless.

6. In this situation, do not pull over in a dark or secluded area. Drive to an area with lots of people around. Note the license number of the other vehicle if you can.

   If you feel you're in danger, call 911 and explain the situation to the operator.

7. Ask your passenger to call 911 and request assistance for the disabled vehicle. Do not stop to help the car yourself. (Bad people have been known to set traps for young women by pretending to have car troubles. Really.)

   If you're alone, drive away from the vehicle to a place that's safe. Pull over there and call 911 to request help for the disabled car. Keep your doors locked and do not get out of your car. When you finish your call, continue on your way.

From page 208

Driver's Review Crossword Puzzle

Teen ***Passenger*** and Parent Contract

Teen's Promise:

Every year thousands of teens like me get killed or badly injured in car crashes when they ride in vehicles driven by teen-aged friends or relatives.

I know my parents love me and want to protect me. They've made the following rules to keep me safe when I'm riding with other teens.

I have read each rule and initialed beside it to show I understand what it means and agree to obey it.

***I WILL NOT*—**

- Ride in a car I know contains illegal drugs or alcohol. ________
- Ride with a driver I know used illegal drugs or alcohol before driving or while driving. ________
- Ride with a driver who is extremely tired. ________
- Ride with a driver who drives unsafely or breaks the law. ________
- Ride with a driver who uses their cell phone while they're driving ________
- Ride with a driver who texts or reads texts while they're driving. ________
- Ride with a driver who doesn't pay attention to the road. ________
- Ride in a car I know contains any guns, rifles or weapons of any kind. ________
- Do anything to distract the driver or block their vision. ________
- Ride in a car where the music is so loud we can't hear sirens or outside noises ________
- Ride with a driver who drives aggressively or is hostile to other drivers ________
- Deliberately damage any vehicle. ________

***I WILL ALWAYS*—**

- Buckle my seat belt. ________
- Make sure everyone else in the vehicle wears a seatbelt. ________
- Tell you if I am ever in a car that is stopped by the police for any reason ________
- Get your permission **BEFORE** I ride with any teen driver who is not listed in this contract. I will tell you who the perspective driver is, where we are going and who else will be riding in the vehicle. ________
- Get your permission **BEFORE** I ride with any listed (in this contract) teen driver,
  for a reason that isn't listed here. ________

Parent or Guardian's Promise:

I love you and want you to be safe. I know that teens are killed and injured every day because they rode in cars with unsafe teen drivers or in unsafe conditions.

I understand that sometimes things can happen that you can't control. Please call me if you are ever in a dangerous situation and need my help.

Please tell me when you are worried or feel pressured to do anything that makes you uncomfortable. I promise not to judge you and to do my best to help you find a solution.

I would rather you call me and stay alive, than get in a car with someone who has been drinking, using drugs or is driving dangerously. I promise to provide you with the help you need and a safe ride home as outlined in the Safe Passage Clause.

Parent(s)/Guardian(s) initials here: _______

The Safe Passage Clause

If you are ever in a situation that threatens your safety and you contact me for a safe ride home, I promise to pick you up without question. It doesn't matter where you are, what time it is or what the situation is. I would rather drive across town at 3 a.m. to pick you up, than identify your body in the morgue the next day.

I won't yell at you or be angry because I want you to call me if you need help. We will postpone discussions about that situation until we can both discuss the issues in a calm, caring way.

If you can't reach me when you need me, the following people have agreed to help you with advice, or a sober ride home regardless of the time or circumstances—

____

____

Allowed Teen Drivers

We agree that you can ride with the following drivers under the circumstances outlined below: (for example: "Julie Smith—to and from school only")

____

____

Teen Signature _______________________________________

Adult Signature (s) ___________________________________

Date: _______________

Level 1 License (Learner's Permit)

Teen's Promise to Parents:

Every year thousands of new teen drivers like me get killed or badly injured in car crashes. I know you love me and want to protect me. You've made the following rules to keep me safe when I'm driving.

I have read each rule and initialed beside it to show I understand what it means and agree to obey it.

I WILL NEVER—

- Drive without a sober, licensed co-pilot who has been approved by you, in the passenger seat beside me ________
- Drive between the hours of _______ and _________ ________
- Drive on these roads (Please define.) ________

  ____

  ____

  ____
- Drive after using illegal drugs. ________
- Drive after drinking any alcohol. ________
- Drive without my seatbelt fastened. ________
- Allow anyone to ride in my vehicle without a seatbelt. ________
- Talk on a cell phone or text while I am driving. If I need to make a call, I will pull over in a safe location first. ________
- Drive aggressively or show hostile behavior toward other drivers ________
- Race or engage in stunts or other risky behavior ________
- Conceal tickets, warnings or crashes from my parents ________
- Allow anyone else to drive the car without my parent's permission ________
- Get in a car with a driver who is under the influence of drugs or alcohol ________
- Wear headphones when I'm driving. ________
- Eat, drink or smoke while I'm driving. ________
- Allow anyone else to smoke in the car. ________
- **The consequences for failure to abide by these rules will be: (Be specific.)**

  ____

  ____

  ____

I WILL ALWAYS—

- Obey all speed limits, traffic signs and traffic lights. ________
- Do my best to tell you when I feel pressured to do things that make me uncomfortable or worry me ________
- Let you know where I'm going, who I'm with, when I will arrive and when I will return. If my plans change, I will let you know as soon as I can. ________
- Keep the music and noise at a level where I can still hear noises like sirens. ________
- Try to make a plan for how I'll get home safely, before I go out ________

The consequences for failure to abide by these rules will be: (Be specific.)

____

____

____

Parent/Guardian's Promise to Teen:

Because I love and trust you and want you to be safe.

I WILL NOT—

- Drive under the influence of alcohol or drugs. ________
- Ride with a driver who has had too much to drink ________
- Use my cell phone or text when I drive. ________

I WILL –

- Provide and maintain a safe vehicle for your driving practice ________
- Pay (or co-pay) for your driving lessons and materials ________
- Be available for driving practice for at least (an average of) 2 hours per week (or arrange for an alternate coach to do so) ________
- Provide practice on a variety of road types and driving conditions ________
- Share my observations and coaching in a calm, respectful manner ________
- Wear my seatbelt and require everyone in my vehicle to wear theirs. ________
- Avoid making decisions that will jeopardize my health and safety or cause you to lose your trust in me. ________
- Provide you with Safe Passage as defined below ________

The consequences for failure to abide by these rules will be:

____

____

____

The Safe Passage Clause

If you are ever in a situation that threatens your safety, ***please*** contact me for a safe ride home. I promise to pick you up without question. It doesn't matter where you are, what time it is or what the situation is. I would rather drive across town at 3 a.m. to pick you up, than identify your body in the morgue the next morning.

I won't yell at you or be angry because I want you to call me if you need help. We will postpone discussions about that situation until we can both discuss the issues in a calm, caring way.

If you can't reach me when you need me, the following people have agreed to help you with advice, or a sober ride home regardless of the time or circumstances—

____

____

____

Allowed Teen Drivers

We agree that you can ride with the following drivers under the circumstances outlined below: (for example: "Julie Smith—to and from school only)

I understand that the terms of our Teen <u>Passenger</u>-Parent Contract also apply.

____

____

____

____

Teen Signature _______________________________________

Parent/Guardian's Signature (s)______________________________

Date: ________________

Provisional (Restricted) License

Teen's Promise to Parents:

Every year thousands of new teen drivers like me get killed or badly injured in car crashes. I know you love me and want to protect me. You've made the following rules to keep me safe when I'm driving.

I have read each rule and initialed beside it to show I understand what it means and agree to obey it.

I WILL NEVER—

- Drive between the hours of _______ and _________. _________
- Drive on these roads (Please define.) _________

  ____

  ____
- Drive with teen passengers in my vehicle. _________
- Drive after using illegal drugs _________
- Drive after drinking any alcohol. _________
- Drive without my seatbelt fastened. _________
- Allow anyone to ride in my vehicle without a seatbelt. _________
- Talk on a cell phone, text or read texts while I am driving. _________
- Drive aggressively or show hostile behavior toward other drivers _________
- Race or engage in stunts or other risky behavior _________
- Conceal tickets, warnings or crashes from my parents _________
- Allow anyone else to drive the car. _________
- Get in a car with a driver who is under the influence of drugs or alcohol. _________
- Wear headphones when I'm driving and I'll keep the music and noise at a level where I can still hear noises like sirens. _________
- Eat, drink or smoke while I'm driving. _________
- Allow anyone else to smoke in the car. _________

The consequences for failure to abide by these rules will be: (Be specific.)

____

____

____

I WILL ALWAYS—

- Obey all speed limits, traffic signs and traffic lights. ________
- Do my best to tell you when I feel pressured to do things that make me uncomfortable or worry me ________
- Let you know where I'm going, who I'm with, when I will arrive and when I'll return. If my plans change, I'll let you know as soon as I can. ________
- Pull over in a safe location if I need to make a call. ________
- Try to make a plan for how I'll get home safely, before I go out ________

The consequences for failure to abide by these rules will be: (Be specific.)

____

____

____

Parent/Guardian's Promise to Teen:

Because I love and trust you and want you to be safe:

I WILL NOT—

- Drive under the influence of alcohol or drugs. ________
- Ride with a driver who has had too much to drink ________
- Use my cell phone or text when I drive. ________

I WILL—

- Provide and maintain a safe vehicle for your driving practice ________
- Pay or co-pay for your driving lessons and materials. ________
- Find safe transportation home if I am ever in a situation where I've had too much to drink ________
- Wear my seatbelt and require everyone in my vehicle to do the same. ________
- Avoid making decisions that will jeopardize my health and safety or cause you to lose your trust in me. ________
- Provide you with Safe Passage as defined below. ________

The consequences for failure to abide by these rules will be:

____

____

____

The Safe Passage Clause

If you are ever in a situation that threatens your safety, ***please*** contact me for a safe ride home. I promise to pick you up without question. It doesn't matter where you are, what time it is or what the situation is. I would rather drive across town at 3 a.m. to pick you up, than identify your body in the morgue the next morning.

I won't yell at you or be angry because I want you to call me if you need help. We will postpone discussions about that situation until we can both discuss the issues in a calm, caring way.

If you can't reach me when you need me, the following people have agreed to help you with advice, or a sober ride home regardless of the time or circumstances—

____

____

____

Allowed Teen Drivers

We agree that you can ride with the following drivers under the circumstances outlined below: (for example: "Julie Smith—to and from school only")

I understand that the terms of our Teen Passenger-Parent Contract also apply.

____

____

____

____

Teen Signature ________________________________

Parent/Guardian's Signature (s) __________________________

Date: _______________

Full License

Parent/Guardian's Message to Teen:

I understand that you're getting older and need more independence now. Driving is still dangerous and I worry because so many young people your age die in crashes every year. You are so precious to me. Even though you may be moving away to go to college or work, I still want you to be safe.

Teen's Promise to Parents:

Every year thousands of teen and young adult drivers like me get killed or badly injured in car crashes. I know you love me and want to protect me. You've made the following rules to keep me safe when I'm driving.

I have read each rule and initialed beside it to show I understand what it means and agree to obey it.

***I WILL NEVER*—**

- Drive after using illegal drugs ________
- Drive after drinking any alcohol. ________
- Drive without my seatbelt fastened. ________
- Allow anyone to ride in my vehicle without a seatbelt. ________
- Talk on a cell phone, text or read texts while I am driving. ________
- Drive aggressively or show hostile behavior toward other drivers ________
- Race or engage in stunts or other risky behavior ________
- Conceal tickets, warnings or crashes from my parents ________
- Allow anyone else to drive the car. ________
- Get in a car with a driver who is under the influence of drugs or alcohol. ________
- Wear headphones when I'm driving and I'll keep the music and noise at a level where I can still hear noises like sirens. ________
- Allow anyone else to smoke in the car. ________
- Drive when I am exhausted. ________

The consequences for failure to abide by these rules will be: (Be specific.)

____

____

____

I WILL ALWAYS—

- Obey all speed limits, traffic signs and traffic lights. ________
- Pull over in a safe location if I need to make a call. ________
- Do my best to tell you when I feel pressured to do things that make me uncomfortable or worry me ________
- Let you or someone else I trust know where I'm going, who I'm with, and when to expect me back. ________
- Try to make a plan for how I'll get home safely, before I go out ________

The consequences for failure to abide by these rules will be: (Be specific.)

____

____

____

Parent/Guardian's Promise to Teen:

I understand that you're getting older and need more independence now. I still worry because so many young people your age die in crashes every year and you are so precious to me. Because I love and trust you and want you to be safe:

I WILL NOT—

- Drive under the influence of alcohol or drugs. ________
- Ride with a driver who has had too much to drink ________
- Use my cell phone or text when I drive. ________

I WILL—

- Find safe transportation home if I am ever in a situation where I've had too much to drink. ________
- Wear my seatbelt and require everyone in my vehicle to do the same. ________
- Avoid making decisions that will jeopardize my health and safety or cause you to lose your trust in me ________
- Provide you with Safe Passage as defined below ________

The consequences for failure to abide by these rules will be:

____

____

____

The Safe Passage Clause

If you are ever in a situation that threatens your safety, ***please*** contact me for a safe ride home. I promise to pick you up without question. It doesn't matter where you are, what time it is or what the situation is. I would rather drive across town at 3 a.m. to pick you up, than identify your body in the morgue the next morning.

I won't yell at you or be angry because I want you to call me if you need help. We will postpone discussions about that situation until we can both discuss the issues in a calm, caring way.

If you are too far away to call me for help, please find friends you can count on to help you.

Teen Signature ____

Parent/Guardian's Signature (s) ______________________________________

Date: ________________

Checklists for Your Driving Sessions

If you choose to follow the Lesson Plan that's provided in this workbook, you'll automatically be covering the items included in the checklists below.

However, if you choose to design your own Lesson Plan, these checklists will help ensure that you cover all the bases.

They include checklists to cover:

- Start-Up
- Basic and Advanced Skills
- Conditions
- Situations

Start-up Checklist

Copy this start-up checklist on cardstock and cut it out. Attach it to the underside of the driver's visor in your car. Flip the visor down to review your checklist, each time you drive your car.

Note: Check your windshield washer fluid under the hood, before you get in the car.

START-UP CHECKLIST

1	Check your windshield washer fluid.	7	Adjust your steering wheel.
2	Walk around your vehicle.	8	Turn off your cell phone.
3	Check your gas gauge.	9	Secure any loose objects.
4	Adjust your seat.	10	Buckle your seatbelt and make sure your passengers buckle-up too.
5	Adjust your mirrors.		
6	Adjust your headrest.	11	Lock the doors.

BASIC SKILLS CHECKLIST

- ☐ Start the engine.
- ☐ Turn headlights on and off.
- ☐ Move forward smoothly.
- ☐ Stop smoothly.
- ☐ Maintain a constant speed.
- ☐ Make safe right-hand turns - including signalling.
- ☐ Make safe left-hand turns - including signalling.
- ☐ Shift gears (standard transmission).
- ☐ Back up (straight back).
- ☐ Back up while turning right.
- ☐ Back up while turning left.
- ☐ Scanning skills - who's in front, beside and behind?
- ☐ Maintain a safe cushion around the vehicle in traffic.
- ☐ Safely cross railroad tracks.

MANEUVERING ON THE ROAD

Once you've mastered the basic skills, it's time to move onto the road and interact with other drivers.

- ☐ Change lanes.
- ☐ Encountering emergency vehicles with lights and/or sirens on.
- ☐ Encountering emergency vehicles with lights and sirens off.
- ☐ Maintaing safe driving distances at various speeds.
- ☐ 360-degree awareness of the vehicles around you.
- ☐ Leaving a "safe cushion" around your vehicle.
- ☐ Safe U-turns and when to make them
- ☐ Safe 3-point turns and when to make them.

Dealing with intersections:

- ☐ No lights or signs
- ☐ Stop sign in your direction
- ☐ Stop sign in other direction
- ☐ 4-way stop
- ☐ Traffic light
- ☐ Traffic light not working
- ☐ Other types of intersections

PARKING CHECKLIST

- ☐ 90-degree Parking
- ☐ Angle Parking
- ☐ Parallel Parking
- ☐ Underground Parking
- ☐ Where to locate parking restriction signs
- ☐ Dealing wih parking meters and windshield 'ticket' parking
- ☐ Dealing with parking lots
- ☐ Dealing with parking tickets

FUELING YOUR VEHICLE

- [ ] Locate the gas cap.
- [ ] Is there an icon on the dashboard that shows which side the gas cap is on?
- [ ] Locate the fuel gauge.
- [ ] Talk about static electricity and how to avoid a spark.
- [ ] Check the oil.
- [ ] Clean the windshield.
- [ ] Clean the headlights.
- [ ] Inflate your tires if necessary.
- [ ] Add gas to your tank.

ADVANCED SKILLS CHECKLIST

- [ ] High speed freeway driving
- [ ] Handling curves ('cornering') at high speeds
- [ ] Maintain safe distances from other cars
- [ ] Merging
- [ ] Showing courtesy to other merging drivers
- [ ] Night driving
- [ ] Driving in snow and/or wet conditions
- [ ] Towing

CONDITIONS CHECKLIST		
ROAD CONDITIONS	**WEATHER CONDITIONS**	**LIGHT CONDITIONS**
☐ Driveway	☐ Dry	☐ Sunny
☐ Large, deserted parking lot	☐ Drizzle/ Light rain	☐ Foggy
☐ Quiet residential area	☐ Heavy rain	☐ Dusk
☐ Busier residential area	☐ Snowing	☐ Dark
☐ Main street	☐ Icy road	☐ Dark with street lights
☐ 2-lane highway		
☐ Multi-lane highway		
☐ Gravel road		
☐ Dirt road		

EMERGENCY SITUATIONS DRILLS

Talk about how you would deal with these tricky situations:

- ☐ Fender bender.
- ☐ Accident involving injuries.
- ☐ Out of gas.
- ☐ Dead battery.
- ☐ Flat tire.
- ☐ High wind driving.
- ☐ Downed power lines nearby.
- ☐ Lock keys in car.
- ☐ Designated driver is impaired.

Driving School Tips

(Thanks to Lauren Pearce, Certified Driving Instructor, for her help with this section)

How to Choose the Right Driving School

One driving school is not the same as the next. There are 2 basic types:

- Schools that provide new drivers with the basic skills they'll need to become safe, responsible drivers. These schools encourage parents to reinforce the lessons through structured practice sessions with their teens.
- Schools that train drivers to pass their driver's test and get their license.

> ***Food for Thought:***
>
> Lauren suggests that teens learn in their own cars, if possible. (This way you have the added security of knowing the vehicle is roadworthy.)
>
> On the other hand, most schools provide vehicles with dual controls, so the instructor can take over if the student makes a serious mistake or loses control of the car.

The objective of the second type was highlighted by a recent local newspaper article about driving schools that are ferrying teens 3 to 4 hours from the city to rural DMV offices to take their road tests. They do it because there's less traffic there so the road test is easier and teens are far more likely to pass on their first try.

The problem with this approach is, of course, that these new drivers will not be driving on rural roads with very little traffic. They'll be driving on complex city streets with plenty of noise and multiple lanes of speeding cars. Passing the rural test will give them increased confidence in their driving skills even though those skills aren't adequate to keep them safe on the roads they'll actually be driving. The result could be disastrous.

And driving schools aren't even as regulated as your local restaurants. At least those restaurants have signs in the window that tell you how they did in their latest review by the Board of Health or licensing authority. There's no such thing for driving schools. Even if the schools were reviewed, it's near impossible for parents to find out how they fared. (To read Lauren's blogpost on this topic, go to http://teendrivingblog.wordpress.com/2009/11/19/how-can-parents-find-safe-driving-schools/)

And—considering the important job they do, you'd think there would be strict standards that apply to all driving schools, but there aren't. Some schools operate within DMV guidelines, others don't. Some don't even ensure that their cars are road-worthy. (Again—read Lauren's blogpost, above.)

So—what CAN parents do to find a good driving school for their teens?

Your teen's high school may offer a driving course. Check that one out first.

Look for a course that includes in-car segments on a closed course, like a parking lot, where teens can learn without worrying about other cars.

Parents should also look at the backgrounds and training of the instructors. Lauren suggests that retired police officers know the rules of the road best and professional racecar drivers have the most driving experience and driver training.

The driving programs should also have a number of elements. AAA (the American Automobile Association) suggests that driving courses:

- Provide significant supervised in-car instruction over an extended period of time because teens take time to learn
- Have a performance-based curriculum that includes:
  - Risk management skills
  - Decision-making skills
  - Visual training
  - Nighttime driving
- Involve parents/guardians and encourage collaboration between them and instructors
- Use a multi-media approach that includes computer-based methods, simulations, demonstrations, and gaming
- Provide consistent, appropriate messages
- Deliver their program at an affordable cost

Guidelines for Choosing a Driving School

Check out the school:

1. How long have they been in operation?
   a) What is their BBB (Better Business Bureau) rating?
   b) What do their facilities look like?
   c) If they provide cars for the teens to drive, look at the cars and see if they are in good shape. (Take someone with you who knows about cars)
   d) What certifications do they hold?
2. Ask about the training of the instructors. What certifications do they have? (Ask to meet the instructors if possible.)
3. Do they have (or use) a closed course for some of the lessons?
4. Do they teach in-car and in the classroom? (How many hours of each?)
5. Do they provide cars or allow teens to drive their own vehicles?
6. Have they surveyed past students to determine the effectiveness of their program?
7. Do they use computers in their program?
8. How many students do they have in a class?
9. What is the student-to-instructor ratio? How many are in the car during the driving practice?
10. Is the school recognized by your insurance company? (Will they provide a discount on insurance when your teen passes the course?)
11. If you need more information to make a good decision, ask if you can sit in on part of a class.

Cost

Of course, cost is a factor in choosing the right course, but don't let it be the determining factor. Keep in mind that good courses will provide you with an insurance discount, which will offset part of the expense. (And avoiding one crash is worth the investment—especially if there would have been injuries!)

Also know that the least expensive schools often keep their prices low by having very large classes and providing very little in-car training. They are not a good investment.

Great Low Cost/No Cost Supplementary Programs

Once your teen has taken driver training and spent some time practicing, you might want to consider enrolling them in some of the other great programs that are available. A few of them are listed below according to where they operate. Check the Resources section of our website for details and additional programs that might be available in your area.

- **Tire Rack Street Survival** (www.streetsurvival.org) This one-day course is available in most states. It's aimed at teaching teens the skills they need to stay alive behind the wheel. It's under $100 because it's run by volunteers.
- **Driving Concepts High-Performance Driving School (California)** (www. drvingconcepts.com) The one-day Teen Car Control Clinic is designed to equip students with the skills to handle emergency situations and avoid accidents. It includes 4 hours of classroom, 4 hours of on-course driving exercises, and a reference manual for home study.
- **Start Smart** (http://www.chp.ca.gov/community/startsmart.html) This innovative 2 hour safety program is offered for teens and their parents/guardians by California's Highway Patrol.
- **Bridgestone Winter Driving School (Colorado)** (www. winterdrive.com) This is a great course for teens who will be driving in winter conditions. Driving practice is on a closed course to make the environment as safe as possible.
- **Every15Minutes.com (U.S. Nationwide)** This is a driver safety program, not a driving course. It takes place at schools and involves local emergency service teams. It helps teens realize the consequences of crashes caused by impaired and distracted drivers.
- **Every 15 Minutes/California** In California, the Highway Patrol runs this program.

TIP: Contact your local police or highway patrol office to see if they offer similar courses.

Your Driving Practice Log

In the first year, new drivers need at least 100 hours of practice on the road. That works out to about 2 hours per week, which is difficult to do in our already over-scheduled world.

But this practice is very important. It's the only way new drivers can develop reflexive driving skills, so schedule your sessions and stick to the schedule as well as you can. If you miss a lesson, schedule a make-up lesson right away.

Use the log to keep track of your time and the skills you're developing.

How to Use Your Driving Practice Log

You have enough Driving Practice Logs to last for your first year because your structured practice should last that long. Afterwards, keep driving and talking with your coach but it isn't as important to track how much time you're spending.

Instructions

1. Fill in the month.
2. Complete an entry every time you drive, as shown.
3. At the end of each month, add up the total hours you have practiced that month.
4. Add the total from the previous month to the total for this month to find out how much practice you've done to-date.

Remember: Your goal is 100 hours of practice during the first year.

WK	Day	# Hrs.	Co-Pilot	Location	Principles Practiced	Road Conditions	Time of Day
1	Sat	0.5	Dad	Parking Lot	starting	good/clear	afternoon
	Sun	1	Dad	Parking Lot	starting/stopping	good/clear	afternoon
	Mon	1	Dad	Parking Lot	emergency stops	good/clear	afternoon

Following are the headings on each chart, with sample entries.

This is what the headings mean:

WK: Keep track of your practice time by giving each week a number. (Week 1, Week 2 to Week 52)

Day: This is the day of the week that you practiced driving.

 # Hrs: This is the number of hours you spent practicing driving on this day.(example: If you practice for 1 hour in the morning, then eat lunch and later, practice for 1 more hour , you'll show "2 hours" in this column)

Co-Pilot: Parent (or acceptable adult driver, according to license restrictions) initials here at the end of each session

Location: This is where you practiced. The location should change and involve more difficult driving locations as you gain practice and confidence.

Principles Practiced: What did you concentrate on during this driving session?

Road Conditions: What are the road conditions? Clear and dry? Wet and slippery? You'll need exposure to all kinds of conditions before you take your road test.

Time of Day: You'll need practice driving in all levels of light and at all times of day (except those restricted by your Level 1 or Level 2 licenses)

Driving Practice Log Month 1 and Month 2

MONTH: ______

WK	Day	# Hrs.	Co-Pilot	Location	Principles Practiced	Road Conditions	Time of Day
1							
2							
3							
4							

______ Total Hrs This Month ______ Total Hrs to Date

MONTH: ______

WK	Day	# Hrs.	Co-Pilot	Location	Principles Practiced	Road Conditions	Time of Day
1							
2							
3							
4							

______ Total Hrs This Month ______ Total Hrs to Date

Driving Practice Log Month 3 and Month 4

MONTH: ______

WK	Day	# Hrs.	Co-Pilot	Location	Principles Practiced	Road Conditions	Time of Day
1							
2							
3							
4							

______Total Hrs This Month ______ Total Hrs to Date

MONTH: ______

WK	Day	# Hrs.	Co-Pilot	Location	Principles Practiced	Road Conditions	Time of Day
1							
2							
3							
4							

______Total Hrs This Month ______ Total Hrs to Date

Driving Practice Log Month 5 and Month 6

MONTH: ______

WK	Day	# Hrs.	Co-Pilot	Location	Principles Practiced	Road Conditions	Time of Day
1							
2							
3							
4							

_____ Total Hrs This Month ____________ Total Hrs to Date

MONTH: ______

WK	Day	# Hrs.	Co-Pilot	Location	Principles Practiced	Road Conditions	Time of Day
1							
2							
3							
4							

_____ Total Hrs This Month ____________ Total Hrs to Date

Driving Practice Log Month 7 and Month 8

MONTH: ______

WK	Day	# Hrs.	Co-Pilot	Location	Principles Practiced	Road Conditions	Time of Day
1							
2							
3							
4							

______ Total Hrs This Month ______ Total Hrs to Date

MONTH: ______

WK	Day	# Hrs.	Co-Pilot	Location	Principles Practiced	Road Conditions	Time of Day
1							
2							
3							
4							

______ Total Hrs This Month ______ Total Hrs to Date

Driving Practice Log Month 9 and Month 10

MONTH: ____

WK	Day	# Hrs.	Co-Pilot	Location	Principles Practiced	Road Conditions	Time of Day
1							
2							
3							
4							

____ Total Hrs This Month ____ Total Hrs to Date

MONTH: ____

WK	Day	# Hrs.	Co-Pilot	Location	Principles Practiced	Road Conditions	Time of Day
1							
2							
3							
4							

____ Total Hrs This Month ____ Total Hrs to Date

Driving Practice Log Month 11 and Month 12

MONTH: ________

WK	Day	# Hrs.	Co-Pilot	Location	Principles Practiced	Road Conditions	Time of Day
1							
2							
3							
4							

______Total Hrs This Month ____________ Total Hrs to Date

MONTH: ________

WK	Day	# Hrs.	Co-Pilot	Location	Principles Practiced	Road Conditions	Time of Day
1							
2							
3							
4							

______Total Hrs This Month ____________ Total Hrs to Date

Instruction Card for Jumper Cables

Directions for Making the Instruction Card for Your Jumper Cables

1. Cut out the cards on the previous page.
2. Glue them back-to-back. Laminate them. (An office supply store like Staples or Business Depot can do this for you.)
3. Punch a hole at the top (where the circle is.)
4. Trim around the card, leaving ¼ inch around the outside so the lamination will stay intact.
5. Attach this card to your jumper cables using a plastic cable or string so it's handy when you need it. Remove it when you need to read the instructions.

If you're involved in a crash (fender-bender or multi-car collision), this form will help you capture all the important details. Keep it for your own records.

Side 1

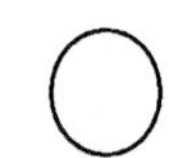

HOW TO ATTACH JUMPER CABLES

- Engines in both cars are **OFF.**
- **DO NOT** touch the claws together.
- **DO NOT** touch any white, powdery substance on the battery.

1. ***At the DEAD Battery:***
   Attach Red claw to Positive terminal.
   The Positive terminal is marked with a "+" (plus) sign.
2. ***At the BOOSTER Battery:***
   Attach Red claw to Positive terminal.
   The Positive terminal is marked with a "+" (plus) sign.
3. ***At the BOOSTER Battery:***
   Attach Black claw to Negative terminal.
   The Negative terminal is marked with a "-" (minus) sign.
4. ***At the DEAD Battery:***
   Attach Black claw to a Ground.
   A Ground is any piece of metal on the engine.

NOW - Start the BOOSTER car and let it run for a few minutes.
THEN - Start the DEAD car.

Side 2

HOW TO REMOVE JUMPER CABLES

- **DO NOT touch the claws together.**

1. ***At the DEAD Battery:***
   Remove Black claw from Ground.
   A Ground is any piece of metal on the engine.
2. ***At the BOOSTER Battery:***
   Remove Black claw from Negative terminal.
   The Negative terminal is marked with a "-" (minus) sign.
3. **At the BOOSTER Battery:**
   Remove Red claw from Positive terminal.
   The Positive terminal is marked with a "+" (plus) sign.
4. **At the DEAD Battery:**
   Remove Red claw from Positive terminal.
   The Positive terminal is marked with a "+" (plus) sign.

Run the engine for 20 minutes to recharge the battery.

TeensLearntoDrive.com

Accident Report

About The Other Driver:

Name: ______________________________ Date of Birth ____________

Address: ______________________________

Home Phone # (___) ____________ Business Phone # (___) ____________

Driver's License #: ____________ State/Prov ____________

About Their Insurer: (You'll get this information from his "Proof of Insurance")

Insurance Co: ____________ Policy #: ____________

About Their Vehicle: (Check their "Vehicle Registration Certificate")

License Plate # ____________ State/Prov ____________

Make: ____________ Model: ____________ Year: ____________

VIN # ______________________________

Vehicle Owner's Name (if Different than driver): ____________

Address: ______________________________

Home Phone # (___) ____________ Business Phone # (___) ____________

About Their Passengers:

Name: ______________________________ Date of Birth ____________

Address: ______________________________

Home Phone # (___) ____________ Business Phone # (___) ____________

About the Witnesses: (in other cars or pedestrians)

Witness #1:

Name: ______________________________

Address: ______________________________

Home Phone # (___) ____________ Business Phone # (___) ____________

License Plate # ______________________________

☐ Vehicle was involved ☐ Vehicle was not involved ☐ Pedestrian

Witness #2:

Name: ______________________________

Address: ______________________________

Home Phone # (___) ____________________ Business Phone # (___) ______________

License Plate # ____

☐ Vehicle was involved ☐ Vehicle was not involved ☐ Pedestrian

About the Police Investigation: File #: ______________________________

Police Officer's Name: ______________________________________

Badge Number: ________________________ Department ________________________

Address: ______________________________ Phone #: __________________________

Did police charge you? ☐ YES ☐ NO

Details: ____

____

____

Was the other driver charged? ☐ YES ☐ NO

Details: ____

____

____

Road Conditions	Weather	Light Conditions	Other
☐ Straight Road	☐ Clear	☐ Dawn	☐ Stop Sign
☐ Curved	☐ Sunny	☐ Daytime	☐ Stop Light
☐ Level	☐ Glare	☐ Dusk	☐ Slow Zone
☐ Sloped	☐ Cloudy	☐ Dark, Street Lights	☐
☐ Dry	☐ Fog	☐ Dark, No Street Lights	
☐ Wet	☐ Snowing	**Road Conditions**	
☐ Muddy	☐ Raining	☐ Potholes	
☐ Icy	☐	☐ Bumps	
☐ Snowy		☐ Gravel	
☐		☐ Paved	
		☐	

About YOUR Insurance Company:

Name of Person you reported the incident to: ______________________

File #: ______________________________ Date Reported: ______________

Keep this paper in a safe place with any photos of the scene and the vehicles.

BUY A SHARE OF THE FUTURE IN YOUR COMMUNITY

These certificates make great holiday, graduation and birthday gifts that can be personalized with the recipient's name. The cost of one S.H.A.R.E. or one square foot is $54.17. The personalized certificate is suitable for framing and will state the number of shares purchased and the amount of each share, as well as the recipient's name. The home that you participate in "building" will last for many years and will continue to grow in value.

Here is a sample SHARE certificate:

THIS CERTIFIES THAT

YOUR NAME HERE

HAS INVESTED IN A HOME FOR A DESERVING FAMILY

1985-2010

TWENTY-FIVE YEARS OF BUILDING FUTURES
IN OUR COMMUNITY ONE HOME AT A TIME

1200 SQUARE FOOT HOUSE @ $65,000 = $54.17 PER SQUARE FOOT
This certificate represents a tax deductible donation. It has no cash value.

YES, I WOULD LIKE TO HELP!

I support the work that Habitat for Humanity does and I want to be part of the excitement! As a donor, I will receive periodic updates on your construction activities but, more importantly, I know my gift will help a family in our community realize the dream of homeownership. ***I would like to SHARE in your efforts against substandard housing in my community!*** *(Please print below)*

PLEASE SEND ME __________ SHARES at $54.17 EACH = $ $__________

In Honor Of: ____________________

Occasion: *(Circle One)* *HOLIDAY* *BIRTHDAY* *ANNIVERSARY*

OTHER: ____________________

Address of Recipient: ____________________

Gift From: ______________ ***Donor Address:*** ____________________

Donor Email: ____________________

I AM ENCLOSING A CHECK FOR $ $____________ PAYABLE TO HABITAT FOR HUMANITY OR PLEASE CHARGE MY VISA OR MASTERCARD *(CIRCLE ONE)*

Card Number ____________________ Expiration Date: __________

Name as it appears on Credit Card ______________ Charge Amount $ __________

Signature ____________________

Billing Address ____________________

Telephone # Day ______________ Eve ______________

PLEASE NOTE: Your contribution is tax-deductible to the fullest extent allowed by law.

Habitat for Humanity • P.O. Box 1443 • Newport News, VA 23601 • 757-596-5553

www.HelpHabitatforHumanity.org

Notes

CPSIA information can be obtained at www.ICGtesting.com
Printed in the USA
LVOW021624290911

248446LV00004B/9/P